✳ THE LIVING OF MAISIE WARD

Maisie Ward
Courtesy of Rosemary Sheed Middleton

The

Living

of

Maisie Ward

✳ Dana Greene

University of Notre Dame Press
Notre Dame and London

The author and the publisher are grateful to the following
for permission to reproduce photographs:
Rosemary Sheed Middleton
Maria Darlington
The Archives of the University of Notre Dame

Library of Congress Cataloging-in-Publication Data

Greene, Dana.
    The living of Maisie Ward / Dana Greene.
        p.   cm.
    Includes bibliographical references and index.
    ISBN 0-268-01311-X (alk. paper)
    1. Ward, Maisie, 1889–   . 2. Catholics—England—Biography.
I. Title.
BX4705.W287G74   1997
282'.092—dc20   96-30396
    [B]   CIP

*The paper used in this publication meets the minimum requirements of the
American National Standard for Information Sciences—Permanence of Paper for
Printing Library Materials, ANSI Z39.48-1984.*

✻ DEDICATED TO
my teachers at the College of New Rochelle
who first taught me the connection
between heart and mind

✳ "The glory of God is (wo)man fully alive."

—Irenaeus

Contents

Acknowledgments   xi

Introduction   1

1. The Ties That Bind   7

2. Through the Calm   25

3. "The Years the Locusts Have Eaten"   39

4. "A Future . . . Almost Too Bright to Look At"   49

5. "The Blissful Catholic Summer of the Twenties"   69

6. A Transatlantic Life   85

7. "This Burning Heat"   97

8. England Revisited   123

9. "Chaos, Shot Through with the Brightest Delights"   141

10. Hitting Her Stride   155

11. "A Rest Is Needed"   169

12. "A Refuge in Browning"   183

13. "Hope in Near-hopelessness"   195

Epilogue   209

Notes   211

Bibliography   231

Index   243

Acknowledgments

✳ ALTHOUGH WRITING A BOOK is solitary work, one does not write it alone. This is a better book for the support and help given me by many persons and institutions on both sides of the Atlantic. I am particularly grateful to Rosemary Sheed Middleton, who was immensely generous with her time, knowledge, and hospitality, and to Wilfrid Sheed, who allowed me to use the voluminous materials in the Sheed and Ward Papers. The financial support of the Cushwa Center of the University of Notre Dame, St. Catherine's College, the College of Preachers at the Washington National Cathedral, and St. Mary's College of Maryland is gratefully appreciated, as is the hospitality of Moreau Seminary at the University of Notre Dame and the inspiration of my colleagues in the Association for Religion and Intellectual Life. I thank Allyson Faith McGill, Don Stabile, Gail Dean, Rebecca DeBoer, and Maria Darlington for help with the manuscript, and the staffs of the Archives of the University of Notre Dame, particularly Kevin Cawley, and St. Mary's College of Maryland for their expertise. Patrick Allitt, Alice Gallin, Karen Kennelly, and Dolores Leckey gave their personal encouragement as did the thirty persons who allowed me to interview them for this book (see bibliography) and who reflected so vividly the openness and generosity which characterized the life of Maisie Ward. In all cases, I take full responsibility for what is written here even while I thank these informants for our differences of opinion. Finally, I am grateful to my daughters—Kristin, Justin, Lauren, Ryan—my husband, Richard, and Jackie Leclerc who endured this book for many years. Their love has made all the difference.

Dana Greene
St. Mary's City, Md.

Introduction

❋ Egypt House faces the sea. Fortresslike, with turrets and towers, its high brick wall insulates its inhabitants, protecting them from the rest of the Isle of Wight. This house was the property of the Ward family, who owned much of the town of Cowes and more than a third of the island. Prominent and moneyed, the Wards were nonetheless set apart. As Catholics, they were members of a tiny minority among the English, most of whom traced their ancestry back to sixteenth-century martyrs. But the Wards were converts and hence zealous. Fellow papists who lived their faith discreetly found them suspect.

In late April, Egypt House is beautiful. The lawns are green and slope down toward The Solent. With the fruit trees in flower it is a perfect site for a wedding. Here the first-born daughter of Wilfrid Ward, Catholic intellectual and biographer, and of Josephine Hope Ward, novelist and relative of the Duke of Norfolk, the first among English Catholics, celebrated her marriage. Vows were exchanged at the simple church of St. Thomas of Canterbury, where school children with flowers lined the stairs of this former house-church. The bride, Mary Josephine, was not young. At thirty-seven, her marriage to Francis Sheed, an Australian eight years her junior, was greeted with apprehension. If her father had been alive it is unlikely that Sheed would have been an acceptable match. After all, Maisie, as she was known, was heir to a long and rich intellectual tradition. Frank was the grandson of a sea captain, and his law degree from the University of Sydney did not count for much in Ward circles; but he was Catholic, and there were no other suitors in waiting. The perceived awkwardness of the match of

Ward and Sheed was eased by the contentment of Maisie and the charisma of Frank, who charmed everyone who came to celebrate at Egypt House. No one could possibly have known in that April of 1926 the success, either in marriage or work, that these two would create. What bound them was religion, not contemplative or quietistic religion, but religion proclaimed: this became their vocation and the basis of their life together.

The Sheeds were an institution that perdured for almost fifty years. As publishers, lecturers, writers, and street-preachers, they shaped twentieth-century Catholicism in the English-speaking world. What was born of this April wedding was not merely the Sheeds, but Maisie Ward. The creation of Mrs. Francis Sheed allowed Maisie Ward to be realized. Of course the elements were already there: the intellectual talent, the religious faith, the perceptiveness, the energy and vitality. But Frank would be the catalyst, the friend-in-arms with whom she could take up the "war" from which "there was no discharge." She had no way of knowing the trajectory of her life, the slow arc that would reach its zenith when she was in her seventies and transport her from the Isle of Wight to Jersey City, passing through three continents on the way.

Neither could others imagine her future. They might expect that she would write—she came from a family of writers—but how could they foresee that her unique talent as a platform speaker would bring her to Times Square and lecture halls throughout America? Could they envision her as a publisher who would help form the reading habits of educated Catholics for more than four decades, exposing them to the best in theological writing? Could they believe that given her conviction to "pass on the Good News and harbour the harbourless," she would found the Catholic Housing Aid Society in postwar Britain or that she would support the efforts of the Catholic Worker and Friendship House in the United States, the Maritime cooperatives of Canada, the priest-worker movement of France, experimental Christian farming communities on both sides of the Atlantic, and land reform efforts in India? Ward had neither official role nor sanction for this work. It would be unapproved, self-created, and taken up in response to the needs of her own

Maisie's wedding, April 1926, at Egypt House. Left to right,
Lady Catherine Howard, bridesmaid, Gravernor Hewins, best man,
Frank Sheed, and Maisie Ward.
Courtesy of Rosemary Sheed Middleton

time. As a lay person and a woman she would be excluded from approved theological discourse, but she would find other ways to express her religious conviction and her moral voice.

On her marriage day Maisie did not know the obstacles that would confront her or the many points at which she could be derailed. She knew only that she loved Frank, and he, her. And she knew the liabilities of being a single woman. She must also have had some intimations of the negative consequences of her family's powerful emotional bonds. She loved her relatives, but unless she married, their hold on her would be relentless. Frank offered escape from their suffocating insularity; he also offered ballast. Bound to him she could take risks she would have never undertaken alone. Through marriage she could become a public person. But Frank would force compromise as well.

It was a wonderful match on both sides. Frank was ecstatic to be marrying Maisie and delighted to ally himself with her family of intellectuals. Although he would be surrounded by adoring women for much of his public life, Maisie would be his center. At his death the telegram she sent agreeing to marry him was found in his coat pocket, a reminder of her love. Frank needed Maisie as much as she needed him.

But Maisie needed more than Frank to lead her unique life. Her drive and talent were trapped by female expectations of herself, and of her society's for her. Seemingly unconscious of this dilemma, she would make her own way. Completely undomestic, Maisie depended heavily on others. Her Australian mother-in-law, her friends, her daughter, her secretaries, all were necessary elements for Maisie's successful life. Although in theory she revered family life, she was incapable or unwilling to give it much material help. There was another allegiance that was more powerful.

Maisie Ward came of age emotionally later than most of the ardent, intellectual Englishwomen who were her contemporaries, such as Vera Brittain, Dorothy L. Sayers, Virginia Woolf, Evelyn Underhill, and Antonia White. Immense changes were thrust on all of them, but unlike many of her generation, Maisie was protected, traditional, and insular. Catholicism cut her off from broad intellectual interaction, and her family's political conservatism led her to see change as threatening. Her assets for making a contribution to a confused and chaotic age seemed few. But both her parents had given her a tradition of intellectual commitment and belief, and her mother one of social responsibility. These values would express themselves in Maisie's conviction that intellectual life and belief were not abstract but must be acted on and lived existentially.

In the mid-1920s no one could have imagined the changes that would erupt in that most unchanging of institutions, the Roman Catholic Church. Yet Maisie Ward would give direction to that tumultuous change. As the Catholic intellectual revival unfolded in the 1930s, 1940s, and 1950s, she found herself at its center. She pushed that change further, arguing that the life of the mind must spill over into Catholic action in the world. When she gave voice in her writing and lecturing to the latent desire for transformation in Catholicism, she did so as a traditional woman, wife, and mother. While offering no feminist critique, her life would nonetheless belie the traditional rhetoric about woman's place. To women, the most dedicated and numerous participants in the Catholic revival, Maisie Ward offered an example; articulate and committed, she gave them liberty to think and act independent of clergy and with or without husbands.

As an increasingly public person she fostered no self-aggrandizement. She neither gathered devotees nor encouraged adulation but remained utterly single-minded. Indifferent to circumstance, she cared not one whit what she wore or ate or where she lived or whom she impressed. Her incapacity for small talk became legendary. Her forthrightness was both disarming and irritating. Demanding of others, she was more demanding of herself. What was important were ideas, their realization, and the people who believed in them.

Maisie Ward was a woman of remarkable talent, boundless energy, and strong conviction, who linked her warrior characteristics to the command, "Go and preach." She had already begun to act on that command when she met Frank, and their life together became an embodiment of that mandate. From their initial work as preachers would grow their activities as publishers and writers. But it was Maisie who insisted that an idea had to be realized, had to become actual and incarnate. It had to change the world. As an inveterate admirer of farming, she thought of ideas as seeds that needed to be planted, watered, nurtured, and harvested, and then their fruit brought to the table so many could eat.

As a woman who acted in a world of men, Maisie saw reality whole, and that was her strength and her weakness. As a woman, connection and relationship were important; as a Christian, inspired by the newly reasserted doctrine of the Mystical Body, her womanly instincts were confirmed by powerful religious imagery. She spent her life broadening her circle of inclusion; in the end this "granddaughter of the Oxford Movement" would defend Australian aborigines, African Americans, conscientious objectors to war, and Indian harijan. Both in her inclusivity and her effort to live belief, Maisie Ward's life represents an important contribution to the history of twentieth-century Roman Catholicism.

Yet on this day of her wedding, as she moved among family and friends at Egypt House, there was no sense of the meaning of her future life but only the happiness of the moment and the hope that after decades she was at last moving in a new direction.

ONE

The Ties That Bind

There are four ways to write a woman's life: the woman herself may tell it, in what she chooses to call an autobiography; she may tell it in what she chooses to call fiction; a biographer, woman or man, may write the woman's life in what is called a biography; or the woman may write her own life in advance of living it, unconsciously, and without recognizing or naming the process.[1]

✳ MAISIE WARD WROTE HER LIFE IN TWO WAYS: She created it in advance, unconsciously, and she interpreted it in three autobiographies.[2] Her acting and her telling are only part of her story. The rest lies beyond the parameters she knew in life and links her to the future in ways she could not have imagined. What she did understand was her connection to the past. It was in that past that she began her story, and it is there that anyone who hopes to understand her must begin.

In every life, genetics and culture conspire to confine. To break through these constraints is perilous; few take such risks. Wanting protection, most people persist within narrow limits. For some few others, the alternative is to maneuver, to slowly pull the legacies of biology and history in a new direction, and if long life is given, to create a final form altogether different from what was inherited. The life of Maisie Ward is one such maneuver. Although biology and culture conjoined in a particularly lethal combination to incapacitate many of the Wards, Maisie escaped.[3] Incapable of rebellion or passivity, she took her original inheritance and forged it gradually into an unusual life. In this way, she transmitted the Ward legacy to the future, albeit with her own particular stamp.

7

The web of loyalties into which Maisie Ward was born was given form and structure by family and church. It is easy to imagine a formidable loyalty to family, but when family allegiance is merely a specific instance of some more universal religious devotion, as it was for the Wards, the emotional and intellectual consequences are far-reaching. It is impossible to understand Maisie Ward's life independently of the English Catholic Church. The point at which the history of that church and the Ward family coincided was the conversion to Rome in 1845 of Maisie's grandfather, the eccentric William George Ward. He was the first of the Oxford Movement converts who would dramatically influence English Catholicism in the nineteenth century.

The church that Ward joined was insular and cut off from national life. John Henry Newman, the most famous of the Oxford Movement converts, described how others saw it, not as a community or a sect, but as the "detritus of the great deluge":

> Such were Catholics in England, found in corners and alleys, and cellars, and the housetops, or in the recesses of the country; shut off from the populous world around them, and dimly seen as if through a mist, or in a twilight, as ghosts flitting to and fro, by the high Protestant lords of the earth. At length so feeble did they become, so utterly contemptible, that contempt gave birth to pity, and the more generous of their tyrants actually began to wish to bestow upon them some favor, under the notion that their opinions were simply too absurd ever to spread again, and that they themselves were they but raised in civil importance, would soon unlearn and be ashamed of them.[4]

In the post-Reformation period, English Catholicism was carried on in the great country houses of the north of England. Clergy were generally poor, itinerant, and dependent on wealthy gentry to sustain them. By the eighteenth century, martyrdom and clandestine religious activity were replaced by discreet expressions of faith. As a tiny minority, English Catholics represented no threat to the nation, but public perception persisted that they were subservient, unpatriotic, and superstitious. Wealthy Catholics had a certain deference extended them, but all Catholics were legally excluded from serving in Parliament and the professions.

The gradual removal of the penal laws and disabilities culminating in the Catholic Emancipation Act of 1829 ended the most obvious forms of discrimination against Papists. In the nineteenth century their numbers were augmented by Irish immigration. The original English Catholics, who could trace their lineage back before the Reformation, were melded with new converts from the Oxford Movement of 1833–1845. Once an official Roman Catholic hierarchy was reestablished in England in 1850, the church was more centralized and clericalized, and ties with Rome were stronger. Although tension over Papal influence and openness to secular life continued, Catholics were optimistic that their degraded state had ended and that, in Newman's words, English Catholicism would experience a "Second Spring."

Against this backdrop of profound change in English Catholicism, the Ward family came to prominence in the persons of William George Ward and his son Wilfrid. These two laymen profoundly shaped nineteenth-century English Catholicism and handed their legacy on to Maisie Ward and her generation. As the self-proclaimed "grandchild of the Oxford Movement," she understood that legacy. Her life was sculpted decades before she was born by the decision of her grandfather to "go over to Rome."

William George Ward, professor of mathematics and logic at Balliol, was a Tractarian and a colleague of Newman. When the latter published Tract 90, which suggested that one could subscribe to the Thirty-Nine Articles of the Anglican Church but put a Catholic interpretation on some of them, Ward came to his defense. As a result Ward was forced to resign his Oxford position. In 1844 he published, *The Ideal of the Christian Church*, which was condemned by the Anglicans as unorthodox. The following year "Ideal" Ward was stripped of his Oxford degrees, and he subsequently joined the Roman Catholic Church.

Self-described as "very strong and very narrow," Ward claimed he had "the mind of an archangel in the body of a rhinoceros."[5] Others saw him as extreme in his positions and eccentric in manner; he was dubbed "the buffoon of the Oxford Movement." Removed from his Oxford professorship, he became Professor of Dogmatic Theology at St. Edmund's College, Ware, a Catholic institution. His financial position was fairly precarious until 1849, when his uncle died without a male heir and left him the inheritance of vast Isle of Wight properties. In 1860 Ward was appointed the editor of the *Dublin Review*, a position he held for twenty-eight years and one he used to forward his views on strong papal authority against Liberals such as Acton and moderates like Newman.

Ward represented the most conservative wing of English Roman Catholicism. He believed that the church embodied the principles of right and truth and as such was a bulwark against the corrosive currents of modern thought. Although he had a personal devotion to Newman, Ward considered him representative of the Old Catholic position and therefore an opponent of Ward's Ultramontanism. As a staunch defender of the pope, Ward allowed that he would be delighted to have a daily papal bull at breakfast along with his *London Times*.

Ward despised the inroads of secular thought on religion and was one of those who influenced Cardinal Manning to oppose the matriculation of Roman Catholics at Oxford and Cambridge when it became legally possible. This meant that his own sons would be denied the opportunities of education that had been open to him. Driven by a sense of duty, detached from wealth and success, Ward lived to promote principle and the truth of the church of his conversion. With his wife Frances, also a convert, he created a household dominated by ecclesiastical concerns. Elaborate daily prayer services were carried out by the family. Each room of their home was dedicated to a patron saint, and Mrs. Ward often wore the habit of a Third Order Franciscan, much like a prioress of a young congregation. Cardinal Vaughan, Frances Ward's spiritual advisor, instilled in all the children a desire to serve the church. Of the eight Ward children, three, Mary, Margaret, and Agnes, became nuns and one, Bernard, a priest and later a bishop and historian of English Catholicism. Two of the daughters, Emily and Gertrude, were invalids and remained unmarried. The eldest son, Edmund, was heir to the Ward estates, but Edmund's marriage ended because of nonconsummation, and he spent his life dedicated to ecclesiastical ceremony. Only Wilfrid, biographer and editor, produced progeny and heirs.

Wilfrid and his siblings suffered under their mother's suspicion of schools. Consequently, Wilfrid did not begin formal education until the age of twelve, when he was sent first to school at Downside and then to St. Edmund's College. Later, reflecting on his narrow but secure life, he wrote: "This feeling of perfect security was engendered by the nature of our life as children. Thus in a sense the very narrowness of my early training told for breadth in the long run—because the narrowness meant the exclusiveness which gives depth and stability to belief."[6] But if the narrowness of his early life might have positive consequences for the intellectual battles he was to confront at mid-life, it did not prepare him for adult choices. Wilfrid was totally undirected professionally. His passions were for music and drama, particularly the opera. His beautiful baritone voice was his most evident asset, but a profession on the stage was unthinkable for a Ward, even a second son. Preoccupied with intellectual and religious concerns, William George was incapable of offering any advice to his son except that Wilfrid become a priest. Wilfrid considered this choice and even went to Rome for study, but he ultimately rejected the priesthood. He began the study of law but his heart was not in that, either. At the time of his father's death he was still floundering. Wilfrid believed his father's high ideals were to blame, at least in part, for his indecision:

And as I had no practicable programme set before me, my father's ideals really tended to prevent my doing anything useful at all. But I do not wish to deny that it was largely my own fault that I was so unsuccessful for years in finding a definite path in life that should be at once practical and useful. I only set down the obstacles which a stronger will and a different temperament might have overcome better than I did, because I think that there are many, who, like

me, would suffer if the unpractical unworldliness of the Oxford
Movement prevailed as the only motive set up for a young man's
inspiration.[7]

Ward's comment is almost prescient of the vocational dilemma
his daughter Maisie would confront years later.

Soon after William George's death, Wilfrid sought to heal
relationships between the Wards and those whom his father
had alienated, especially Baron Friedrich von Hügel and John
Henry Newman. He also found his life's work as a Catholic
apologist. Through biographies of the church's intellectuals
and prelates, Wilfrid would chronicle the contributions of
nineteenth-century English Catholicism. He began with his father. *William George Ward and the Oxford Movement* was published
in 1889, and *William George Ward and the Catholic Revival* appeared four years later. Although these were works of filial
piety, they were also intellectual histories of English Catholicism
in the early part of the nineteenth century.

Wilfrid's attempts to present Catholicism in a new light
could not have come at a better time. The pontificate of Leo
XIII brought with it a greater openness between the English
Catholic Church and the world. Wilfrid Ward saw this as a time
of opportunity. The state of siege that had preoccupied the
Catholic church since the Reformation had ended. Protestant-
ism, the old enemy, was now no enemy at all. All Christians must
unite against the new opponent, atheism in its myriad forms.
Catholic intellectuals like himself must respond to this great
transition by presenting Catholicism in a new, less defensive
manner. Since he was not a theologian, Ward would reveal the
greatness of the English church through her sons. He lionized
his father's contribution to the revival of Catholic thought, told
the story of the reestablishment of the English Catholic hierarchy in his biography of Cardinal Wiseman, and illustrated the
power and dedication of the greatest English Catholic thinker,
Cardinal Newman, as the one best able to bridge Catholicism
and modern thought.

At thirty-one, five years after his father's death, Ward married Josephine Hope, heeding Cardinal Vaughan's admonition

that he marry well and ensure his ability to serve the church. Their marriage was not easily made; Wilfrid was rebuffed on his first two proposals. Josephine accepted the third time and they were married in 1887. The links between the families were through Catholicism. Wilfrid's godmother, the Duchess of Norfolk, was also the grandmother of Josephine. Their formal introduction as adults came when the Duchess invited the young Ward to sing Holy Week services at Arundel Castle, the Duke's ancestral home in West Sussex. He was immediately taken with Josephine and decided that he wanted her as his wife.

Josephine's family was wealthy and well connected. Like Wilfrid's parents, hers were Oxford Movement converts to Catholicism. Josephine's mother, Victoria Howard, was the daughter of Minna Lyons, the Duchess of Norfolk. When Minna Lyons converted to Roman Catholicism, her ten-year-old daughter, Victoria, decided after some initial hesitation to "go over to Rome" as well. Josephine's father, James Hope, was a Tractarian who also joined the Church. His first wife, who had died soon after their marriage, was the granddaughter of Sir Walter Scott. James Hope-Scott, who had added her surname at marriage, then married Victoria Howard and with her had four surviving children—Josephine, Minna, Theresa, and James. At the birth of their youngest, Victoria died; a few years later so did James, leaving the four children orphaned. Their maternal grandmother, the widowed Duchess of Norfolk, adopted them, and they were cared for by her unmarried daughters, Mary and Margaret Howard, at Arundel Castle. Josephine would name her firstborn Mary Josephine after the Aunt Mary who became a mother to her.

Much like Wilfrid Ward, Josephine spent her childhood in the company of adults. In society, she and her sisters were the Misses Hope, who often appeared with the Duchess of Norfolk and the Ladies Howard. Like the Wards, the Howard household was dedicated to religion, not so much in intellectual but in practical expression. Theology was important as it applied to life. The Howards opened a public chapel and established settlement houses for the poor. They believed that poverty and social ills could be alleviated through the work of individuals acting on Christian principle. The Howards' sense of personal responsibility arising from religious commitment would be transmitted from them, through Josephine, to her daughter Maisie.

Although Josephine's education was broader than Wilfrid's, they shared a narrow Catholic upbringing. The Howard household had a full program of religious practices—daily Mass, meditation, spiritual reading. The objective was to spiritualize everything and attack worldliness. No money was to be spent on amusements and everything must be approached with grave otherworldliness. Victorian earnestness and Jansenistic scrupulosity were religious and family values. Given this environment of piety, it is understandable that at one point Josephine considered entering the convent.

When Josephine Hope finally agreed to marry Wilfrid Ward, her relatives were delighted. Their marriage was the joining of the children of four ardent Oxford Movement converts. In the union of Wilfrid and Josephine, intellectual commitment and artistic expression would combine in service to the Church. Theirs was the Catholic marriage par excellence.

Both Josephine and Wilfrid saw marriage as a way of consecrating their lives to God. Marriage was a holy state and God was primary in their relationship. Both spent several days in separate retreats before their wedding day. Their vocation was marriage and their career was writing, his as a biographer and editor and hers as a novelist. At the time of their marriage both were published authors. In *The Wish to Believe* Wilfrid explored the nature of belief, while Josephine's novel *In the Way* portrayed the poor of Sussex. As a couple their livelihood was made possible by Josephine's inheritance and the proceeds from a sale of property that Edmund Ward had given to them. Although not wealthy, they were independent and free to write in support of the church and to examine religious questions.

The Wards began their married life in a small house on the Isle of Wight near Weston Manor. Edmund lived nearby in Freshwater, and although he traveled frequently to Catholic colleges in England and on the continent, his presence was a strain. He was wildly eccentric and often in the company of clerics, serving as master of ceremonies in their prolonged liturgical services. Within two years Wilfrid and Josephine would move to Hampstead. But before the family left the Isle of Wight, Josephine gave birth to their first child, Mary Josephine, on January 4, 1889, a little over a year after their marriage. As her confinement neared its end, Josephine chose the milder climate of Shanklin, at the island's far southeastern end, for her delivery. She returned to Weston Manor in mid-March. After the birth, Josephine's mother-in-law gave her a prayer book and told her to prepare for death—supposedly, her life's work had been accomplished! The new baby, known as Maisie, was introduced to the Ward's most illustrious neighbor, Alfred Lord Tennyson, who on seeing her announced: "She's exactly like Henry VIII."[8] One can only imagine that it was the squareness of her tiny face that was reminiscent of the king's. Or perhaps Tennyson had some premonition that she too would be a "Defender of the Faith."

The Wards were busy in the early years of marriage. Wilfrid published his first volume on his father's life and in 1890 he was appointed a lecturer in philosophy at Ushaw, the Catholic ecclesiastical college near Durham, and an examiner in Mental and Moral Philosophy at the Royal University of Ireland. While he was away from home, Josephine and Maisie visited the Howard aunts. In October 1890 Wilfrid, known as "Boy," was born, and eleven months later came Theresa, who was called Tetta. In that same year, 1891, the family moved to Eastbourne to permanently escape the influence of Edmund. They first lived in a furnished house in Jevington Gardens and then at Molescroft, their home for the next nine years. The strain of the move and the presence of three small children was made worse by the death of Josephine's youngest and most beloved of sisters, Theresa, a Carmelite nun, in November 1891. Two years later, in 1893, Wilfrid's youngest and favorite sister, Margaret, another Carmelite, also died. The loss of such young women pressed on them. Josephine's suffering contributed to the writing of her first major novel, *One Poor Scruple,* published in 1899.

Family responsibilities did not stunt Wilfrid Ward's literary productivity. His career as a biographer was well underway in

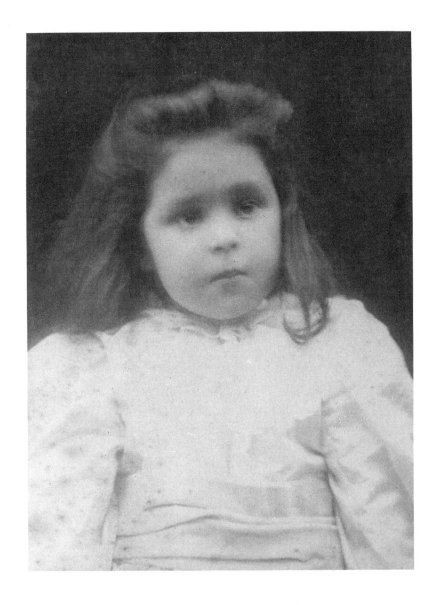

Maisie Ward around the age of four.
Courtesy of the Archives of the University of Notre Dame

the early years of his marriage. His second volume on his father and the Catholic revival came out in 1893. Even before its release he was at work on a two-volume biography of Cardinal Wiseman that Cardinal Vaughan had asked him to write. Josephine had persuaded him to accept this request. Five years in the making, the Wiseman biography won acclaim for Wilfrid and his election to the Athenaeum, the London male club for the intellectual elite. As a Catholic layman of considerable reputation, in 1894 and 1895 he helped obtain permission from Cardinal Vaughan for Catholics to attend the national universities. Having been denied that opportunity himself, he could now offer it to his sons. He would ensure that his sons, Herbert and Leo, born in 1894 and 1896, would attend Balliol and Christ Church, two of the Oxford colleges with which William George Ward had been associated.

In the last decade of the century, it appeared as if the siege were really over and that Catholics could enter into dialogue with other Christians. In 1896 Wilfrid Ward, along with Arthur Balfour, the prominent philosopher and statesmen, founded the Synthetic Society to promote dialogue among Catholics, Anglicans, and Nonconformists. A distinguished group of colleagues, including Henry Sidgwick, Thomas Huxley, Friedrich von Hügel and Father George Tyrrell, met together to find a "working philosophy of religious belief." All this was part of the realization of Ward's hope that Catholic intellectual life and arts could flourish and that the more important battle against anarchy and infidelity would be taken on by all Christians.

The years at Eastbourne were quiet and tranquil ones in spite of a household of five young children and demands for literary productivity. The Wards did not carry on an extensive social life. Eastbourne was out of the way, and among its residents there were few whom the Wards considered their social equals. An exception was Professor Huxley and his wife who lived nearby; although the families had intellectual and religious differences, they became fast friends. Anatole von Hügel, the brother of Friedrich von Hügel, and his wife Isy Froude von Hügel also visited frequently. Anatole was the Curator of the

Museum of Archaeology and Ethnology at Cambridge University, and Isy, a great friend, read all of Josephine's novels in manuscript. A local Catholic family, the Williams, were also visitors. Generally, the Wards wanted to protect themselves from social interaction that distracted them from work. Josephine believed that one should return all social calls, refuse all invitations, and give none. Of course, relatives visited, and there were occasional trips to London, but usually the Wards were at home. Both Wilfrid and Josephine had some limited involvement in the community. Wilfrid trained the choir at the Eastbourne church, and Josephine instructed converts and founded and worked at St. Margaret's, a local settlement house. Their participation in politics was also very circumscribed. They were right of the Tory party, but their great sense of personal responsibility aligned them with political positions that sometimes were akin to that of an older radical tradition. Like most others they believed that the Empire was a power for good, and in the Boer War they were strong jingoists who supported British imperial claims against the Afrikaners.

Maisie spent most of her childhood at Molescroft, where family life followed a set routine. Her father worked four hours in the morning and regularly walked or played golf in the afternoons. He reserved the evening for reading aloud and playing and singing with his children, after which he retired early. He and his wife shared a common dedication to the Church through the vocation of marriage and a common intellectual life expressed in different forms. They read their work aloud to each other and constantly discussed how ideas worked to shape the character and destiny of an individual in biography or in fiction. They were devoted to Newman and from him learned the principles of psychology that they used to explain the Catholic position in their respective genres.

Josephine was busy with motherhood. Her five pregnancies were difficult and she had to retreat to bed with each of them. Yet she managed to be a productive novelist, at least in part to earn extra money for the family. In these early days her work went slowly. She could only steal away to a spare room for two or three hours a day to write. Since Catholic writing in England had been treated with contempt for several centuries, the work of any writer with the Catholic perspective was suspect. Additionally, since the novel was a post-Reformation genre, Josephine had few Catholic models she could follow. She patterned her writing on the English novelists, but they did not share her belief in grace as a power operating in life. By dint of hard work she became a pioneer in a new arena of literary expression, the Catholic novel. Her first major success in this genre, *One Poor Scruple* (1899), took seven years to finish. In it she articulated her conviction that grace was a sanctifying power that suffused all of existence. As a deeply religious woman she used the novel, an accepted form of female expression, as a vehicle for her own theological statement. By doing this she challenged the widely held opinion that women had no place in theological discussion, a position articulated clearly by John Ruskin when he wrote:

> There *is* one dangerous science for women—one which they must indeed beware how they profanely touch—that of theology. Strange, . . . that while they are modest enough to doubt their powers, and pause at the threshold of sciences where every step is demonstrable and sure, they will plunge headlong, and without one thought of incompetency, into that science in which the greatest men have trembled, and the wisest erred.[9]

Although Josephine was a prolific Catholic novelist, she remained a minor figure in English literature, one often confused with the more famous Mrs. Humphrey Ward.

Molescroft was a large, sturdy house with a less-than-adequate garden for children's play. Life at the house went on with the help of a bevy of servants. Old Nanna, the nursery maid, was half Cornish and half Irish. She and the cook tyrannized the rest of the household staff—the housemaid, parlor maid, kitchen maid, and knife-and-boot boy. Although Nanna had considerable authority, Wilfrid and Josephine were involved in the lives of their children much more than was customary among parents of their time and station. "Mumma" read aloud to the children, and taught them reading and religion, which she always tried to make interesting. "Puppa" enlivened evenings with singing, especially the family's great favorites, Gilbert and Sullivan. Both parents took the children on walks over the downs to the sea, which was only fifteen minutes from Molescroft.

Birthdays were favorite celebrations. The birthday child was queen or king for the day and got to choose a special dinner and decide what games were played. Some parts of the year were particularly festive: October and November were the birthday months of Wilfrid and Tetta, Christmas followed in December, and Maisie's birthday fell in January.

Maisie and Boy had a permanent governess for a short time, and the three younger children were cared for by Nanna. Eventually Boy attended a day school, and Maisie and Tetta took lessons from Miss Williams, their Catholic neighbor.

Maisie and her siblings led a protected, tranquil life punctuated by visits to their relatives. There were obligatory calls on Uncle Edmund and invalid Aunts Emily and Gertrude, Wilfrid's sisters. The children would also see Uncle Bernard, their uncle-priest and president of St. Edmund's College, and Agnes, the Abbess of a Benedictine community, who was a great friend of Josephine. With the exception of Mary, a Dominican who founded a convent in Australia and died there, and Margaret, who had died earlier, the Ward children were in contact with all of their aunts and uncles on their father's side. Grandmother Ward lived until 1898 and saw the birth of all five of her grandchildren.

Of the two families, the Ward children preferred the Howards. The Howard household was comprised of Aunt Mary, who kept house for her widower brother Henry and his disabled son, and Aunt Margaret (Peggy), now an invalid. The children loved to visit them at Arundel, particularly at Christmas time when the place was festively decorated. Uncle Henry, the Duke of Norfolk, let them have the run of this huge medieval Gothic castle with its towers, battlements, and vast rooms.

But however warm and affectionate Maisie's family life was, it was lived out in dedication to the dead William George Ward. Important things were required of those who carried his name. A Ward lived by principle, and that meant a life of earnestness and religious scrupulosity. Nonetheless, Maisie's

above. Maisie on swing
with Tetta and "Boy."
Courtesy of
Rosemary Sheed Middleton

left. Maisie at
Freshwater Bay, the
Isle of Wight.
Courtesy of
Rosemary Sheed Middleton

memories of her childhood were generally fond ones,[10] but her inability to be critical of family probably colors her recollections. Her happiness undoubtedly resulted from her sense of security and the attentiveness given her. She especially loved her mother. As a young child she wrote Josephine, "I'm supposed to love mother and father equally, but I love you more than Papa and I can't help it."[11] She considered her mother her confidant, and Josephine regarded Maisie as her eyes and ears among the younger children. Maisie spoke easily of her affection for her mother. "I not only liked my mother, I loved her a great deal better than my father or than anyone in the world. . . . She understood everything and always had time to spare for a long and satisfying conversation."[12] Her relationship with her father was different. Her recollections of him were a mixture of light and darkness: one could have fun with him—with his stories, mimicry, and recitation—but he was also "violent in temperament," "vehement," "rash," and "very excitable."

At the age of six Maisie acquired what was called by some of her Ward relatives that "horrid Howard habit of reading." She was addicted to storybooks, especially Elizabeth Wetheral's *Queechy* and *Wide, Wide World*. In both these books she liked how grownups talked to children about religion, and especially how the young American Methodist heroine of *Queechy*, Fleda, converted a rich English atheist. Scott and Dickens were read aloud to her, and she read them to herself. Her favorite author during these Eastbourne years was Jane Austen, but she also enjoyed Charlotte Yonge and Anthony Trollope.

By her own description, Maisie was a "very conformist child . . . [who wanted] to be a boy—but only because they seemed to have more fun and it was so much easier to climb in knickers than in a skirt."[13] She saw herself as an uncomplicated child. "My own stream flowed . . . placidly. I felt no deep emotions as I said my prayers. I doubt if I ever acquired a complex. I could cry heartily if upset, but it was all over in a few minutes. I accepted my parents' infallibility as well as that of the Church but was not deeply concerned with either."[14] This link between parental and religious authority was pervasive in her life. At the time of her first communion at the age of eleven she spent two days on retreat in a local convent; Josephine went with her.

However golden Maisie's early life, there are nonetheless clues of tension. Maisie adored her mother, but the apple of Josephine's eye was not this eldest daughter on whom she depended, but Boy. His tragic death occurred when Maisie was only thirteen years old. However, in Maisie's formative years her mother's love and hopes centered on the charming Boy. In later life Josephine admitted that he had been her favorite child. His passing created such grief in her life that she was nearly broken. Maisie's desire to please and win the affection of Josephine was played out against her mother's more utilitarian view of her. What Maisie wanted above all else, the devotion of Josephine, she never got. Instead Josephine, who was herself motherless from an early age, turned to her daughter to "mother" her.[15] That inverted relationship formed and bound Maisie for the next quarter of a century.

If Maisie was overshadowed by Boy in her younger years, during adolescence she was upstaged by Tetta, who was more rebellious and who looked to her father for affirmation. Tetta and Maisie were often compared, with Tetta being the "pretty" Miss Ward and Maisie the "clever" one. Herbert, one of the last of the little ones that Maisie watched over, was, like Tetta, rebellious. In adulthood he would have serious problems with alcohol; Tetta would struggle with severe depression.

Leo, the youngest, was more like Maisie in his compliance. Religious and ardent, he wanted to be a priest from the age of eight and after several false starts would be ordained. Following the death of Boy, Josephine transferred her principal affection to Leo, who seemed to have such promise. Ultimately, Leo too would prove psychologically fragile. A recurrent nervous disorder frequently incapacitated him in adulthood, and he frequently required the care of Josephine and Maisie. Leo's mental instability was never diagnosed, although Maisie believed its cause lay in Leo's harsh treatment by the Jesuits.

As Maisie matured she increasingly served as a substitute for her mother. She accompanied her father on social visits and served as his secretary and traveling companion. Intellectually, this would provide her great benefits, but her utilitarian role in the family would also be further solidified.

Maisie admitted that she was a conformist child who obeyed the dictates of parents and culture. Childhood experience also clarified for her the restrictions on females. They should be devout and either enter the convent or marry. Since they did not think of a career, education would be limited. Boys had more fun and their education was more important. These differing gender expectations were lived out in the Ward household. Boy was soon sent from his day school to a boarding school, while Maisie and Tetta first had a day teacher and subsequently attended a local school. Although much was expected of Maisie as a Ward, the restrictions on her as a young woman were clear.

A nursery environment pervaded the Ward household for a long time, and Maisie, the oldest, was influenced accordingly. All that would change in 1901 when, after eleven years in Eastbourne, the family moved to "Lotus" in the town of Dorking in Surrey, a half-way point between London and Arundel. For the next fifteen years Lotus provided Wilfrid and Josephine, both in their prime, with direct access to intellectual and social currents. It would be an exciting and anxious time for them, and the end of Maisie's placid childhood.

TWO

Through the Calm

✳ MAISIE, TETTA, AND THE TWO SMALL BOYS came with their parents to Dorking, but Boy stayed on at his boarding school in Eastbourne. A few months after the move, Boy became sick with influenza that quickly turned into meningitis. Josephine and Wilfrid rushed to Eastbourne, leaving their children in the care of Maude Petre, Josephine's friend. Maisie was determined to see her brother and convinced Maude to bring her to visit him. Maisie saw Boy, but within a few days the seemingly impossible happened; her charming and humorous brother was dead at the age of eleven. This sudden death of a young and beloved child was difficult for everyone, but the loss devastated Josephine. Her suffering was intense; she took to drinking. She later confided to Maisie that she feared she might become an alcoholic in her grief.[1]

Boy died in February 1902. In the spring Mary Howard gave Josephine and Wilfrid a trip to Rome to help them recover. There, in the eternal city, Josephine tried to deal with the meaning of her suffering. Her meditation would become part of her next novel, *Out of Due Time*. While her parents were in Rome, Maisie visited Isy von Hügel and her husband in Cambridge. Their idyllic home, Croft Cottage, was a center of learning and intellectual exchange for students and dons. Although still suffering from her brother's death, Maisie loved being with the von Hügels. She had no sense that she would return to Cambridge as a student in a small convent school a few years later.

The sorrow at Boy's death was great. There was an additional sense of loss of what he might have been—the heir to the

Ward tradition. Baron Friedrich von Hügel captured this feeling in his letter of condolence to Wilfrid:

> I have many a time wondered, with affectionate interest, as to what "Ideal Ward's" grandson and Wilfrid Ward's son, and eldest grandson and son, would turn into. Would he turn out like his grandfather or like his father, in what they had of different qualities and tendencies; or would he be like them both in what they had of likeness; or would he be like some previous progenitor, or some collateral relative, or again, would he be, for the most part, like your wife's, his mother's, or some one of her relations' character and outlook; or would he simply be like himself, starting a more or less fresh Wardian tradition?[2]

With the death of Boy, it must have been assumed that Herbert, but more likely Leo, who was more serious and pious, would carry on the Ward tradition. It never occurred to anyone that Maisie would take up this role.

As was the custom, Josephine, Maisie, and Tetta wore black for a year of mourning. Boy's bedroom became a chapel where visiting priests said mass. One of these priests was Father William Maturin, who had known Boy at school and came to comfort his family. Maturin was an extraordinary preacher and spiritual guide, an Irish convert and former Anglican priest and Cowley father. He became a confidant of the Wards and one of Maisie's earliest mentors. Maturin's magical voice and superb delivery of sermons produced an unforgettable effect on his hearers. He portrayed God as a loving creator who could overcome human malice. This positive theology was paralleled by an optimistic psychology that saw sin as the misuse of God-given power. For Maturin, a Christian should affirm rather than flee life. He preached of vocation and the need of God for each person's work. He advocated a philosophy of integralism that saw the various human faculties of heart, will, and intellect functioning as a whole. In sum, Maturin represented a fresh approach to theology and moral life.

Maisie was mesmerized by Maturin the preacher. Although she did not have a full sense of the implications of his theology, she was aware of his religious and personal vitality. His dramatic

The Ward family.
Left to right, Josephine Ward, Herbert, Leo, Maisie, Wilfrid Ward, and Tetta.
Courtesy of Rosemary Sheed Middleton

death in the sinking of the Lusitania in 1915 (he gave his life belt away so that another might be saved) guaranteed that his memory would endure. Even in death he continued to have an impact on Maisie. When her father died in 1916 she continued his work of editing Maturin's letters; four decades later her abiding interest in Maturin would result in a long biographical piece on him.[3]

As the pain of loss faded, domestic tranquility and intellectual life were restored. Lotus itself was a gracious and pleasant environment for the Wards. The house was roomy and provided a lovely view of the Surrey hills. The big yard was a special delight; azaleas, roses, bamboo, and silver birch trees filled its terraces. As an avid gardener, Josephine loved the place. Here she could try out new seed varieties for planting and establish the cuttings that Anatole von Hügel brought from his exquisite garden in Cambridge. Lotus represented the spaciousness of country-house living. Its large staff offered the Wards and their many house guests a leisured life. Its good location, twenty-five miles from London and twenty-five from Arundel, ensured that there would be many visitors, some of whom would stay as long as a week.

It was in this environment that Wilfrid, now in his mid-forties, and Josephine, nearing forty, carried on their intellectual and domestic life. Wilfrid published *Problems and Persons* in 1902. For the first time he had help with his work in the person of Stuart Dodgson Collingwood, a self-described "scriba privates" and nephew of Lewis Carroll (Charles Dodgson). The book that followed in 1904, *Aubrey De Vere: A Memoir,* was a study of the Irish convert poet and friend of Newman and Wordsworth. This was easy writing compared to the large biography of Cardinal Wiseman published in 1898. When Ward finished the Wiseman book, he had begun to work intermittently on a biography of Newman, but access to important materials was denied him until 1905. Only then did he begin writing in earnest.

The importance of Newman to Ward cannot be overestimated. To Ward, Newman represented Catholic theology at its best and as a bridge to contemporary thought. In his enthusiasm for his subject, Ward could not forsee the many obstacles that would confront him as he was caught up in the larger battle of Modernism, that attempt to bring together the Catholic faith with the methods and assumptions of modern thought.[4]

On the one hand, the situation for English Catholics around 1900 looked better than it had in centuries. The pontificate of Leo XIII (1878–1903) did much good in opening the church to new ideas. The coming of Edward VII to the throne in 1901 meant that, for the first time since the Stuarts, the king was not anti-Catholic. The English Catholic population was growing and its institutional organization was strong. Yet even in the years before the Modernist storm broke in 1907, there were intimations that the free discussion of ideas within the church would not be tolerated. A papal encyclical in 1893 set limits to wide-ranging biblical criticism by Catholics. In 1900 the English Catholic hierarchy issued a joint pastoral letter condemning excessive liberal Catholicism and demanding obedience from the laity.

While Modernism made inroads among Catholic intellectuals, it was never a powerful force among ordinary people. Neither was it as pervasive in England as it was on the continent. Modernist thinking infiltrated Roman Catholicism very gradually. As it did, the orthodoxy of its proponents was challenged. Wilfrid Ward was directly in the center of this controversy, not because he was a Modernist but because he was associated with Father Tyrrell, Maude Petre, and Friedrich von Hügel, the principal actors in English Modernism.

By instinct and intellectual conviction Ward was a conservative. As early as 1903 the liberal Friedrich von Hügel summed up his view of Ward's fundamental orientation. He wrote to him:

> I have quite a number of *living* Catholic scholars and thinkers whom I work with and for, and with whom I am fully prepared to be identified, and by the working with whom I learned so much, even purely spiritually . . . whereas you have some such figures among the dead, but not I think the living, and I do not find that the dead can develop one in the ways I mean.[5]

Later Father Cuthbert, who called Wilfrid Ward "a philosopher of the Church's constitution," wrote of him:

> He could hardly have been a liberal in thought even had he tried, any more than he could have been a democrat in politics. By temperament he was essentially conservative; it required the full weight of his intellectual ability to make him an open-minded conservative, that is to say, a conservative who believes the world has a future as well as a past.[6]

Although conservative, Ward was not a reactionary; he believed the upper classes were natural leaders and that change must be gradual and congruent with the past. Cautious and suspicious of the Modernists, he nonetheless supported free discussion. However the vitriolic encyclical *Pascendi,* which condemned Modernism, left him little room to maneuver.

Since the Ward household was filled with discussion of Modernism, the adolescent Maisie was aware of the parameters of the debate. But her focus was on school and the concerns of youth. Her family and her Catholic convent school at Dorking insulated her from the larger world. Social barriers severely limited her interaction, although Josephine insisted that those barriers be lowered for people who worked within the church. Throughout her life Maisie assumed equality with those who were allies in faith.

Maisie's pleasures outside school consisted of reading, acting in plays, walking, and singing. Since she was tone-deaf, her musical achievement was limited. Creating and acting in plays was another matter. With the help of their father, the Ward children revised the children's stories of "Sleeping Beauty" and "Cinderella," weaving into them quotes from Shakespeare, Sheridan, Pope, and Tennyson. The plays were then performed at Lotus, Arundel Castle, in London, and in Cambridge for small audiences of family and friends. Above all, Maisie loved to read. This love had been nurtured by her parents. The reading aloud of Dickens and other authors by Josephine or Wilfrid was a family ritual, carried out continuously during the years at Molescroft and Lotus. It was an observance that brought alive characters and the values they embodied, such as Dickens' Sissy Jupe:

But, happy Sissy's happy children loving her; all children loving her; she, grown learned in childish lore; thinking no innocent and pretty fancy ever to be despised; trying hard to know her humbler fellow-creatures, and to beautify their lives of machinery and reality with those imaginative graces and delights without which the heart of infancy will wither up, the sturdiest physical manhood will be morally stark death, and the plainest national prosperity figures can show will be the Writing on the Wall—she holding this course as part of no fantastic vow, or bond, or brotherhood, or sisterhood, or pledge, or covenant, or fancy dress, or fancy fair, but simply as a duty to be done.[7]

Maisie's favorite authors, Dickens, the Brontës, and Jane Austen, remained her favorites throughout her life. She loved Dickens' attacks against poverty and injustice and his understanding of society as a unified whole—a social, physical, moral organism in which all parts interacted and influenced all others. She admired the Brontës for their critique of the position of women. Like Dickens, they offered no remedies, but they raised the question and forced society to think about the condition of single women. Jane Austen's *Pride and Prejudice* was, to her lights, the greatest novel ever written. In it the hard reality of life for single women was confronted with optimism and courage:

> Without thinking highly either of men or of matrimony, marriage had always been her object; it was the only honourable provision for well-educated young women of small fortune, and however uncertain of giving happiness, must be their pleasantest preservative from want.[8]

As she moved into young adulthood it became increasingly clear to Maisie that the single life was a real liability for women. Marriage, however, was still a remote ideal; in practice she knew nothing of men, romance, or sex. The latter was never discussed at home. The one indication that she understood romantic love, at least intellectually, was her devotion to Robert Browning's poetry. She took up its study at the age of twelve and learned much of it by heart. Browning remained a lifelong interest of hers and became the subject of a two-volume biography she wrote in her late seventies.

When the Wards moved to Lotus in 1901, Maisie and Tetta enrolled at the nearby convent school as day students. Soon afterwards Josephine wrote to Aunt Mary Howard regarding Maisie's reaction. "Maisie has fallen a complete victim to the conventual system and the tone of her voice had changed in a week. She would become the model Convent girl with terrible rapidity."[9] The curriculum at the school was narrow: the study of the Gospels and Acts, French, German, music, and Shakespeare. But Josephine, fearing the convent mentality, where poorly educated nuns refused to vitally discuss religion, insisted that her girls be exempt from classes in religion; instead, she taught them at home. Sister Domitila, the school's head nun, required that her pupils take exams in the assigned subjects. Josephine forbade this, maintaining that she did not want her girls to become competitive. Maisie later complained that examinations might have improved their education, which she came to regard as uniformly inferior.

Maisie's recollections of her early education were dim, although she did recall that she wrote an essay on the fifteenth-century Florentine reformer, Savonarola, her favorite hero. One wonders whether it was his power of oratory, his antimaterialism, or his zealous religiosity that attracted her. Perhaps all three claimed her admiration.

Isy and Anatole von Hügel were frequent visitors at Lotus. In 1905 when Maisie was confirmed as Mary Josephine Paul Francis Philip Ward, Isy was her sponsor. By that time, Maisie's desire to go to a school in Cambridge was strong. When Aunt Anne Kerr and her daughter Minna visited from Scotland in 1903, Maisie and Minna became devoted friends. Subsequently, Minna enrolled at the St. Mary's Convent School in Cambridge. In September 1905, the sixteen-year-old Maisie followed. She was elated.

The Mary Ward nuns of the Institute of the Blessed Virgin Mary who ran the school had come to Cambridge from York.[10] The purpose of their school was to immerse young Catholic women in the atmosphere of a religious community for a few years. The school was small, with about twelve students. Most came from the aristocracy, the upper middle classes, or from abroad and stayed only two or three years. Although the object of this education was principally religious and cultural, it provided remarkably good training in a few subjects. Maisie studied Latin, Scripture, logic, French, and English. She considered Revered Mother Mary Salome, a scholar of the life of Mary Ward, the Institute's foundress, and Sister Mary Aquinas first-rate teachers who inspired her to learn. Monsignor Nolan, her Latin teacher and head of St. Edmund's House, saw great potential in Maisie as a Latin scholar. Under his tutelage she studied Horace and Tacitus; when she gained Distinction in Latin (in addition to logic, French, and English) on the Cambridge Senior, a certifying examination, Monsignor Nolan was delighted.

Although the curriculum at St. Mary's was limited, the one-and-a-half years that Maisie spent there were broadening ones for her, and her parents' influence over her was confronted for the first time. As Revered Mother Salome observed, "If I say anything different from what your parents have told you, your disapproval is very obvious. I like you for this but you will learn in time that there may be two quite good ways of looking at a thing."[11] Maisie's narrowness was also challenged by lectures given by academic friends of the nuns. Concerts, visits to York (the memorial city of Mary Ward), and perhaps archaeological digs and visits to the nearby botanical gardens all expanded her horizons. She also enjoyed the intellectual exchange she encountered at the home of Anatole and Isy von Hügel.

During these brief Cambridge years another powerful influence, that of Father Hugh Benson, shaped Maisie's life. Like Father Maturin, Benson impressed her through his preaching. Son of the Archbishop of Canterbury, a convert, and a superb orator, Benson cast his spell over many ardent students, including Evelyn Underhill and Pierre Tielhard de Chardin. Maisie, hearing him preach at the local parish church and lecture at the convent, wrote home to her mother about him. She constantly compared him with Father Maturin, whom she considered the superior of the two, probably because he was a long-time family friend.

Benson's two books, *Religion of the Plain Man* (1907) and *Christ in the Church* (1913), suggest both the style and content of his sermons, which aimed to enliven in his listeners a desire to know the doctrines of the faith, especially the doctrine of the Mystical Body. While the writings of St. Paul, the church fathers, and the Schoolmen contained this doctrine, since the Protestant Reformation it had lost its prominence as the church struggled to reassert its authority and build up its organization. By the late nineteenth century, however, the doctrine re-emerged. Through it the church was represented as the living mystical body of Christ in which each of its members realized its fulfillment in the whole. This doctrine, which came alive for Maisie in the sermons of Benson, became a central and defining tenet of her religious understanding. Just as Father Maturin had given her a positive theology and psychology, Benson resurrected a doctrine from the church's history that became a means by which she could understand the church, Christ, and her relationship to others.

Also a powerful influence on Maisie during these Cambridge years was that of the life of the founder of the Institute of the Blessed Virgin Mary, Mary Ward.[12] Although Maisie would live to see the vindication of Mary Ward as "an incomparable woman" and a model for women in the lay apostolate, for most of history Mary Ward was reviled and scorned. In the seventeenth century Mary Ward attempted to establish a women's religious order without enclosure. Attacked by Protestants and spurned by the Jesuits and Catholic clergy, she was imprisoned and condemned to death. Although given a reprieve, she died a failure, her religious houses broken up and her nuns scattered. In her suffering she endured what she called "the long loneliness"[13] as she gave her life to sustain Roman Catholicism in England. The influence of this courageous woman impressed the young Maisie, and soon after she left the Cambridge school she reviewed a book about her in the *Dublin Review*. Later she would also write two articles on Mary Ward's thought and life.[14]

Maisie left the convent school in December 1906, having been head girl since the previous summer. She departed not because her education was finished but because she would be eighteen years old in January. It was time to move on to the next stage of female life: presentation at a London social season.

While she had been away in Cambridge, her parents' lives had become more complex and stressful. Wilfrid Ward became the editor of the *Dublin Review* in 1906, when the *Review* was at a low ebb. As such, he was directly in the center of Catholic intellectual life. His intent was to create a vehicle to express a large Christian humanism that would engage both Catholics and non-Catholics, a goal very different from that of his father, who had been editor from 1860 to 1888. While Catholic in intent, the *Review* published articles on science, travel, history, and literature, as well as religious topics. As its editor, Wilfrid Ward usually wrote the lead article and some reviews; for other pieces he enlisted the help of major writers. But Josephine, his brother Bernard, and eventually even Maisie and Tetta contributed.

By the first decade of the 1900s, there was increased tension in intellectual circles about what theological issues Catholics were allowed to discuss. In 1902 the French Modernist Abbé Loisy published *L'Évangile et L'Église*, which aroused strong Church opposition. In England Friedrich von Hügel defended Loisy's right to present his ideas as a Catholic, but the new pope, Pius X, placed all of Loisy's work on the Index. A papal encyclical issued in 1906 condemned insubordination among the Italian clergy, and in England Father George Tyrrell, the leading proponent of Modernist ideas, was dismissed from the Jesuits. The stage was set for a full-scale attack by the papacy on Modernism in the following year. Wilfrid Ward's position both as editor of the *Dublin Review* and as biographer of Newman made him particularly vulnerable to scrutiny. Newman was accused of being a Modernist by anti-Modernists and hailed as a Modernist by Modernist supporters. Ward tried to walk between these two camps but found himself in the thick of controversy.[15]

As a prominent lay Catholic intellectual, Wilfrid Ward grew increasingly anxious. In 1906 he declined Friedrich von Hügel's invitation to join the London Society for the Study of Religion, his argument being that there were fewer Catholics in the group than Anglicans and that public disagreement among Catholic members might lessen respect for the Church. His trepidation would increase in the next few years.

As Ward's position became more precarious, Josephine, who had nerves of steel, responded by writing about the oblique origins of Modernism in her novel, *Out of Due Time*. Although the novel depicted Félicité de Lamennais, the French priest and philosopher, and an earlier break in the Church in the 1830s, it gave a historical perspective on the impending crisis of Modernism. The novel's theological theme was the power of suffering to sanctify others. As a woman who had endured the deaths of her sister and her young son, Josephine understood the meaning of suffering and its ability to transform.

While Wilfrid and Josephine wrestled with the shifting currents of religious thought and the political and personal implications, Maisie had a decision about her own future to make; lamentably, she did not make it. Instead, she drifted, pushed by convention and her need to please her parents, rather than by her growing awareness of her own capabilities.

When Maisie passed the Latin Cambridge Senior Certificate Examination with Distinction, Monsignor Nolan urged her to study at the university. Her options were restricted. Cambridge University was oriented toward mathematics and science and did not admit women. London University allowed women to matriculate, but it was too secular for a Catholic woman to attend. To go to the university meant to attend Oxford, where at least Catholics had some connection. Women attended Oxford lectures in the first decades of this century, but a chaperon had to accompany them and they could not enroll in a degree-granting program. Dorothy L. Sayers, for example, finished her university studies in 1912 but was not awarded an Oxford degree until 1920. Vera Brittain and other women who had attended Oxford during the war also had to wait to be awarded their degrees.

The Ward family affirmed society's view that a young woman did not need a university education. Such education was the requisite for a profession, and women did not have professions. Moreover, anyone could secure appropriate education through experience. Wilfrid Ward was himself a perfect example of this; he had not attended a university but was considered an intellectual nonetheless. While Josephine might allow her daughter to take competitive examinations in the calm atmosphere of St. Mary's school, she did not think it necessary or proper to be in a university atmosphere with men. Both she and Isy von Hügel believed that men and women should occupy separate spheres. They were repelled by the "bluestocking" female intellectuals they encountered.

On leaving her school at Cambridge, Maisie hoped that some new intellectual horizons would appear. Her parents had controlled every aspect of her life until now, including the selection of her reading material. Hoping for the best, she returned to Dorking with a collection of French and Latin books to be used to prepare for matriculation at Oxford. But she was incapable of moving toward that goal. She waited for direction from her parents, who had no plan for her other than participation in the requisite London social season.

Maisie's parents said she should wait, not that she could never go to Oxford. "I imagine had I fought for it [to go to Oxford] I should have won," she wrote years later.[16] But fighting her parents' wishes was impossible. No matter how much she might want to attend university, she wanted most their approval and support. She did what they suggested and only years later would lament her loss.

In retrospect, Maisie claimed that her father unconsciously made the same mistake with her that his father had made with him; out of fear that their Catholic children would be corrupted by Oxford, they refused them entrance.[17] However valid this might have been in her case, such fear was overcome in the case of her younger brothers, Herbert and Leo, both of whom attended Oxford. Maisie recognized, although she was incapable of saying it forthrightly, that other reasons came into play as well. She discovered in reading about her father's work with the Commission of Higher Education in Ireland that he was the only commissioner who did not ask about women's education.[18] While there was no question that her brothers would attend university, Maisie, a Catholic woman, had to wait on other prospects. Gender and religion combined to decide her fate.

At eighteen, Maisie was ready to be presented to society. What she was not prepared for were the years of indecision, banality, and lack of direction that lay before her. The calm of her youth would be replaced by the ennui of young adulthood.

THREE

"The Years the Locusts Have Eaten"

❋ IN 1907 THE WARDS RENTED A HOUSE in London for several months so that Maisie could participate in the social season. To succeed in this ritual one had to take social life seriously. Maisie did not. She was absolutely hopeless at small talk with either male or female contemporaries. Nor did she work at dressing correctly, maintaining a good figure, or improving her dancing. She went through the motions of the London presentation as was expected of her, but her heart was not in it. Neither was her heart engaged elsewhere. Maisie was without aim or purpose. Her inherited spacious and free life made possible endless desultory activity. She traveled to Constantinople to visit her uncle, who was the British ambassador; the exotic Turkish bazaars and cultural festivities charmed her. She went on to Paris, Brittany, and Florence. Back at home she took up flower–making and embroidery, played tennis, studied the history of Florence and the writings of Dante, volunteered for bazaars, read novels, canvassed for a Conservative party election, and worked at a settlement house at Mile End. This diffuse activity amounted to very little, although at Mile End she met someone who inspired her—Sybil Smyth Piggott, who ardently gave herself to the care of retarded children. Years later Maisie claimed that in Sybil Piggott she saw faith shining through.[1] But on the whole, these were difficult years, "years the locusts have eaten," years in which "the leisured life . . . left too much room for the narrower choices but precluded—unless you were very strong-minded—a large one."[2] For a woman known for her strongmindedness, Maisie's passivity can only be explained by her emotional and social attachment to her parents and her inability to break or even stretch her ties with them. As she waited, presumably for marriage, it was her parents' lives that gave hers structure and meaning. Marriage did not happen, and so she squandered her young adult life.

From 1906 on Wilfrid Ward's two commitments were his massive biography of Newman and the *Dublin Review*. Since he needed help with both, Maisie was enlisted as his personal secretary and traveling companion to conferences abroad. She spent her days in the company of her father and came to understand the world as he did. As a consequence, she was profoundly influenced by his views. Josephine became concerned that her daughter might be overworked, and she saw to it that Maisie's secretarial work was cut back. Still, since Wilfrid needed a traveling companion and Josephine was unwilling to be one, Maisie continued to accompany him on his travels.

Intellectual life dominated the Ward household. There were visits from Hilaire Belloc, who lived close by, Frances and Gilbert Chesterton, who came to have a great impact on Maisie's life, and George Wyndham. For a time, friends—the Reginald Balfour family—and relatives—the O'Conor family—came to live with the Wards. Yet Wilfrid and Josephine's literary output did not flag. Josephine published *The Job Secretary* in 1911 and *Horace Blake* in 1913. Wilfrid produced *Ten Personal Studies* in 1908, the two-volume *Life of John Henry Cardinal Newman* in 1912, and *Men and Matters* in 1914, all the while serving as editor of the *Dublin Review*.

The spirit of John Henry Newman dominated the Ward household throughout these years. Wilfrid had grown up disputing with his father about Newman, but in his own household he and Josephine were devoted to the man whom they considered the greatest Catholic mind of their times. Since the Wards' attitude toward Newman was reverential, it was no wonder that Maisie would revere him as well and, like her father, write his biography.

The weight of being the official interpreter of Newman fell heavily on Wilfrid Ward. He believed that the best biography was written by one who actually knew his subject and who aimed at giving the reader a knowledge of the person that friends had of him in real life. Love and sympathy were needed to portray the greatness of a man.[3] Since Ward was convinced that a biographer must live "in" the person about whom he is writing, his life was increasingly dominated by his subject. Under any circumstances this undertaking would have been monumental, but these were not ordinary times, nor was mere biographical interpretation at stake.

By the time Ward took up the Newman biography in earnest, the Modernist crisis was full-blown and suspicion was cast on all Catholic intellectuals, the living and the dead. Newman came under fire. Was he a Modernist? Some argued yes and faulted Ward for *not* interpreting him as one. Others argued no and criticized Ward *for* interpreting him as one. The outcome was important because Ward had staked his intellectual life on Newman. He had sided with him against his father on the question of papal authority, and he defended Newman as the one great hope to bridge Catholic thought to the secular world. If Newman were a Modernist, so was Ward. The prospect of a condemnation of Newman drove Ward into a frenzy. His emotional balance was threatened, and he continued to have nightmares until the biography was published. His suffering was compounded by the fact that his Modernist friends worked against him.

Ward's intellectual position was untenable. In his mind he needed both to defer to the authority of the church and to defend Newman. Since he believed that the encyclical had condemned Newman's ideas, he tried in both discussion and in writing to separate Newman from Modernist thought. He argued that the doctrines condemned by the encyclical were only those that appeared in Modernist writings per se.[4] While he maintained that one had to accept and obey the encyclical in order to preserve the church, he also believed that church prelates should not give intellectuals instruction. For Ward,

Newman saw far more in Catholicism than the Pope did. Thus Aquinas (too) saw more than Innocent III. Edmund Burke saw more in the English constitution than did George III. It is the thinkers who see the full significance of institutions. . . . The Pope is an official, not a philosopher.[5]

As the individual condemnation of Modernist thinkers began, Ward went into a depression. His own position as editor of the *Dublin Review* was precarious. Heresy-hunting was in full force; many new books were added to the Index and Ward's personal enemies were vocal. It hurt him to be called a "liberal" on the one hand and "an official mind" on the other. He felt very lonely in what he considered his moderate position. He argued that he would not resign from the *Review* because to do so was to acknowledge that he was a Modernist and allow his opponents to gain control of the journal. He considered it his obligation as editor to help his readers through the morass.

Although Ward viewed his position as a middle way, he clearly failed to give decisive leadership as a Catholic intellectual. He urged obedience to orthodoxy and demanded that the encyclical be explained more fully. He felt oppressed, betrayed, and defensive. Maisie internalized these feelings; they would color her subsequent interpretation of her father's life. Josephine took a tough approach. To her mind the Modernists were "confused" and were injuring her husband and threatening his reputation. She blamed Friedrich von Hügel for leading Tyrrell to Modernism in the first place.[6]

Modernism provided the opportunity for a battle between thinkers and officials. The result was an extraordinarily painful episode that curtailed intellectual life among Catholic thinkers for decades and nearly broke Wilfrid Ward. Since Cardinal Bourne was not particularly eager to be a heresy-hunter, he prevented the condemnation of von Hügel and continued, although tepidly, to support Ward as editor of the *Dublin Review*. Gradually the purge ended. Some had been expelled from the church, some left, and others who had been attracted to the church decided not join. Those who remained did so on terms that they obey. The great hope of Newman and Ward to reconnect Catholic belief to modern thought was dashed.

For better or worse, Catholic intellectuals were forced again to turn inward. Exhausted by controversy, they found some consolation in the ascension of Benedict XIV to the papacy in 1914. The new pope urged Catholics to cease condemning fellow believers. By September 1914 the attack of Catholics on Catholics faded as attention turned to the more lethal viciousness of the war engaging all Europe.

Ward continued to work on his biography of Newman throughout the Modernist crisis. *The Life of John Henry, Cardinal Newman,* finally appeared in 1912, some years after the worst of the controversy had passed. It was hailed as a brilliant treatment of Newman, the spiritual and intellectual genius of the nineteenth century. The acclaim brought Ward some sense of relief and vindication after seven years of labor and worry. He traveled that year to Switzerland and to Brittany, and he and Maisie made a special trip to Sienna, where they visited the Italian priest, Don Nazareno Orlandi, who worked with the city's street urchins. This beautiful Tuscan town with its steep hills must have flooded Maisie with thoughts about its most famous saints, Catherine and Bernardino. Two years later she would publish her first book, the biography and sermons of Bernardino, Sienna's most renowned preacher.

Maisie had been asked by a Jesuit, Father Goodier, to write a book on Bernardino as one of a series on saints he was editing for the Herder publishing company. Since she had little else to do, she took up the task eagerly. To be a Ward was to be a writer; the book provided the first opportunity to try out her abilities. Since Herbert had now gone off to Oxford, any hope that her parents would send their older daughter there was irrevocably ended. Anyway, at twenty-four she was too old to begin such study. Since her father was lecturing in America, she was not occupied in assisting him. She plunged into work at the British Museum. She only realized in retrospect her inadequacy in dealing with the source materials she found there.

Her book was both a life of Bernardino and a compilation of some of his sermons, none of which had been published in England. She was determined not to write hagiography but rather to give a vivid picture of this Sienese people's preacher.[7] Like her biographer father, Maisie tried to immerse herself in the life and thought of this popular Franciscan reformer.

Much like Savonarola, Bernardino attacked the pomp and corruption of the towns of early fifteenth-century Italy. Although he was a scholar, his genius was in the simplicity of his preaching, which transformed individuals and ended divisions and hatred. Accused of heresy, he bowed to church authority, only to be cleared of the charges against him. He triumphantly carried the Holy Name of Jesus throughout Italy, where town after town begged him to be its bishop. His mission, however, was to preach and therefore to keep faith alive in the world.

Maisie had resonated with many great preachers in her life—Maturin, Benson, Savonarola, and now Bernardino. Each had captured her imagination, preparing her subliminally for her own future vocation. But at twenty-four she was still without direction. Of course, her parents' hope was that she would meet an appropriate marriage partner. She seemed unconcerned with this matter. The only man in whom she showed the slightest interest was Walter Moberly, whom she visited when she went to Oxford to see Herbert. Moberly was a tutor at Lincoln College and friend of Wilfrid Ward. He had read sections of Ward's biography of Newman in manuscript, and although he was more modern in social outlook than Ward, the older man approved of him. Moberly was an Anglican, and while Maisie admitted that she saw the very best of the Church of England through him, their religious difference may have been an impediment to the development of a permanent relationship. None did develop.

Maisie remembers her mid-twenties as a time of stock-taking. One of her aunts brought her to visit a newly opened Carmelite convent, but she shuddered at the idea of young girls in such places. A religious vocation never seemed to attract her.

"I had everything to make me happy yet really fundamentally I wasn't," she wrote retrospectively about this period. "I enjoyed an immense number of things in life, but I had a vague unsatisfied ambition and . . . time often hung heavy on my hands."[8] After almost seven years, the war intervened and finally give some meaning to what had become a vacuous life.

Wilfrid Ward was in America again in early 1914, giving lectures on Newman and his old friend, Tennyson. He had worked hard to write these lectures and had them critiqued by his family and his brother Bernard. Lecturing was enjoyable, and Ward was thrilled to see his name on the marquee. He only lamented that he had not begun this work years before. His travel took him to cities up and down the east coast and as far west as Cincinnati and Detroit, where he met many prominent American Catholics. In Philadelphia he was introduced to the convert, Maria Brown Bullitt, and a General Smith, both of whose families would welcome Maisie to America years later. Even when war broke out, Ward felt he had to honor his commitment to return to America in 1915, this time to give lectures on the nature of biography at American universities, including Harvard and Yale.

Father Maturin, who had been in Philadelphia for several years, hoped that he and Ward could return to England together. Ward, however, was committed to giving the Royal Institute Lectures that spring and had to sail before his friend. When Maturin returned in May 1915, it was on the ill-fated Lusitania, sunk by the Germans during its crossing. The Wards mourned the loss of this beloved preacher and family friend. As a memorial, Ward devoted himself to arranging Maturin's sermons for publication.

On his return to England, Ward found his family engaged in the war effort. Josephine entertained soldiers at Lotus and later visited hospitals, worked at the Admiralty, and helped reorganize the Catholic Soldiers' Association. Herbert, a member of the Officer's Training Corps at Oxford, had been shipped off to India. Leo was still at school but was eager to volunteer as a soldier the next year. He was rejected because of his health, however, and entered Oxford instead. Tetta worked with refugees in London under the auspices of the Red Cross and later with the Catholic Women's League in France. She would see more of the war than would Maisie, who took up nursing British soldiers in an Italian hospital run by the Sisters of Charity in London. This work was enjoyable even though it introduced her to a life of practicality she had not known previously. She learned how to wash dishes, scrub floors, and make beds. She also came to understand that many of the nuns with whom she worked had found their vocations by default. Her assumption that all nuns had a commitment to piety and service was shattered.

The widespread enthusiasm for the war effort must have been a welcome relief after years of personal aimlessness. However, while the war gave Maisie something to do, it did not broaden or change her. She never saw the war firsthand and, unlike her contemporary Vera Brittain, never experienced a self-transformation because of it. Her world continued to be narrow, hemmed in, and very Catholic.

When Wilfrid arrived home in early 1915 he had more to contend with than his scheduled lectures and a general concern for the war. There was some talk that the *Dublin Review* should have a new editor; ultimately nothing came of it, but the prospect worried him. In the midst of this he also had to publish the next issue of the *Review,* write an article for the *Quarterly,* arrange Maturin's sermons, and work on his own reminiscences. In September 1915 his elder brother Edmund Granville died while undergoing an operation. Within a month of his brother's death, Wilfrid became ill himself, but he gave little attention to his symptoms because of his preoccupation with his brother's will.

Edmund's will awarded huge legacies to various charitable and religious entities, including convents, bishops, and diocesan charities, as well as to various family members—but not to Wilfrid Ward. In order to pay the legacies Wilfrid was forced to sell many of the Isle of Wight properties that he had expected to pass on to his sons. No one understood why Edmund would exclude his brother from an inheritance. In retrospect, Maisie speculated that Edmund had a graphic fear of hell and believed endowing religious institutions would ensure him perpetual prayers. She also believed he might have been driven by revenge: as the eldest son, he was furious at being defined as

Wilfrid Ward's brother. By Edmund's denying Wilfrid any inheritance and by endowing his other siblings himself, Edmund guaranteed that no one would look to Wilfrid. The dead Edmund would be their benefactor.[9] Whatever the reasons for the will, it created a particularly difficult situation for Wilfrid, who by contesting it, placed himself in opposition to Catholic bishops, nuns, and priests, including his Abbess sister and Bishop brother.

The stress on Wilfrid was tremendous and he became physically weak. As his symptoms worsened, the doctors recommended that he enter a nursing home. Further investigation revealed that he had inoperable cancer. The news prompted Maisie to leave the war hospital and Tetta to return from France. Josephine and her daughters took rooms near Wilfrid's nursing home and waited for the end. It came quickly. By April 1916 Wilfrid Ward was dead. No compromise on the will had been reached.

The Ward family was now without its center. Wilfrid's vital and robust personality, his gift for conversation, his singing, his passionate intellectual commitment, were gone. For Maisie, sorrow at her father's death was mixed with indignation at her uncles—Edmund for his will and Bernard for believing that once Wilfrid died his family would cease to contest Edmund's will, which excluded them while it endowed him. Herbert came home from the war to press for a legal compromise among the parties. Although Maisie returned to work at the Italian hospital, she was mentally in a stupor and after a short period left her work there. While visiting her Aunt Emily Ward on the Isle of Wight, her fear of losing the family properties came to the fore. She remembered that, unable to sleep, she randomly opened the New Testament to read from Paul: "We are sons of God. And if sons, heirs also, heirs with Christ." The stupidity of her concern over the estate and the aimlessness of her life rushed before her. She felt deep remorse for the years she had lost.[10]

At the suggestion of her Aunt Gwendy, the Duchess of Norfolk, Maisie took up work in a hospital for incurable soldiers in Littlehampton for six months. This seemed to her like a time of distancing from her past, but no immediate relief was in sight.

The death in February 1917 of Uncle Henry, the Duke of Norfolk and her mother's beloved surrogate father, added to both Josephine and Maisie's despondency. The only good news during this time was that a compromise was finally reached over Edmund's will.[11]

The year 1917 was devastating in terms of war news. New conscripts were needed constantly. Leo, studying at Christ Church, Oxford, was finally called up after several unsuccessful tries. Josephine and Maisie dedicated themselves to making a home for the soldier Leo, first in Cambridge and then in Southhampton. There was no reason to keep Lotus any longer, so Josephine put it up for sale. Symbolically this meant the end of seventeen years of family unity.

By 1918 there was some relief for the family from the ongoing strain. The most happy event was the marriage of Tetta to Francis Blundell of Crosby, a Lancashire Catholic, who would serve later as a Tory M.P. Their home at Little Crosby, the faithful Catholic village, would come to have special meaning for Maisie. With Tetta gone and Herbert and Leo involved in the war, Josephine and Maisie spent the year in a rented house in London. Together they worked to ready for publication Wilfrid's last lectures, along with a memoir of him by Josephine. November mercifully brought the end of the protracted war. Herbert returned to England and took up residence at Egypt House on the Isle of Wight. Leo returned too, and for the interim lived with his mother and sister as he waited to be accepted as a priest in the Westminster diocese. Only Maisie, now twenty-nine, was without direction. But her years of aimlessness were about to end. Finally, her formidable energy would be harnessed to an ideal, and the unique Ward heritage, which well might have ended, would be carried forward in a new direction.

FOUR

"A Future . . . Almost Too Bright to Look At"

❋ ALTHOUGH YEARS OF AIMLESSNESS wearied Maisie Ward, they did not weaken her active and zealous personality. Once she clarified her vocation, she held back nothing. Since her world was centered in Roman Catholicism, the church provided her sole object of dedication. It was for her the vehicle of salvation and the manifestation of the Body of Christ on earth. Maisie's genius was to interpret these beliefs outwardly and thereby reject the stultifying spirituality that kept English Catholics insular and cut off from the larger society. It was inconceivable to her that she could know the truth and keep it to herself.

Although she would become a defender of the faith, her motivation was more apostolic than apologetic, an orientation inherited from her mother, who through her life and writing inculcated this in her daughter. Maisie must have particularly valued this advice in one of Josephine's novels: "I want to ask you to-night," wrote Josephine, "to include the whole world in your ambition. You will never come out of yourself enough to be strong; you will never have faith enough for yourself if you have not faith for others. Never say 'I want to save myself,' say 'I want to save the world.' That is the only horizon worthy of a Christian for it is the horizon of Charity."[1]

Unbelief was not an option for Maisie. Her experience was too narrow, and Catholic doctrine and family culture too emotionally tenacious for her to reject them. Her only options were commitment or tepidity, and Maisie was incapable of the latter. Although cursed with indirection as a young adult, once she

49

found something to which she could give herself, she did it ardently and without reserve.

The personal decisions of Maisie's life were made against the backdrop of postwar Europe. With the Great War ended, many longed for peace and expected spiritual revival. Four years of slaughter of Christian by Christian promoted both a decline in the influence of most churches and a search for spiritual meaning both in and outside institutional religion. True, the condemnation of Modernism ensured that Catholicism continued to be cut off from larger intellectual currents. But the church's devotional life was more robust after the turn of the century, largely because of new emphasis on the Eucharist. This new confidence would express itself in a desire for religious renewal.

Josephine, Maisie, and Leo Ward were all interested in this renewal. At Oxford Leo had met Christopher Dawson and E. I. Watkin. After the war Dawson and Watkin became part of a group organized by Josephine and Algernon Cecil to discuss means to revive postwar spiritual life. Father Cuthbert, a long-time friend of the Wards, headed the group and Maisie was its secretary. In 1920 the group published a collection of essays entitled *God and the Supernatural: A Catholic Statement of the Christian Faith*. Three of its contributors—Dawson, Watkin, and Ronald Knox—were converts, while Fathers Cuthbert, C. C. Martindale and Martin D'Arcy also contributed to the collection. The authors proposed that Catholicism was the answer to the contemporary spiritual malaise because it alone among religious systems adhered to the supernatural as its starting point. Written not for theologians but ordinary believers, *God and the Supernatural* was a precursor of the literature of the Catholic intellectual renaissance that would emerge in the next decade.[2] Although neither Josephine nor Maisie wrote essays for the volume, they must have been greatly influenced by its creation.

Maisie's serious postwar writing project was completing the edition of Father Maturin's letters which her father had begun before his death. Consequently, in the years immediately after the war Maisie was immersed in the life and ideas of this great preacher as well as the ideas of contemporary English Catholic intellectuals attempting to make Catholicism relevant to modern society. Unconsciously she was being prepared for the first important vocational commitment of her life, membership in the Catholic Evidence Guild.

Maisie came to the Guild through Leo, then living in London with her and Josephine prior to going to Rome to study for the priesthood. One day in 1919 he burst into their home with the news that he had encountered a group of Catholics preaching in the park. Maisie went to investigate and soon after signed on as a charter member of the C.E.G. Joining was analogous to conversion; it was like "lifting shutters in my mind" she wrote later. Leo and Josephine soon followed suit.

In November 1920, unbeknownst to Maisie, a young Australian law student, Francis Joseph Sheed, came to England. After finishing two years of law school at the University of Sydney, Sheed had decided to visit England and perhaps "do something" about the Irish question. He planned to return to Australia after a year. Within two weeks of his arrival in London he encountered the Catholic Evidence Guild and was so taken with its mission that he decided to stay on. He joined the Guild and, in order to pay living expenses, secured a position as an organizing secretary of the Catholic Truth Society's Forward Movement, a job he kept for three years.[3] With his small salary he was able to support himself and his mother, whom he had brought over from Australia.

There are two stories about the meeting of Maisie Ward and Frank Sheed, both of which are consistent and connected to the Guild. One is that Frank tried to sell Maisie a pair of defective scissors at a C.E.G bazaar and she turned them down. Another is that Maisie, an experienced speaker, had the newly arrived Australian assigned to her C.E.G. squad. She was impressed with his lecturing ability and the fact that he knew Latin; they struck up a friendship. It was Frank who first knew that he wanted to marry Maisie.[4]

Although they immediately shared much, Frank Sheed was an unlikely match for Maisie Ward. Younger by eight years, he was also emotionally and socially different from her. Whereas Maisie was retiring in social situations, Frank was an extrovert who was always on stage—talking, joking, singing. Women idolized him for his idealism, his charisma, and intelligence. He admired their intelligence. Throughout his life Frank always had a flock of female devotees surrounding him.

Frank's early life was also at complete variance with what Maisie had experienced. Not only was he an Australian of largely Irish descent, he was born into a family in religious conflict. His father was from a Presbyterian background with a particular animosity toward Roman Catholics. John Sheed was a quasi-Marxist who sent Frank and his brother, Jack, to a Methodist Sunday school. Intelligent, charming, and sarcastic, John Sheed was also a boozer, a gambler, and probably a womanizer. In his relationship to his sons, Frank and John (Jack), he was sometimes physically brutal, particularly to the latter.[5] He had married Mary (Min) Maloney, a devoted Irish Catholic woman, who came from England to Australia when she was thirteen. Their marriage was a difficult one, and Min and her sons left John Sheed several times. From his father Frank acquired his intelligence and ability to argue logically. In opposition to him he became a lifelong teetotaler and a believer in fidelity in marriage. From his mother he inherited a tough piety and unswerving faith in the Catholic Church. She ensured that her sons secretly attended mass and received the sacraments. From both his parents he gained a wonderful sense of fun and merriment, although his father's anger always lay under the surface.

Frank was conservative in a different way than Maisie. He thought of the empire and the church as ordering institutions. He distrusted all politicians, believing they were always deceptive. He tried to be apolitical, and except for one Australian election, he never voted. He turned his energies toward the church. In high school in Sydney he read Chesterton and Belloc, who revolutionized his world view. Here were laymen who were intellectual, aggressive, and religious; he loved their fearlessness and their high spirits.

When Frank arrived in London, he too was searching for some meaningful cause. At least for a time he thought vaguely of involving himself in the Irish struggle. Since a career in law had never really captured his imagination, he then toyed with the idea of working toward a Ph.D. and writing a thesis on the

Irish literary contribution.[6] Within weeks he joined the Guild and became fast friends with Maisie. He was intoxicated by this new world which introduced him to a theology he had never heard before. The ideas of the Mystical Body and the supernatural life were completely revolutionary and ignited his evangelical conviction. In the C.E.G. he was in his element.

The Catholic Evidence Guild was a unique organization, founded in 1918 by a New Zealander, Vernon Redwood. Although outdoor platform lecturing was a well-established part of secular English life, it was not until 1894 that Lister Drummond first gave lectures on Catholicism on the platform in Hyde Park.[7] The C.E.G adopted the secular outdoor lecturing format for its own purpose. Following the scriptural command —Go ye and teach—the Guild encouraged Catholics to speak out to overcome centuries of fear and to defuse hostility against them from lapsed Catholics, Protestants, and nonbelievers.

The formation of the Guild in 1918 was part of a much larger movement to enliven Catholicism in England. In 1884 the Catholic Truth Society was founded to distribute Catholic pamphlets of all kinds, and The Catholic Missionary Society was organized eighteen years later to serve Catholic missions in the English countryside. The Guild, with its mission to proclaim the faith outdoors, developed along diocesan lines, had the approval of the local bishop, and involved wide participation of laity.[8]

These Catholic organizations linked themselves to a more robust devotional life that was developing among the faithful after the turn of the century. There was a growing sense of church unity as Catholics became more sacramental in practice and more mystical in doctrine. In some ways this reinforced a triumphalistic view of the church, but in other ways the emphasis on the Eucharist and the Mystical Body opened up the possibility of a unique sense of self-understanding among Roman Catholics. This interest in devotional life, however, coexisted with the prohibition on free discussion of ideas and with continued ecclesiastical authoritarianism.

The reigning spirituality of personal sanctification through individual piety began to be challenged by the doctrine of the church as the Mystical Body of Christ, which promoted a great sense of communal responsibility. Although it was not officially promulgated as a doctrine until the early 1940s, its impact was noticeable in England in the first decade of the century through the preaching of Robert Hugh Benson. Inherent in the doctrine was the notion that participants in that Body, i.e. all Catholics, had a responsibility to act as Christ's body in the world. One strengthened one's participation in the Mystical Body through the Eucharist. Although the implications of lay responsibility, Eucharistic devotion, and the church as the presence of God on earth were only hinted at, they were available in incipient form to believers.[9] Organizations such as the Catholic Evidence Guild were important lay forums in which the implications of these religious beliefs could be examined.

The initial purpose of the C.E.G was to defend the faith in the context of outdoor speaking. Its methodology evolved from defense of Catholicism, to proof of it, to explanation of the faith. In order to achieve its end, Guild members had to undertake religious education. The C.E.G both systematically presented the faith and trained and educated laity. Its greatest success was not the converts it won or the lapsed Catholics it reclaimed but its education of believers.

From the start the Guild's approach was intellectual rather than emotional. While Guild presentations were often highly charged and speakers were heckled, the intent was to explore doctrine and to do so without attacking other religions. While the Guild tried to be open, it existed within a triumphalistic Catholicism. Guild songs illustrated this:

> Come all ye faithful Christian men
> and join the gladsome throng
> of those who hold that time is short,
> Eternity is long.

> The Pope who is infallible
> and seldom goes far wrong
> has always thought that time is short
> Eternity is long.

> And Lambeth thinks there is a sense
> In which 'tis not too strong

To say that time to us seems short,
Eternity seems long.

But some there are who tremble lest,
the march of modern thought
may one day prove that time is long
Eternity is short.

We are the sweet selected few
The rest of you are damned
There's room enough in Hell for you
We can't have Heaven crammed.[10]

Although some clergy participated, the Guild was dominated by lay people. The local bishop was nominal president,
but the organization was run by officers elected by members.
Cardinal Bourne, who oversaw the Guild in the Westminster
diocese in its early days, was very interested in lay organizations
and supported the C.E.G against the hostility of clergy and laity
who feared lay-speaking and evangelical causes.

Guild membership crossed class lines. The poor and the
well-heeled shared the platform. Josephine Ward trained and
lectured, as did the charismatic Louisa Cozens, a self-educated
cockney cleaning woman who subsequently wrote a book on
heresies. Most members were relatively young and unmarried.
Women made up at least half the guild but there was opposition
to them holding office. In 1922 Maisie ran for Chairman of the
Practical Training Committee when there were no men to serve.
She won the race but the opposition to her election was considerable.[11] Nonetheless, to a remarkable degree class and gender
barriers were lower in the Guild than in society at large.[12]

Because Maisie and Frank were both natural speakers and
had joined the Guild soon after its founding, they quickly assumed leadership roles. The theological direction of the Westminster Guild was guided by three clerics: the Dutch priest, Dr.
Arendzen, a scholar and apologist; Father Bevan, an Oratorian
who established a close relationship with Guild members; and
Father Martindale, a Jesuit scholar who moved the Guild from
its early apologetic orientation to a more theological one.[13] All

three became friends of Maisie and Frank, although Fathers
Bevan and Martindale were closest to them.

The demands on Guild members were extensive. They received training at least two nights a week and usually lectured
on a weekday evening and up to three times on the weekend.
Lecturing was exhausting and exhilarating. In all kinds of
weather members had to gather and retain an easily bored and
occasionally aggressive crowd. Although hecklers were distract-
ing and sometimes violent, they played a positive role in holding
a crowd and creating the basis for interaction. Frequent practice
in these arduous circumstances quickly made one an excellent
speaker. Tom Burns, an early C.E.G. member, remembers how
all speakers dreaded taking the platform, but once one's time
was over it was bliss, and the camaraderie among members
was tremendous.[14] All speakers were assigned to squads, which
were responsible for several hours of lecturing each week at a
specific park. Squad members encouraged one another, critiqued performances, and provided fellowship.

Guild members had a marvelous esprit de corps. They spent
much of their free time together—praying, studying, and prac-
tising preaching. The guild was both community and work.
Members often lived with each other. They brought their
friends and family into the Guild and sometimes intermarried.
The Guild became a way of life for all its participants, including
the dedicated Maisie and Frank.

Maisie's active commitment to the Guild continued for
forty-eight years. Membership in the Guild was analogous for
her to a religious vocation. It provided a spiritual discipline that
included the prayer of self-offering and gratitude, daily communion, study and preparation, and the practice of the presence of God. For her, if Guild work were to be done right then
one's whole life had to be dedicated to it, much as if one had
joined a religious order.[15] Maisie obviously craved the dedicated life; in 1921 or even earlier, she also joined the Third
Order Dominicans, an association of lay persons committed to
following the modified rule of the Dominican order.[16]

Maisie and Frank assumed various roles in the C.E.G. over
the years. He was Master of the Guild in the early 1920s, and

she was in charge of training in the classroom and on the street corner. Both helped shape Guild policy. Maisie was particularly adamant that lectures should be nonconfrontational, dialogical, and expository, not defensive.[17] She believed in a positive approach which did not attack an individual but rather attempted to identify what was in the mind of the hearer. She insisted that the Guild develop a rule never to attack another's religion or laugh at a questioner. Since she was always forthright and spoke her mind, she sometimes found herself in the position of having to apologize to a heckler.[18] But her intent was to win over the person rather than to be victor in an argument: "Hence we must try very hard to find out exactly what is in their minds," she wrote. "We must remember all the time [the] immense language barrier. We must engage in dialogue. You are asked a question—but what does it mean? What is in the questioner's mind? There is no such thing as a question, there is only a questioner."[19] "We are perhaps the only Catholics they know: we must give ourselves and with ourselves truth. It is far worse to lose a person than an argument."[20]

According to Maisie, Guild members needed to arouse the crowd's interest in interpreting their own lives and the reason for their existence. Doctrines were to be presented not as mere thoughts or beliefs but as a way of life and an organic totality. In this presentation of Catholicism the most central doctrine was the Supernatural Life, which gives meaning to everything. Supernatural Life needed to be shown in action as it energized the lives of Christ and the saints and as the key to the meaning of ordinary life. Unless this doctrine could be understood, all Catholicism remained opaque.

The theological and practical aspects of Guild training were compiled by Maisie in *The Catholic Evidence Training Outlines*, which was published by the Catholic Truth Society and used to train new members in other parts of England and in the United States.[21] The *Outlines* prepared speakers to know their subject and to deal with a variety of questions from the crowd. The doctrinal issues covered were broad, including the Bible, the church, the pope, the Mystical Body of Christ, the Supernatural Life, the sacraments, the Eucharist, and two favorites of the hecklers—persecution and the Virgin Mary. Although Guild members repeatedly wrestled with the application of doctrine to political and social questions, they ultimately agreed to speak only on doctrine and to bypass its divisive concrete applications.

Training to become a Guild speaker lasted between six and twelve months. This training gave one an Ordinary License, which meant one could speak on limited subjects. Training for five or six years gave one a General License, which permitted one to speak and answer questions on all subjects. All members were asked to study, practice speaking, read Scripture, attempt to understand the crowd, accept criticism, and spend as much time in prayer before the Blessed Sacrament as they spent speaking on the outdoor platform. The objective of the training was to show that "God matters," that belief changes life. Only when the speaker had actually understood the meaning of the doctrine personally could it be translated to the crowd. As Frank claimed, the message and the speaker reached the hearer together. The point was to bring the speaker and hearer together into a union of minds. For him the "outdoor crowd was a school of theology." He saw the speaker as "making love to his audience."[22]

The reality, of course, was something else. The chairman of a squad began an outdoor session with a prayer and then attempted to draw a crowd. There was not much to draw one except for a speaker's podium inscribed with the words—"Catholic Evidence Guild" and an affixed crucifix. The pattern was always the same. The chairman would turn the platform over to the first squad speaker, who would speak for ten to fifteen minutes and then take questions. The next speaker continued in the same way, while other squad members prayed silently. When the crowd died away, or the hecklers got particularly fierce, the chairman would take the platform again. The session concluded with the praying of the Apostles' Creed.

The C.E.G. was a vocation for Maisie Ward and Frank Sheed. It gave direction to their lives, deepened their faith, and enhanced their influence on others; it also made them excellent speakers. The significance of the Guild in Catholic intellectual life is another matter. Numerically it was a tiny movement, reaching its height about 1931 and then declining.[23] Its success in winning over converts or reclaiming lapsed Catholics was not great. However, as a grassroots movement of lay women and men who expounded on the faith in an outdoor setting it was innovative. As a movement of religious education it supported the study of doctrine by ordinary people. The Guild presented Catholicism as an intellectually credible system of belief that could transform lives. Although the word "preaching" was shunned, participants explained doctrine, discussed scripture, and gave witness. In fact, they preached. The Catholic Evidence Guild was an uncommon institution for its time, and it shaped the lives of Maisie and Frank in uncommon ways.

Although most of Maisie's Guild friends were lay people, some were clerics. As a member of the English Catholic gentry, clergy did not awe her. She respected them, but she was unafraid to criticize them. There was nothing that irritated her more than poor sermons given by uninformed priests. Her best relationships with clergy were with the clerics who guided the C.E.G.—Fathers Arendzen, Bevan, Martindale—and the Irish Dominican Vincent McNabb, who was also active in the Guild.

McNabb was another superb preacher who made a profound impact on Maisie. He was a colorful figure who wore his habit when he lectured at Marble Arch, even though it was illegal to do so. With boundless energy, he served a parish, wrote thirty books, and lectured widely in addition to preaching. He had a particular interest in the working class and called for a return to a simple way of life, away from the cities. Like Chesterton and Belloc, McNabb defended the Distributist movement's call for the redistribution of property, the rejection of mechanized labor, and the end to government restriction. Fearful of both capitalism and communism, Distributists urged self-sufficiency through a back-to-the-land movement. McNabb and the Distributists would have a lasting effect on Maisie and influenced her love affair with farming.

During her first years in the Guild, Maisie lived with her mother and three servants at 5 Pelham Place, a fashionable London address. She lectured at least twice a week, trained speakers, organized the Guild's *Outlines,* and worked for the

Catholic Truth Society as an honorary librarian and editor of publications. With Josephine, she also tried to keep up family ties. Tetta was living with her husband at Little Crosby, and for the moment all seemed well with them. Herbert lived on the Isle of Wight, where he was involved in a variety of civic causes. Maisie knew of his increasing addiction to alcohol and tried to convince him to seek a cure; meanwhile she kept this information from Josephine. Leo was training as a novice at the Jesuit seminary. He presented no concern to Maisie and Josephine until 1923, when he had a complete nervous collapse and left the order.

In order to recover, Leo went to Switzerland, where Maisie visited him. When he returned to Freshwater on the Isle of Wight in 1924, Josephine nursed him back to health. For the time being, Leo gave up the idea of becoming a priest and actually proposed marriage to a woman, but she turned him down. He began to work for the Catholic Truth Society and hoped to return to lecturing with the Guild when his health improved. His psychological fragility took its toll on his family. Maisie, until the very last years of her life, carried a resentment toward the Jesuits for what she believed they had done to Leo by demanding too much of him in the exact practice of the Ignatian Spiritual Exercises.

By the fall of 1924 Frank had been in England for three years. If he were to finish his law degree he would need to return to Australia soon. He had stayed in England because of the Guild and Maisie. As early as 1921 it was clear to Maisie that their friendship was very special. "I won't face the suggestion that our friendship is only for the summer," she wrote him at the end of 1921.[24]

What was it that this woman, inheritor of the Ward tradition, saw in this young, admittedly charming Aussie of no particular pedigree? Frank ignited in her a renewed commitment to the ideals she cherished. "I know you sympathize profoundly in my passionate wish to be a Catholic first and everything else afterwards," she wrote.[25] They shared a commitment to Catholicism and a vocation, outdoor-speaking for the faith. "I'm going to try to and I want you to try to write a prayer for us to say every morning of self-offering and utter dependence on God. Also, gratitude for being allowed to do this work."[26] Sometimes she was unbelieving of Frank's affection. At one point she asked straight out, "Am I what you want?"[27] Apparently she was, because Frank proposed on August 15, 1924, the Feast of the Assumption. Two and a half months later he sailed with his mother back to Australia. When he left, Maisie had not yet responded to his proposal. She needed time.

Frank returned to Australia via America, where he had lecturing engagements in Ontario, New York, Washington, Chicago, Portland, San Francisco, and Oklahoma. His outdoor lecturing in London had attracted the attention of several American clerics, who arranged these tours. Frank had no sense of the role America would play in his future. In fact, his view of America was not entirely positive. He found American Catholicism divided by politics and ethnic rivalries. Even the religious orders competed with each other. In his estimate this was not a hospitable environment for the development of the C.E.G.[28]

Frank returned to Sydney and persuaded the law school officials to allow him to cram his remaining two years of course work into one. He supported himself by teaching two hours every morning at St. Aloysius College and twice a week at night at the Workers' Educational Association. He spent his spare time founding the Catholic Evidence Guild in Sydney. It soon became evident to him that although he had skill as a lawyer, he did not love the law as much as the Guild. But while the Guild was his calling, it did not earn money. His problem was professional, vocational, and geographical. What was he to do and where?

While Frank was in Australia, Maisie and Josephine kept up their outdoor lecturing in London. Since the end of the war Josephine had been preoccupied with the weariness which had come over the nation. Two of her postwar novels, *Not Known Here* (1921) and *The Plague of His Own Heart* (1925), dealt with this theme. Early in the 1920s she visited Italy and became fascinated by Mussolini. His ability to keep ideals alive in Italy and to offer an alternative to the futility of other nations was captured in *The Shadow of Mussolini,* which she published in

1927. These novels, her Guild work, and her organization of the group that produced *God and the Supernatural* all showed her preoccupation with the need to revivify spiritual ideals. The best way to achieve that goal had yet to be found.

With Frank's departure, Josephine and Maisie went to Lourdes to pray over the marriage proposal. Tetta had married well enough, but Francis Sheed was not Francis Blundell. Even though Josephine liked Frank, the hiatus between his proposal and Maisie's acceptance indicates that the marriage needed discussion between mother and daughter. Josephine had agreed to her own marriage reluctantly, but then made it a means of vocation to the intellectual life of the Church. Could Maisie do likewise?

Maisie was thirty-five years old when Frank proposed. She had never had a marriage offer and there were no other suitors at hand.[29] She had no desire to enter a convent and no desire to marry for marriage's sake, although she was convinced that life was unfair to single women.[30] It was marriage to Frank or nothing at all. And Maisie's acceptance would be difficult for Josephine, since she would lose her daughter's constant companionship. Then there was the additional problem of the couple's location. Where would Maisie and Frank live? Australia, America, England? Frank felt they had to spend at least the first couple of years in Australia or perhaps America, where he could practice law, but that later they could return to England permanently.[31] Josephine wanted her daughter, who for decades had acted as her mother, settled nearby. After Frank announced his intention to marry her daughter, Josephine wrote to him: "That cable does not only change your life & Maisie's but my own and your mother's not a little. The fact is that Maisie has mothered me ever since I lost my eldest boy when she suddenly grew up & undertook me."[32] If Maisie were to stay in England, then suitable work for Frank had to be found. The question was how to arrange this.

Maisie's letters to Frank in Australia are filled with the details of daily life. She writes endlessly of problems in the Guild, of Herbert who is drinking too much, of her weight gain, of

Leo's nerves. She rejoices in her lightheartedness, something she hardly knew before she met him. She encourages him to pray, to go to mass, and to offer it for their love. She jokingly says others think she has refused many offers of marriage and that she better let him think that too so as to enhance her value in his eyes. She speaks frequently of her conflict of duties to her mother and the Guild and how difficult it would be to fulfill those duties if she went to live in Australia or America.

By March 1925 Maisie had reached a decision. For Frank's birthday she sent a telegram to Sydney. "Yes[,] Carisseme. Happy Birthday." Maisie had agreed to marry; her affirmation meant everything to him. And his meant everything to her. Although Maisie had the confidence and security of her family lineage and the certitude of religious belief, it was Frank's love that made all the difference.

Her letters to Frank in 1925 and 1926 are ardent and full of eagerness for him. Having recently read her mother's pamphlet, *Marriage: A Dialogue,* which ends with a discussion of marriage as a sacrament, Maisie was sure she knew the secret of marital bliss. She wrote to Frank: "Dear, we have got that secret."[33] "No, Frank, I don't believe we could have married apart from the church, etc. You see that is what has made us and we should have been different beings without it."[34] She knew from the start it would be a wonderful marriage and almost prophetically she wrote: ". . . [O]ne glorious thing is that we shall have all our lives one series of honeymoons[,] for every trip we can snatch in busy lives will be a honeymoon."[35]

However elated she was at the prospect of marrying Frank, Maisie felt it was necessary to assure Frank's mother of her devotion to her son. "There is no one good enough for Frank," she wrote Min, "but I will try. I do want to make you happy."[36] The immediate questions of where to live and what work to do were not yet resolved. "I'm tempted," she wrote Frank, "to wish for money so we could live anywhere and work for the church always[,] but temptation passes."[37] She was sure that since their own happiness was not in doubt, they could make the church, the Guild, and their mothers their top priorities.[38] Guild work was paramount; it "is the biggest and most glorious thing on earth," she wrote, "and God is very good to us to let us belong to it."[39] But how were they to support themselves? Maisie was not sure whether Frank just wanted a law degree or whether he actually intended to use it.[40] As for place, she seemed willing to go to Australia or America, but how then would she fulfill her responsibilities to the Guild and her mother?

These questions about work and locale were answered in April 1925 when Josephine proposed that Frank join with Leo to start a publishing business.[41] From Josephine's point of view this resolved the dilemma of employment both for her son-in-law and her son and would also keep her daughter close by. If the publishing business did not work out, Frank could pursue it part-time or fall back on the law. Since the priesthood seemed no longer an option for Leo after his nervous collapse, he could be a publisher of Catholic books. Josephine felt sure that the team of Frank and Leo would be a good one,[42] and she was willing to put up the capital for the venture. Furthermore, a Catholic publishing firm which produced books rather than prayer manuals and rosaries would help stimulate a Catholic intellectual revival in England. As a novelist Josephine knew the loneliness and isolation of Catholic writers. Most, like herself, published with non-Catholic firms. If a Catholic house were established, it would unify Catholic publishing and encourage authors. Additionally, the excellent continental Catholic writing could be translated and would reach English audiences.

As a writer and a friend of writers, Josephine was knowledgeable about the publishing business. In considering her idea she talked to a variety of publishers, including a Mr. Thring of the Authors' Society, who insisted that what was needed was "flair." Both Josephine and Maisie agreed that Frank had that.[43] Writing was a Ward's business, so why not a firm to produce what one wrote? As it turned out, Josephine's last two books would be published by Sheed & Ward. Tetta Blundell, publishing under the pseudonym Wingfield Hope, would also bring out several books under that imprint. Leo's one book, *The Catholic Church and the Appeal to Reason*, was published by MacMillan in 1926, before Sheed & Ward began its operation.

The original vision of Sheed & Ward was Josephine's. With Ward contacts and capital and Frank's "flair," it was an idea with promise. It followed logically from Guild work in which Frank, Maisie, Leo, and Josephine had all been engaged. In order to grow in faith one had to read, and to that end shouldn't one read the very best in English and continental theological writing? Frank was delighted to undertake the project. He wrote to Maisie telling her how this offer fit into his aspirations for global service.

> I'm returning to that old dream of mine: that you and I may yet work in *all* the English speaking countries: spending a certain time in each place, and working on the Guild and the schools & even the C.T.S. [Catholic Truth Society]. The dream seems a little nearer realization for the publishing scheme. Truly I think we have a wonderful future of useful work for the Faith. . . .[44]

Frank and Maisie were concerned about Leo, however. He lacked business acumen, and Maisie was worried that he wanted to publish apologetic material. It soon became obvious that Leo was not up to the work. Sheed & Ward quickly evolved to include the other Ward, namely Maisie, who had experience as a writer and as an editor of Catholic Truth publications.

As soon as Maisie agreed to Frank's proposal of marriage in March 1925, he sent an engagement ring through the mail. Their marriage was officially announced in November 1925. In the meantime Maisie set to work to make arrangements for the wedding and for the return of Frank, which was still a year off.

Even though she had joined the Guild before she met Frank, everyone, including Maisie, believed that he had rescued her, a plain woman, from spinsterhood and a desultory existence. For the rest of her life she was grateful to him for having saved her and for having made a new and larger life possible. But it was not only Maisie who considered herself saved. For Frank, marriage had been unthinkable before he met Maisie.[45] The fact that she was thirty-six years old did not seem to bother him. He told her to think of herself as twenty-six.[46] Frank also valued the fact that he would be connected by marriage to the Wards and to the Duke of Norfolk. By association he gained what he himself did not have—a certain status among Catholic intellectuals.[47] The son of John and Min Sheed had done well indeed.

The love letters of Maisie and Frank are filled with testaments of their affection for each other and often closed with the Latin, "In aeterum et ultra"—i.a.e.u., to eternity and beyond. Maisie told Frank that she could only marry a man superior to herself in all respects, one who was more than Maisie Ward's husband.[48] He felt pressed to achieve a notoriety of his own so that she might become an appendage to it.[49] Maisie's letters to Frank are filled with confessions of her inadequacies. "Dear I had a lot of heart searching yesterday. I realized I wasn't praying properly & I linked that on with my general disagreeableness. Frank I solemnly know I'm not nearly good enough for you—and the woman ought to be the best!! especially the most pious. I've been trying to make resolutions & I'm looking to your improving me."[50] In these letters she admits her many domestic shortcomings and indicates that she thought about taking a course at a School of Domestic Science, but she never got around to it. In fact, for the rest of her life Maisie would never get around to domesticity; there were too many other things that were more important. It is her eager anticipation of their life together that dominates these letters. The idea of the publishing firm excited her because that would mean they could share almost all of their work. She asked whether she should look for a home with an office. By July she found a flat at 68 Albany Mansions and secured the services of a maid, a fellow Guild member. Her dream of a little cottage for the two of them would have to wait.[51]

The wedding was planned for the end of April 1926. William T. Cotter, the very Irish Bishop of Portsmouth, had agreed to officiate, and the young Lady Catherine Howard (later Phillips) and Gravernor Hewins, son of the founder of the London School of Economics, able lawyer and Master of the Guild, were bridesmaid and best man. Herbert would give Maisie away.

Frank finished his law examinations in April and arrived in Plymouth on April 21, six days before the wedding. He was awarded his law degree in absentia from the University of Sydney on April 24. In order to meet him, Maisie, in Cowes for wedding preparations, had to travel to London and then to Plymouth. Frank stopped in London to inspect their flat and to meet with Hilaire Belloc, who was very excited about the establishment of the publishing firm. Belloc, a great friend of Josephine and Frank, agreed to give them a manuscript of his poems for publication, and Father Martindale presented the manuscript of his *Christ is King* as a wedding gift. Josephine promised to come aboard as an author as soon as she was free from existing publishing commitments. Surely Chesterton could be persuaded to participate as well.

On the eve of their wedding Frank met some twenty new relatives; he charmed them all. On that same night Maisie, who had been schooled in Victorian prudery and otherworldliness, was told of the facts of life, which somehow had escaped her all these years.[52] If Frank is to be believed, her emotional development was prepubescent when they first met,[53] but her love apparently overcame these initial limitations.

Their wedding day was sunny, and the small, dignified church of St. Thomas of Canterbury was a lovely setting for the marriage. The reception that followed at Egypt House was a lively affair. The parting of Maisie and her mother was difficult, however. Josephine admitted that she felt jealousy at the loss of her daughter,[54] but she was gaining a son-in-law she respected and Maisie was not lost to Australia or America.

Maisie and Frank's honeymoon first took them to Paris, and then to Venice, Rome, and the Italian lake country. This was the beginning of the honeymoon that Maisie hoped would last for the rest of her life. Previously she had told Frank that what she liked best in his letters was him saying over and over again how much he loved her.[55] Now she had his love permanently, and as she had told him years earlier, his love and friendship gave her "a sense of peace and security."[56] The love of Frank was the missing piece in Maisie's life; once she found it there was no turning back. Several years before, she had written words that now seemed to be coming true: "What a future we have ahead of us; almost too bright to look at."[57]

FIVE

"The Blissful Catholic Summer of the Twenties"

✳ The bright future Maisie Ward expected arrived almost immediately. The founding of Sheed & Ward in October 1926 catapulted her and Frank into the Catholic intellectual revival that was in full force on the Continent. These were heady and exhilarating times as their firm became the means by which that revival made its way to England and later to America.

Sheed & Ward began inauspiciously with an office in Paternoster Row in the shadow of St. Paul's Cathedral. The company had 2,600 pounds in capital, no telephone or electricity, packing crates for office furniture, and only Herbert's car to distribute its wares. From the beginning its ownership was a family affair.[1] The staff included Frank, a clerk, a salesman, a manager, a business manager, and some packers, none of whom knew anything about publishing. Hilaire Belloc was brought on as an adviser and for his name.[2] Unfortunately, none of his counsel was helpful. The only useful advice came from Stanley Unwin's recently published *The Truth About Publishing* that Frank read for its pragmatic suggestions on how to run a publishing business.

Sheed & Ward attracted energetic and spirited people who worked fiendishly hard and received little pay. Characterized as a cross between "a sweat-shop and a university,"[3] the firm was known for its "Catholic gaiety." The "wit, humor and high spirits" of the staff bespoke Catholic confidence.[4] No matter the conditions, long hours, and low compensation, the work of Sheed & Ward was considered a noble cause by its staff, and that made all the difference.

The connection between C.E.G. and Sheed & Ward was strong from the beginning. Tom Burns, the managing editor for ten years, and Edward Connor, the no-nonsense business manager who stayed on for decades, were both Guild members. Many Sheed & Ward staff would bridge these two organizations; once engaged with one, they signed on with the other.

The firm's audience was a specific one. As Frank said, they aimed "just above the middle of the brow"[5]—that is, at the educated lay person and the clergy who liked to read. Their only Catholic competitor was Burns, Oates and Washbourne, but it dealt mostly with official church publications and devotional books. Major publishers like Longmans sometimes published Catholic writers, but there was no all-Catholic publishing house. Sheed & Ward filled the gap not with religious books per se, but books written by thinking Catholics. To Catholics and non-Catholics alike it offered the best in Catholic writing. Its publication list soon included philosophy, biography, history, poetry, essays, novels, drama, short stories, sociology, devotional writing, morals and scripture—but initially not much theology. These publications reflected the historical reality of the condemnation of Modernism, which meant that Catholic intellectual life was forced to find modes of expression that avoided head-on confrontation on theological issues.

Frank called this period "the blissful Catholic summer of the twenties." The spiritual revival that began after World War I brought numbers of converts to Catholicism, many of whom were intellectuals who used their literary skills in the service of their new belief. In France, where the revival began, the writings of Leon Bloy, Paul Claudel, Charles Péguy, Jacques Maritain, and Étienne Gilson served as a resource for Catholic intellectual life. Their influence spread to German theologians such as Romano Guardini and Karl Adam, and finally to England, where Sheed & Ward made available translations of these continental writers while simultaneously encouraging English ones.

This infusion of foreign literature helped stimulate English Catholic writers, who had their own insular and defensive history to contend with. During the twenties the most influential were Gilbert Chesterton and Hilaire Belloc who, while different in orientation, were seen from the outside as representing a triumphalistic, high-spirited Catholicism that reveled in contradiction. Their aggressive style was maintained by a celebrated rivalry between George Bernard Shaw and Chesterton in one camp, and H. G. Wells and Belloc in the other. On all sides there was a certitude of the rightness of one's position. The Chester-Belloc spirit infected Sheed & Ward and was evident in its very first publication, Belloc's attack against Wells' *Outline History of the World.* Belloc's *A Companion to Mr. Wells' Outline of History* (1926) criticized Wells' work and exposed its anti-Catholic sentiments.

But the Chester-Belloc spirit was not the only one operative at Sheed & Ward. From the very beginning, C. C. Martindale, Ronald Knox, Christopher Dawson, and E. I. Watkin were also influential.[6] These men, each of whom had contributed to *God and the Supernatural,* became Sheed & Ward authors. Theirs was a less combative spirit that placed emphasis on the spiritual, especially the importance of the supernatural life and the doctrine of the Mystical Body. Martindale was the first to become associated with the firm, with the publication of his manuscript of *Christ is King* (1926), his wedding gift to the Sheeds. Knox, who began publishing with the firm in 1927, continued as one of its authors for thirty years; he had more books on the Sheed & Ward list than any other author. Dawson and Watkin were prolific writers and great friends of Maisie, who sought their advice on all of her manuscripts. In fact, Maisie claimed that while her early intellectual life was shaped by Browning, Newman, and Chesterton, the most powerful influence on her thinking at middle age was Christopher Dawson.[7]

The triumphalism of Chesterton and Belloc was challenged in the late 1920s by Tom Burns, who, independent of Sheed & Ward, organized a Catholic salon including Dawson, Father D'Arcy, Bernard Wall, Alick Dru, Harmon Grisewood, and the poet David Jones, among others.[8] Under Burns' leadership the group, joined by the likes of Eric Gill, brought out in little more than a year five issues of a new magazine called *Order.* Its purpose was to counter the general sectarian and narrow religious press and to support publication of all kinds of intellectual and creative work, no matter what its denominational character. Dawson, D'Arcy, Wall, Dru, Grisewood, Jones, and Gill each became associated subsequently with Sheed & Ward. Although *Order* was short-lived, it prompted Burns and Dawson to coedit a series, *Essays in Order,* under the auspices of Sheed & Ward. The series began in 1931 with Maritain's *Religion and Culture* and continued until 1934 with thirteen other publications. Each was stamped with the woodcut of a "stag set free," a colophon created by David Jones. The series' purpose as laid out by Dawson in his introduction was

> to attempt to face the problems which arise from this new situation [the collapse of the old order] and to examine the possibilities of co-operation and of conflict that exist between the Catholic order and the new world. . . . Yet it would be equally impossible to dismiss the problems of the modern world as though they had no meaning for those whose lives were based on the supernatural certitude of the Christian faith. The Puritan or the sectarian Christian can isolate himself from the age in which he lives and construct a private world in harmony with his religious convictions. But for the Catholic this should be impossible. Catholicism stands essentially for a universal order in which every good and every truth of the natural or the social order can find a place."[9]

The promise of this series was to help Catholics engage with the modern world and to assure them that Catholicism, an ordering and unifying system of thought and belief, offered the way out of the modern dilemma. Much as in *God and the Supernatural, Essays in Order* suggested that Catholicism was the key to human meaning in the contemporary world.

In its early years Sheed & Ward expanded rapidly. To start with, a backlog of French and German books waited to be translated. In addition, the postwar converts who poured into the church, many of whom were intellectuals, were eager to write about their belief. In little over a year after its founding, Sheed & Ward had almost one hundred titles in print. In 1928 it began the first Catholic Book of the Month Club, and in 1931 it listed almost two hundred books.[10] By founding Sheed & Ward, Maisie and Frank created another institution dedicated to the conversion of England. As the Guild won believers through the spoken word, Sheed & Ward would do it through the written one. Their successes gave them reason for euphoria.

The goal of Sheed & Ward was to provide books that awakened the reader to truth. "And as publishers," Maisie wrote, "we felt always that our choice of books must be such as to build a deeper awareness of God among Christians and try to awaken it from the depths of those pagan minds which, after all, were God's creation."[11] But neither the nobility of this goal nor the availability of books ensured financial success. During its early years the firm was always financially precarious. In part this stemmed from policy. "If Frank Sheed and I had anything in common," wrote Tom Burns, "it was the conviction that the quality and relevance of a book were what counted in the decision to publish or not to publish. Its financial prospects came second."[12] Maisie attributed their financial difficulties to the fact of their rapid success. They published too much, too fast, and were always in need of liquid capital that they did not have.[13]

Maisie, as the vice president of the company, spent her time selecting, editing, and translating manuscripts, cultivating authors, and drawing up their contracts. She did not involve herself in financial matters directly. Only gradually did people realize that the Ward of Sheed & Ward was a woman. Beachcomber's [J. B. Morton] comic column in the *Daily Express* ran this confused jingle during the firm's early years: "When I am in my direst need; I seek the help of Mr. Sheed. But much prefer when I am bored, the company of Mr. Ward."[14]

Several months after the founding of Sheed & Ward, Maisie became pregnant. Before her marriage she hoped that given her age and the fact that there are so many other things to do she would not have children. But she came to realize that "marriage makes one desire children."[15] The pregnancy was difficult. She grew enormously large and almost had a miscarriage. She and Frank, and virtually everyone who knew their desire, hoped for a boy to carry on in Wilfrid Ward and Frank Sheed's steps. But in 1927 on October 18, the feast of St. Luke, Rosemary Luke was born at home. Min was named godmother and Herbert godfather. Congratulatory letters poured in, lamenting the baby's gender but consoling Maisie that she had reproduced herself in Rosemary. Tetta wrote overjoyed that Maisie had a daughter and a pretty one at that.[16]

Immediately after the birth Maisie became very ill. The baby was taken to Josephine's home. Blood clots developed in Maisie's legs and arm and in a lung, which collapsed. Her temperature rose to dangerous levels. Her only comfort was in the morphine that allowed her to sleep and in Frank reading Dickens, the author who always brought her solace. Maisie spent a month in bed under the care of Helen McQuaid, the doctor who had delivered Rosemary. She lost a considerable amount of weight and was very weak. Her fine-textured hair fell out, never to grow in again. For the rest of her life she was forced to wear a wig. For five long months she recuperated; armies of people prayed for her recovery. Gradually she healed without the need of surgery. Only in April 1928 did she venture out of her flat. The illness left her with a scar on her lungs, one shoulder higher than the other because of the collapsed lung, and phlebitis in her legs.

For five months Maisie did not see Rosemary, her new baby. A nanny cared for her at Joesphine's home, and Min, Frank's mother, who had come to live with the couple, ran the household. Since Maisie was ill and knew nothing of domestic work, Min was an invaluable help. The Sheed household could not have included two more different women. Although intelligent, Min was self-educated and narrow in her outlook. She could be very merry, but also had dark moods. Her situation was a difficult one. John Sheed had left her years before, and Jack, her younger son, had died. If Frank and Maisie had enough money, they might have arranged other quarters for her, but money was scarce. Although Min hated the horrible weather, she had to stay in England. She had no money and earned her keep by overseeing Frank and Maisie's home. She was an inveterate traveler who frequently returned to Australia to visit, but until her death in 1953 her son and his wife were her only means of support.

Min and Frank shared a mutual admiration for each other. Min believed that her son was a perfect man and was totally devoted to him. Frank thought his mother the perfect woman until he met Maisie, who was also a perfect woman but one who was both religious *and* intellectual. The devotion of Frank and Min for each other was complete and played a major role in how Frank and Maisie lived out their lives.

The fact that Frank had married someone so remote from her must have been painful for Min. In her eyes, Maisie's redeeming quality was that she was a Catholic and devoted to Frank. Maisie had little in common with Min. Nonetheless, she accepted her as Frank's mother. Min was "queen of the kitchen," and Maisie praised her for this contribution. Both Maisie and Min needed each other, but that did not make living together easy. Frank served as negotiator in the unspoken problems between these two women. When he was not home, which was much of the time, there was a truce between them.

As Maisie recuperated from the illness brought on by childbirth, she translated M. J. LaGrange's *Christ and Renan* (1926), one of the first pieces of Continental literature to appear on the Sheed & Ward list. Gradually she regained her strength. This was the first time in her life that she experienced severe physical suffering, and her response was one of gratitude to be alive. In an act of thanksgiving, Maisie and Frank decided to open a public chapel in Surrey, which they would run and support. The Southwark diocese, eager to accommodate the burgeoning Catholic population, gave them two hundred pounds to realize this project. Maisie and Frank needed to move from their flat at Albany Mansions; serious flooding had made life difficult there. Josephine encouraged them to leave as well. They scoured the countryside looking for an appropriate place and found a large house with outbuildings at Horley, about twenty-six miles from both London and Brighton. The property included fruit trees, a vegetable garden, and an old stable, which they envisioned as the future chapel. Maisie bought the place with her own money and they moved in 1928 into their new home, Chestnuts, named for the large horse-chestnut trees that grew at the gate. During this time Maisie became pregnant again, but she soon miscarried. A second miscarriage would follow.

Life in the country was very different from life in London, but Frank kept up his Guild activities by attending classes twice a week and lecturing on Sundays. Maisie was largely cut off

from contact with the Guild. She spent much of her time working in the vegetable and flower garden and dealing with those
who stopped to ask for food and work. When Rosemary was not
being cared for by her nanny, Maisie played with her. She also
selected and edited manuscripts for publication and organized
the growing community that began to develop around the
newly renovated chapel. Min supervised the household staff of
two maids and a cleaning lady. The distance to London did not
keep Maisie from seeing her mother, who lived at Pelham Place
exclusively after 1929 when Herbert married and moved to
Egypt House. She also saw Tetta and Leo, who was again training for the priesthood, this time at the Oratory in Birmingham.
Leo had developed an interest in missionary activity in Japan,
but he was unwilling to go there because it meant leaving his
mother. His chance to evangelize in Japan would come soon,
however.

Sheed & Ward continued to expand. In early 1929 Frank
had an opportunity to go to America to lecture and promote the
firm's publications. Maisie decided to go with him. She left
Rosemary with Josephine in London. The lecture tour was exciting, and the warmth and eagerness of their audiences were
appealing. Both Maisie and Frank believed they were contributing to some larger purpose and that great things would result
from these lectures. Surely hearers would read and reflect
more, and study groups might develop. They spoke at Catholic
colleges and high schools, at Newman Centers at state universities, at communion breakfasts, and all kinds of parish gather-
ings. They traveled from Toronto to New York, Chicago, Min-
nesota and Oklahoma. They stopped at Sacred Heart convents
everywhere and especially enjoyed their visit with Mother Dam-
mon at Manhattanville College. Maisie met friends along the
way, including Dr. Helen Ingleby, who had been a fellow student at her convent school in Cambridge. Outside Philadelphia
in Torresdale, Frank and Maisie met Grace Smith, the daughter
of the General Smith who had entertained Wilfrid Ward years
earlier. Grace Smith's next-door neighbors were Jean Bullitt
Darlington, daughter of Maria Brown Bullitt, and her husband
Bill. The Sheeds delighted in this hospitality; they had no sense

of where their relationship with the Darlingtons might one day
lead.

Lecturing invigorated Maisie, who had been largely removed from public life since the move to Horley. Still, although
indoor lecturing would increasingly become important to her, it
was not as exciting as the outdoor platform. Inside,

> [b]oth lecturer and audience become a trifle over-civilized; it is
> valuable for the lecturer to realize that his audience is not a captive
> one, for the listeners to feel free to walk away. Yet there are
> balancing advantages; a universal sympathy is more readily estab-
> lished and questioners and lecturer are not distracted by a dozen
> irrelevant questions all shouted together.[17]

It was clear to her that she must continue to lecture, indoors or
out.

> [A] long space without a lecture leaves me played out. Lecturing
> can be tiring but not to lecture can be utterly exhausting; the
> details of the day pile up into a dusty heap of depression. The only
> alleviation is writing—or reading in preparation for a book. Writ-
> ing, too is a form of expression—but lecturing is more: it is an
> exchange of ideas, a meeting of minds, a friendly clash of person-
> alities. In short, it is life.[18]

The Sheeds enjoyed their trip to America immensely, but
even though Frank had a dream of working throughout the
English-speaking world, it did not occur to them to move to
America. Maisie was committed to their work in building up the
Catholic community in Horley, and the thought of leaving her
mother was incomprehensible. They returned to a busy life in
England, and by spring Maisie was pregnant again. On Decem-
ber 27, 1930, the feast of St. John, the much-longed-for boy,
Wilfrid John Joseph, was born at Josephine's home on Pelham
Place. Chesterton was chosen as godfather and Tetta as god-
mother. After four weeks of rest, Maisie returned to Chestnuts
at the end of January 1931.

Maisie's principal efforts after Wilfred's birth were devoted
to the young chapel community. Although traditional English
Catholic gentry had chapels in their home, the experiment at

Horley was not undertaken to ensure family devotion but to provide sacramental life for a community. Catholics in the local area were increasing in numbers, and the four-mile trip into either Redhill or Crawley for mass meant that many did not go to the sacraments. Non-Catholics who might be interested in joining the church had little access to organized religious life. Initially, the old stable was renovated to serve as a chapel for about forty people, but the congregation quickly expanded. When it reached sixty, the space was overcrowded and a second sung mass was begun. Frank instructed the congregation in singing the *Missa de Angelis* and Maisie taught prayers and translated from the Latin. A priest offered religious instruction for children, and Maisie worked with adult converts individually. The lively liturgies included the boys from Farmfield, a local institution for mentally deficient young men who had been in trouble with the law.

Horley was a lay-run congregation, and much like the C.E.G. it offered opportunities for leadership. Everything but the sacraments themselves was in the care of Maisie, Frank, or other lay people. Since the local clergy showed no interest in the Horley experiment, Frank and Maisie invited priests from London to come on Saturday for confessions and stay through two masses and benediction on Sunday. The priests who came, especially Fathers Fennessey and Healy, became fast friends of Maisie. John Healy, a straightforward, intelligent diocesan priest, became her confessor.

Although Maisie came from a family of liturgical enthusiasts—her father, grandfather, uncle, and brother Herbert qualified as such—she claimed that it was in the chapel at Horley that she learned real participation in the mass.[19] Increasingly, her participation in the Eucharistic service became her means of prayer. It fulfilled her needs to adore, to thank, to ask forgiveness, to intercede. She rejoiced if she could participate in more than one mass a day. It was the singing at Horley that impressed her most. She saw it as a form of congregational dialogue and a means by which the distance between priest and people was diminished. Although she was totally unmusical, hearing the

Gloria, Creed, and responses sung by the people gave her a new understanding of the meaning of the mass and its place in the larger context of the Divine Office.[20] This new experience of worship was to expand and deepen in the coming years.

The experiment at Horley continued and flourished. Meanwhile, Frank continued with Guild work, publishing, writing, and travel. Although he always missed his family when he was away, he traveled to the United States again in late 1931. The possibility of opening an American branch must have been in his mind, but he dismissed it as too personally costly. He wrote to Maisie: "One thing I'm clear about: if I were offered the money now to start an American branch, I should refuse it at once, if it meant spending a part of each year here. I am not going to be parted from you again. I should die if this went on."[21] Of course, Frank did not know the future. Within thirteen months money would become available and he would open an American branch of Sheed & Ward.

Provoked by questions from street-corner hecklers, Frank published *Nullity of Marriage* in 1931. The book dealt with the differences between divorce and the Catholic concept of nullity. *A Map of Life*, a book on Catholic life and doctrine, came out the following year. But all was not well. The world-wide economic depression of the 1930s affected publishers, and selling books became increasingly difficult. Sheed & Ward was no exception. Initially, Frank kept this depressing news from Maisie.[22] Since Frank did not take a salary from the company, the family lived on royalties and lecture fees, which at this point were minimal. Maisie, worried about household expenses, decided to grow greater quantities of vegetables and to raise chickens and rabbits for family consumption. Her love of the land had been nurtured by Josephine and developed by her association with Chesterton, Belloc, McNabb, and the Distributists.

The Distributists' goal was spiritual: to promote an organic, unified society through a return to agrarian life. For them, land should be redistributed and mechanization and government intervention shunned. These ideas were not new but had their proximate origins in the Catholic ruralist movement, which had been in existence for over a decade, in particular in the rural religious community of Ditchling overseen by Maisie's friend, Father McNabb.

In 1931 Maisie joined the Scottish Catholic Land Association, which urged people to grow their own foodstuffs so as to increase the availability of food and drive prices down. To forward this goal, the Association provided interested parties with a farm manager and young male workers from the slums of Glasgow. Frank was not enthusiastic, but in that same year Maisie used her inherited money to purchase a nearby farm in Upper Prestwood. She bought cows, a horse for plowing, and a sow. She then tried to learn farming from a book.

The Sheeds had agreed to share any profits from the farm with the staff. But there were no profits. "Misery" farm, as Frank dubbed it, was an unmitigated disaster. Everything that could go wrong, did. To make the place work, the family moved there and rented out Chestnuts. Conditions were primitive. Since there were no baths at Upper Prestwood, they had to go to Chestnuts or Pelham Place in London to clean up. As they soon came to realize, a farm could not be run on Christian principles if no one knew anything about the techniques of farming. Upper Prestwood was not merely a failure, it was a "farce." Maisie's idealism, belief in self-help, and fear of government solutions, as well as her desire to "do something" about the worsening economic condition of her family and England led her to this catastrophe. But the lure of a small, agrarian Christian community was a powerful force in her life; "Misery" farm was not the last of it.

In the fall of 1932 Frank and Maisie were off again to America on a lecture tour. Rosemary and Wilfrid, ages five and two respectively, stayed with Josephine. Frank gave a lecture at Manhattanville College that was heard by a Father John Hartigan, who decided right then that Sheed & Ward had to come to America. His encouragement obviously meant a great deal to Frank, who convinced Maisie that a New York office should be opened. But the excitement dimmed when Maisie received a telegram in November that her mother was very ill and needed an operation. Maisie immediately cut short her trip and booked

Left. Frank and Maisie with Rosemary and baby Wilfrid, 1931.
Courtesy of
Rosemary Sheed Middleton

Right. Maisie in the 1930s.
Courtesy of
Rosemary Sheed Middleton

ship passage back to England, but she was too late: on board she received a radiogram that Josephine had died of bowel cancer. Since Frank had been unable to make the travel connection, Maisie, in deep grief, sailed back to England alone. It was then that she decided to write her mother's life history. That goal was soon enlarged to include both her parents and to set their lives within a history of the Ward family. It would be Maisie's first major writing project, one spurred on by death and sorrow.

Frank soon rejoined Maisie in England, but directly after Christmas 1932, he returned to America for two months. Min was in Australia. Maisie, still grieving over the death of her mother and with no one to help with the children, took Rosemary and Wilfrid with her to stay with her friend Catherine Ashburnham. Her sorrow was gradually healed in the family chapel at Ashburnham, where she was comforted by the belief in the communion of saints. "I have always thought," she wrote, "that in the Communion of Saints, God allows those dearest to us to help us very specially by their prayers when He has taken them to Himself. After Boy's death we had been aware of it, after my father's and now again."[23]

This sadness marked the beginning of a new chapter in Maisie's life. Her profound grief at the death of her mother was poured into her first major writing project. With it, she launched a writing career that would involve editing or authoring twenty-nine volumes. And with her inheritance, she and Frank launched the American branch of Sheed & Ward. In late January 1933, Frank signed a lease on an office in a brownstone on Fifth Avenue in New York City. A permanent connection across the Atlantic was established, and Frank's dream of working in all the English-speaking countries would begin to be realized. Without the influx of inherited money from Josephine's estate, this expansion could not have been undertaken. Although Sheed & Ward had succeeded in its mission to bring the fruits of Continental Catholic intellectual revival to England,[24] its financial success was not great; in fact, the early 1930s, particularly 1931, were financially precarious. Furthermore, if Frank and Maisie had understood their firm strictly as a business rather than as a vocation, they might not have taken this chance. The Depression was deep, and any business expansion was highly risky. Nonetheless, it was a moment of decision. If it had not been seized, the future of Maisie and Frank would have been very different. As it was, Sheed & Ward grew, and Maisie emerged as a writer and a woman with a mission in America. She was on the verge of the happiest time of her life.

SIX

A Transatlantic Life

✳ SHEED & WARD IN AMERICA—the idea had fired Frank's imagination for a long time. With start-up capital, contacts, and six years of experience, the Sheeds had confidence that they could succeed. Frank opened the American branch in March 1933. It did not go unnoticed that its founding occurred during the one-hundredth anniversary year of the Oxford Movement.[1] To start with, $10,000 worth of British books were transferred to the New York office and $20,000 deposited in an account.[2] Letters of support and introduction were supplied by Sigrid Undset, Ronald Knox, C. C. Martindale, Jacques Maritain, and Alfred Noyes. Tom Burns was sent over to get the office running, and a few weeks later Hubert Howard, a young, energetic and intelligent manager took over.[3] The fact that neither Howard nor anyone else in New York had publishing experience did not seem to bother Frank, who also was self-taught in the trade. When Howard left after six months, it was expected that Burns would manage operations on both sides of the Atlantic. If the general financial situation were bleak, hopes were high that the burgeoning American Catholic population would buy books. The market looked big enough for competition. And they had that. Two other Catholic firms, Bruce Publishing Company and Newman, emerged in the 1930s, and Prentice Hall and McGraw-Hill added Catholic lines.

The American venture came at the right moment. In England, Roman Catholicism had reached an apex.[4] Although its numbers continued to grow slowly, and there was an extraordinary outpouring of Catholic literature, the difficult history of the English Catholic church left a mixed legacy. Its intellectual elite was small, and Catholic institutions, most of which developed in the nineteenth century, allied English Catholics closely with Rome. Since the Catholic press, parties, and education system were young, it was difficult for the church to reach deeply into the lives of believers. The expectation that a Catholic intellectual revival would enliven the ecclesiastical-supported Catholic Action movement did not materialize; in fact, lay activity remained stunted. If Sheed & Ward had not branched out beyond England at this time, its history might have been quite different. The company would have its greatest success in America.

Of course, neither Maisie nor Frank knew what lay ahead. When the early months of 1933 did not bring financial improvement to the London firm, Frank responded by cutting staff in the home office and betting on increased profits from the American branch.[5] His strategy was to begin by publishing the English list in America. Fortunately, three big sellers—Leon Bloy's *The Woman Who Was Poor,* François Mauriac's *God and Mammon,* and Paul Claudel's *The Satin Slipper*—all were released in the first year, and hopes were renewed that hard times might be ending.

Frank returned from America in the spring of 1933. Maisie and the children had left Ashburnham and moved into Josephine's home at Pelham Place. A year later the family returned to Chestnuts at Horley; Upper Prestwood had been rented out. The pattern of the Sheeds' lives was now set. Frank would travel extensively and Maisie would join him when she could, which turned out to be infrequently.

Frank had little time with his family. It took almost a week on a fast boat to get to America, where he would look after the business and lecture every chance he got. In America, unlike England, lecturing meant book sales. On the American lecture circuit one could promote books, find authors, and generally advertise the new firm. In England Frank did Guild work, publishing, and writing. His *A Map of Life* (1933) was followed by *Communism and Man,* published in 1938.

In 1933 Maisie was forty-four, the mother of two young children. During the year she suffered the sorrow of another miscarriage.[6] Given Frank's preoccupations and frequent absence, and the resolve she had formed following her mother's death, it was no wonder she immediately turned to writing. Writing gave her a sense of balance. "I would advise all temperamental women," she wrote years later, "especially those condemned to much separation from husband or children, to have on hand the kind of reading one does when a book is in the head. [I]t is a wonderful steadier for the imagination and prevents the emotions from taking a dangerous control over the reason."[7]

Her two-volume *The Wilfrid Wards and the Transition* was a massive undertaking, but her familiarity with the subject made it a manageable project. She had tried her hand at writing previously, but her efforts were minor compared to this. Before she could begin in earnest, however, she finished editing *The English Way: Studies in English Sanctity from St. Bede to Newman*. The volume's contributors included some of Sheed & Ward's regular writers—Chesterton, David Knowles, Belloc, Watkin, Dawson, Martindale, and D'Arcy. Each contributor painted a portrait of an English Catholic and showed how he or she expressed Christianity in a specific historical time. Bede and Newman framed the two ends of the book, which included chapters on Boniface, Alcium, Alfred, Thomas of Canterbury, Julian of Norwich, John Fisher, Thomas More, and Edmund Campion. Maisie's contribution was a chapter on Mary Ward, her mentor from her youth. She presented Mary Ward within the difficult circumstances of seventeenth-century England and showed her betrayal by Jesuits, Vatican officials, and her own nuns. For Maisie, Mary Ward was the personification of a woman who was totally Catholic yet given to England. This dual commitment was one cherished by Maisie herself.

The Sheeds' lives were very busy with Maisie's writing and Frank's travel, lecturing and publishing, but the young family tried to take long vacations together. Christmas time and its festivities were treasured by Maisie. She loved to decorate the tree and to give presents, which she would select with great care. Many summers were spent at Crosby Hall visiting Tetta and her family. The village of Little Crosby, enclave of Old Catholics, served as a tranquil haven. There were daily Masses, long walks in the woods, and games in the garden with Rosemary and Wilfrid and their cousins, Nick, Hester, and Richard. Conversation with Tetta and Francis was a great pleasure. Through long talks with Francis, who was not only a conservative M.P. from Ormskirk but author of *The Agricultural Problem,* and an expert farmer, Maisie was able to reassess the extreme positions of the Distributists who had influenced her for so long.

These were happy years for Maisie when the emotional support of family and the intellectual excitement of writing coalesced. Her most intimate friends, now as always, were members of her family. First was Frank, who was without equal in her life. After Frank, Tetta was Maisie's closest confidant. The rest of the family were scattered. Herbert, recently married, was occupied with local affairs on the Isle of Wight. Leo was in Japan. After Josephine's death, he fulfilled his dream of becoming a missionary, and with the blessing of Cardinal Bourne left for Japan in 1933, later serving under a Japanese archbishop. He visited England for the last time in 1937.

The research and writing of the family history dominated the middle years of the 1930s. Volume one, subtitled *The Nineteenth Century,* appeared in 1934; volume two, *Insurrection versus Resurrection,* in 1937. Ironically, Maisie's initial intent, to write her mother's life, was not realized in these books; Josephine was very much a secondary character. *The Wilfrid Wards and the Transition* was a biography of her father, and a family, institutional, and intellectual history. It was a form of autobiography as well. Maisie's childhood was chronicled and set in the long Ward family tradition that shaped English Catholicism. In writings these books, the granddaughter of the Oxford Movement memorialized her family and accepted the mantle as heir to that tradition. There was no other Ward to accept such responsibility.

Positive reviews of the first volume of the book poured in. It was not only the story of Wilfrid Ward, a lay Catholic intellectual during a period of enormous change, but the story of English Catholicism itself told through the life of a family. In the first volume Maisie plunged back into the nineteenth century to explore the world of her grandfather and Newman, as well as the first half of her father's life. She mapped her father's relationship with his father, their differences over Newman, Wilfrid Ward's associations with friends and family, and his contribution to the English church. She built her narrative around long extracts from her father's reminiscences, which made the book stylistically reflect its nineteenth-century subject matter. Although written seventeen years after Wilfrid Ward's death, its tone was apologetic and defensive. Given the continued insularity of Catholicism and Maisie's nature, it would have been difficult to be otherwise. Maisie found it almost impossible to be critical of her father and presented every issue from his point of view. When forced to admit that his course was not the best one, she adverted to the belief that a good end had resulted from his actions nonetheless. By late twentieth-century standards, her work was too adulatory and uncritical. By Maisie's standards, it was as biography should be—the life story of a subject as known by his friends.

Volume two of the family history traced her father's life through the Modernist controversy to his death in 1916. In this volume, "Insurrection," the revolt of the Modernists, was balanced by "Resurrection," the state of English Catholicism as it emerged after that controversy. Maisie's defensiveness was exacerbated here because she had to deal with the Modernist crisis and her father's attempts to walk the middle way between heresy-hunters and heretics. The suffering of Wilfrid Ward in the Modernist crisis was deeply felt by Maisie. More than fifty years after his death she wrote, "looking at this past moves me more deeply than anyone can understand who did not live through it."[8]

Ward's position as biographer of Newman and editor of *The Dublin Review* had placed him in peril. Although he garnered little support and was condemned by both sides in the Modernist controversy, Maisie saw him vindicated by history. She believed that because Modernism was crushed, revealed faith could live on. In churches where Modernism was not suppressed, that faith died. Like her father, Maisie maintained that "Revelation" had to be saved. "Better far an uncritical, unscholarly Church," she wrote, "holding fast the divine truth to a Church of scholars which had let go the one thing necessary."[9] The positive outcome, now that the crisis had passed, was that a Catholic intellectual revival was possible. *Pascendi,* she wrote, "had been one of those terrible but salutary blows under which, according to Newman, the Catholic intellect thrives and strengthens. But it must needs be followed by a period of growth and peaceful silence. Through the war clouds might already be seen, by anyone detached enough to see it, the dawn of the Catholic intellectual revival."[10] Her thesis was clear: Although Wilfrid Ward was unpopular in his time, he was on the winning side. He had helped make possible the Catholic revival. Through this interpretation she established her family at the center of English Catholicism and linked it to the contemporary intellectual revival. Written only two decades after the death of Wilfrid Ward, the book was apologetic. Apologetics was not an affliction merely of Maisie or Catholic writing in general; it was the method of choice of most biographers who had not yet come under the critical influence of Lytton Strachey, whose acerbic wit transformed that genre. In *The Wilfrid Wards and the Transition* Maisie both vindicated her family and confirmed herself as heir to their tradition. As publisher and now writer, she could build on the Ward legacy and redirect it into the future.

Maisie held that the greatest influence on her intellectually at this middle life juncture was Christopher Dawson, who, she said, saved Frank and her from a parochial Eurocentric religious view.[11] Dawson was also a valued friend and adviser; he read all of Maisie's manuscripts and later urged her to study the early Greek fathers of the church and to write her autobiography.

Dawson's principal thesis was that modern Western civilization had detached itself from its religious roots and that the consequence was political, moral, and cultural breakdown.[12] He advised not a return to the values of the medieval past but an examination of those values so they might be used in the present. Because he was a historian, he was suspect to the Neo-Thomistic philosophers who came to dominate the Catholic revival. It was his historical insight, however, that united him to

Maisie, who was more the historian than the philosopher or theologian. Dawson's influence coincided with Maisie's own developing interest in social questions.[13] It was she who increasingly insisted that Sheed & Ward publish books that explored social questions and Christian responsibility to ameliorate the world.

The chaotic start-up of the New York office and the departure of Tom Burns from the London office in 1936 meant more preoccupation with business matters for Frank. Although he conceived of himself as a businessman,[14] it is unclear how good he was at running a business. Frank's strength was clearly in energizing people. He encouraged writers and actively sought manuscripts. As a charismatic lecturer, he stimulated his hearers both to write and to buy books. For most of its history, Sheed & Ward was a closely held corporation; that is, Frank and Maisie controlled everything—the assets and all editorial and marketing decisions.[15] Frank was not a man to look after details and much of the time business operations were chaotic; procedures were few, pensions nonexistent, royalties to authors and debts to suppliers were often not paid on time. The firm was kept going by a small, enthusiastic, and dedicated staff, most of whom were female and many of whom were young; they worked exceedingly hard. There were complaints that the staff was exploited, but Frank and Maisie and most of the staff conceived of their work in vocational terms. Sheed & Ward flourished, particularly in America, not because of Frank's business acumen but because the time was right for their venture. As Frank said: "We did what needed doing." He added in typical Sheedwardian style, "[a]nd we had a lot of fun doing it."[16]

The 1930s were difficult years economically. As the world economic depression continued, keeping a publishing business alive on both sides of the Atlantic was no mean feat. The political events of the thirties were also challenging for the Sheeds, who since the early days of the Guild refused to enter political debate. Maisie, and especially Frank, insisted on principle that their statements be apolitical. They maintained that the church's social teachings followed from her doctrine and did not need to be applied in specific political instances; to do so was to be divisive. Frank distrusted all politicians and by all accounts remained totally uninterested in either English or American politics. Maisie well may have been less convinced on this point, but she went along with Frank.

The rise of authoritarian governments in the 1930s challenged the Sheeds' apolitical orientation. What guided them above all was their religious allegiance.[17] They would have no truck with communism because it was blatantly atheistic. Generally, English Catholics were highly individualistic and opposed to collectivism of any sort. Chesterton, Belloc, and most of the Distributists reflected that position. Hence the rise of Mussolini and Franco presented problems. Their regimes were overtly anticommunist, and they shared with English Catholics an anti-modern tendency. They believed that bourgeois, liberal, secular, and materialistic society was responsible for the destruction of an organic, agrarian, spiritual past. And ostensibly they were Catholic.

The initial idealism of Mussolini and his willingness to allow religion to operate more freely in Italy appealed to English Catholics. When the papacy gave a benediction to his regime, English Catholics were tentatively supportive. Josephine Ward was greatly impressed with Mussolini after her visit to Italy. In 1935, with the Italian invasion of Abyssinia, however, suspicions were raised against Mussolini, but Catholic opposition to him was not clear until Hitler, who had allied with Mussolini in 1936, became the enemy of Britain. The case of Franco was different; there was very little English opposition to him at all during the Spanish Civil War. Among Catholic publications only *Blackfriars* opposed him. Like so many others, Maisie and Frank supported Franco as the lesser of two evils. In short, English Catholics, for a variety of reasons, tilted toward the authoritarian right in Italy and Spain and showed an unwillingness to condemn those regimes because they were sympathetic to Catholicism and its values. This world view was summed up by Robert Speaight, an associate of Sheed & Ward:

> We were concerned to sacralise the world, not to secularise the Church. We were anti-modernist and even, except in esthetics,

anti-moderns; radicals only in the sense that we wanted to get down to roots, not in the sense that we wanted to pull them up. We were more anxious to preserve the values of an ancient civilisation than to set about the construction of a new one.

. . . [W]e were not revolutionaries. Such anti-clericalism as we professed was merely skin-deep, and we were so impatient with the shibboleths of the Left that the sophistries of the Right, except in their crudest forms, left us relatively undisturbed. Nevertheless the cracks began to appear with Mussolini's Ethiopian adventure, only to be closed with General Franco's crusade. The mystique of 'order' was worked for considerable more than it was worth, with an illegitimate extrapolation from the theological to the political field.[18]

In 1936 Francis Blundell died, leaving Tetta to raise her children alone. At his funeral the entire village of Little Crosby turned out to show their affection for their Catholic squire and former M.P. Tetta in her grief came down to Horley to be with her sister. The death of Chesterton in June increased Maisie's sorrow. It was hard to accept that the old loveable Chesterton whom she had known for so long had passed from life. One of his last acts in Maisie's behalf was to do a radio review of her first volume of the family history. After he died his wife, Frances, and his secretary, Dorothy Collins, asked Maisie to write his biography. She agreed, knowing that this project, like the family history, was personal to her; she had the motivation and ability to complete it. Since she was still working on *Insurrection versus Resurrection,* however, she delayed research. Mrs. Chesterton wanted the biography to be "the final and definitive" one. It took Maisie six years to complete it. This massive undertaking proved to be her most successful venture as an author.

After the family history was published in 1937, Maisie proceeded slowly with her next major project. There were family moves to be dealt with; in 1937 the family settled in Ealing, a London suburb, then returned to Horley, where they stayed until mid-1940. Although Maisie began research and interviews for the Chesterton biography, she also had other minor writing projects. She wrote a small booklet, *The Oxford Groups* (1937), in which she examined this evangelical religious group and its challenge to Catholicism.[19] She also published "A Kingly People" (1938), a piece in which she described the church as a deeply democratic institution whose sacred doctrines were not the secret possession of a clergy-elite but were open to all, as was its leadership.[20] It never occurred to her to qualify this statement to mean male leadership. Maisie was caught up with the idea of the spiritual equality of all believers, but she was quick to balance that with the principle of authority that she found just as necessary for the church.

In the midst of these projects Maisie began to agitate for the leasing of land allotments to residents of the town of Horley. In a short article on this problem published in *The Weekly Review* shortly after the outbreak of war in 1939, she pointed out the urgent need for land allotment in order for people to grow food. The article clearly showed her continuing enthusiasm for gardening and farming and her exasperation with a government bureaucracy that blocked individual initiative.[21]

The first months of the war gave Maisie the opportunity to see the economic conditions of her neighbors and fellow Catholics and to enter into a "Prayer Front."[22] This Front was organized by the Grail, a secular institute for women which devoted itself to apostolic activities. The outbreak of war did not mean an end to travel for Frank or for her, however. Leaving Min and the children at Horley, they left for America for four months in January 1940. Their travel route was circuitous: by land to Paris and then to Lisbon where they sailed on the Vulcania to New York. Among the passengers were Vera Brittain and nine hundred refugees.[23] In April they returned to Europe, landing in Naples and proceeding by land back to England, barely missing the German invasion of the Low Countries in May. Back at Chestnuts they had to consider what would be the most sensible course given the escalation of the war. Should they all stay in England, all move to America, or let Frank travel between two continents? Several American friends urged them to send the children over to safety. Finally, they decided to go to America together. Chestnuts would be turned over to an East End boys' orphanage for the duration.

In early summer 1940, all five of the Sheeds sailed on the Dutch ship Volendam to New York. It was an uneventful trip, although they almost struck a mine as they passed out of the English Channel. Unbeknownst to them this was the Volendam's last voyage; the ship was destroyed by a submarine during its next sailing. When the Sheeds arrived in New York, expired visas forced them to stay at Ellis Island for the night before debarking. Wilfrid and Frank went to one dormitory, Maisie, Min, and Rosemary to another. Ultimately, they worked their way through the labyrinth of immigration and began a new life in America. Their five years in the United States would have a great impact on them all. Wilfrid would ally himself with his new country. Rosemary, on the other hand, would learn that her roots were deeply English. Frank, and particularly Maisie, became redefined by their new mission to American Catholics.

The Catholic church they encountered in America was very different from the church they had known. Although American Catholics made up only about 17 percent of the population, they were growing in numbers, wealth, and influence.[24] An elaborate network of Catholic institutions gave structure and unity to the church's ethnic diversity. The papacy had initiated Catholic Action as the laity's participation in the work of the hierarchy, but much of the activity of American Catholics in the 1930s and 1940s took place outside the bounds of ecclesiastical control. The interwar period saw the establishment in America not only of Sheed & Ward but the Catholic Worker movement, Friendship House, The Catholic Evidence Guild, and the Grail. These lay-controlled and lay-led organizations impelled members to live out in the world the implications of membership in the Mystical Body.

The Catholicism of America was increasingly robust and optimistic. Rooted in a revived Thomistic philosophy, Catholicism offered a return to reason and God and an alternative to secular skepticism and irrationalism.[25] Philosophically and theologically, the church offered meaning at a time of disillusionment. If the church was democratic and all believers were valued; if participation in the church meant being linked to the communion of saints and to the ongoing work of Christ in the world; if reason confirmed the dictates of faith; if Catholic thought led to action and action to thought, then Catholicism represented a total way of life, a unity of thought, belief, and action that stood as a counter to disintegrating contemporary life.

The inclusivity, unity, and critique of contemporary society offered by this Catholic world view were attractive to many. While self-sacrifice and dedication were required, the reward was a sense of belonging to the universal church. The desire to commit oneself to sanctity was at its heart. For Leon Bloy and for others, the only unhappiness was not to be a saint. This vibrant Catholicism appealed especially to the young and ardent, and particularly to educated Catholic women who, blocked from positions of leadership in the church, found in this revival a world of personal meaning. The Catholic revival in America was preeminently a movement of women.[26]

Maisie entered this dynamic American Catholicism first as an occasional lecturer and then as a permanent if peripatetic resident beginning in 1940. As a lecturer, writer, and publisher she would direct and augment the Catholic revival in a particular way. In her person and lineage she represented the educated and cultivated influence of England in America. Although some American Catholics would be irritated by the presence of this foreign woman, and others find her quaint, she served nonetheless as a link to a European heritage that Americans both disdained and admired. Dowdy in appearance, her cultivated manner of speaking nonetheless connected her listeners and readers back through the long tradition of Catholic intellectual life. Maisie was a bridge to the religious and intellectual life of Europe. This was a role she, but not Frank, could play.[27] American Catholicism would reap the benefits.

SEVEN

"This Burning Heat"

✳ THE WAR YEARS BROUGHT AN ACCELERATION to Maisie's life; she lectured and wrote more, and subtly her energies were redirected. She also suffered in new ways. The war tested her optimism, and the death of her brother Leo in 1942 and illness of her son in 1944 deepened her sense of tragedy. Her friendships with Dorothy Day, Catherine de Hueck, and Caryll Houselander challenged her understanding of faith as well. It was as if finally, at mid-life, Maisie was able to move beyond her Victorian optimism and enter into the anguish of the twentieth century.

The six years spent in the states between 1940 and 1946, three in Torresdale and three in New York City, marked a richly prolific period. Maisie lectured all over the country and wrote three books, each of which was in some sense connected to the war. *This Burning Heat* was her first. Feeling guilt that she and her children were safe in America, she compiled this book as her small contribution to the war effort, with royalties from its sale going to the Grail and the Catholic Worker in England. In these collected letters from friends in England she showed people determined to survive and to help each other under drastic circumstances. The hope was that her American audience, still removed from the war, would see these sacrifices positively.

This Burning Heat was written out of immediate need to respond to the war effort. It was completed rapidly and easily. Maisie then began work in earnest on what would be her most popular book, a biography of Chesterton.[1] In all, she worked on the manuscript for six years. In one respect this biography was

97

firmly connected to her earlier life. Chesterton was a family friend whom she had known for a long time. Since he was one of her most important early intellectual influences, to take him on as a subject was to explore her own intellectual development vicariously. But Chesterton belonged to all the English people and represented values that they were defending in war. This biography of an extraordinary Englishman and Christian was a kind of contribution to national morale.

The Splendor of the Rosary, the third book she wrote in America, might too easily be classified as devotional writing.[2] It was that, but much more. John Walker, Director of the National Gallery of Art in Washington, D.C. and her cousin, sent Maisie copies of a series of paintings by Fra Angelico and suggested that they might be reproduced as illustrations of the mysteries of the rosary. She took on the project and secured the agreement of Caryll Houselander to do companion prayers. The book was Maisie's attempt to bring together theology and prayer and to rejuvenate an ancient devotional practice with new intellectual vigor. She worked on the manuscript during the last year of the war as her thirteen-year-old son, Wilfrid, lay stricken with polio. The rosary became her prayer through war and personal suffering.

When the family first arrived in America in 1940, Rosemary and Wilfrid were sent to visit the Ross Hoffman family in Rye, New York, and then went on to Bill and Jean Darlington's for a month in West Chester, Pennsylvania. Their parents joined them there. The Ward connection to the Darlington family went back to early World War I, when Wilfrid Ward came to Philadelphia to lecture. During the 1930s, Frank occasionally stayed with the Darlingtons when he was in the states. In 1932, Frank and Maisie became in absentia the godparents of Bill and Jean Darlington's daughter, Maria (Missie) Darlington. When Maisie, Frank, Rosemary, Wilfrid, and Min finally settled down, it was at Birdwood, a large stone house in Torresdale lent them by the Darlingtons. Birdwood was the same house in which Maria Brown Bullitt had entertained Wilfrid Ward years earlier. The children found the early nineteenth-century house "gloomy," but Maisie loved the place. It had a large yard, dense with foliage, that still allowed room for a victory garden and bee hives. In Birdwood there was plenty of space for the entire family to spread out, and it was quiet and secluded on the banks of the Delaware River. But Rosemary and Wilfrid were bored. There were no children around, and they felt trapped in the great old house. Next door lived Grace and Kilby Smith. Mrs. Smith, a Catholic philanthropist, was a friend and sister-in-law of Mother Katherine Drexel who established educational opportunities for black children. In their interlude in Torresdale, the well-connected Smiths became the Sheed's fast friends.

During the school year Rosemary attended nearby Eden Hall, a very strict convent school run by the Religious of the Sacred Heart and a short walk from home. Since the Sheed's personal finances were stretched, Frank and Maisie delivered regular lectures at the school in lieu of tuition. At Eden Hall Rosemary gained the mastery of French that allowed her later to become a Sheed & Ward translator. Initially, Wilfrid attended a coed parochial school, but he hated it and his parents moved him to a Benedictine boarding school, Delbarton, in Morristown, New Jersey. Delbarton was a monastery trying to be a school. By his own account, Wilfrid did not learn much in this eccentric place.[3]

It was difficult for both children to acclimate to their new world. Their parents were so obviously not American, which was important to Wilfrid, and not fashionable, which mattered to Rosemary. Maisie particularly seemed dowdy and old-fashioned. The Sheeds were very evidently a family of limited means who lived in a borrowed house with borrowed furniture and whose daughter wore hand-me-downs to school. Occasionally, Grace Smith brought Rosemary and Wilfrid generous presents, which delighted them no end.

Min did the cooking and ran the kitchen in the household, although such work was difficult when her arthritis flared up. Her pastimes were listening to the radio, knitting, and reading, especially Dickens, whom she adored. An intelligent woman, Min had no formal education, and her narrowness gave evidence of this. Her life had been a hard one. She did not remember her own mother, and her father died when she was twelve.

Her alcoholic husband deserted her and left her to raise two sons. To her credit, Min brought Frank up to be secure and provided him with a good education. For that Maisie loved her, although she was often a difficult woman—nervous, insecure, and riddled with a sense of her inferiority. Min liked boys better than girls, and between her and Rosemary, then a young teenager, there was considerable disagreement. The worst times in their relationship had occurred earlier at Horley, but sometimes war would still break out between them.

The lack of communication between the aging Min and Maisie was exasperating. Maisie wrote to Frank, who was away frequently, that they had to make other living arrangements for Min, who "was sometimes herself and other times not."[4] But Min stayed on. She vented her anger on Rosemary, who gave as good as she got. Maisie, aware that she was incapable of dealing with flare-ups between Min and Rosemary, plunged into work. By American standards, this might be seen as forsaking one's child; by British standards Maisie was far more involved with her children than most of her contemporaries. Moreover, she took her work seriously and was not about to be thrown off course by the squabbles of her children. Min, whom Maisie considered a perpetual child, albeit one she was very fond of, was no companion for her when Frank was away. At least Rosemary at this age could offer some semiadult friendship.

Maisie's routine at home was set. She would rise early in the morning at about four or five a.m., make a big pot of tea, get back in bed, and propped up with pillows, write until about eight on her long, yellow legal sheets. During the day she worked upstairs in the cavernous house, trying to ignore the latest hostility below. A rapid and voracious reader, she would appear at lunch with a book and read through the meal, seemingly oblivious to the world around her. If visitors were present, she would read them what she had written. She assumed they were as interested in her work as she was. Her daily pleasures offered some respite: reading detective stories and drinking— three of four cups of tea or coffee, and later in the day, sherry, old-fashioneds, or manhattans. Frank, a teetotaler, never seemed to mind this habit and would frequently transport some requested alcohol from one continent to another. In the evening Maisie would read aloud to the children, mostly from Dickens and Boswell.

Summer vacations were particularly difficult times. Although visitors came frequently to Birdwood, among them the English actor and writer Robert Speaight and the Trapp family singers, Torresdale was a boring place for children. When Frank was there, things were lively. He would sing, play the piano, and joke. Just being himself was great entertainment for anyone. But more often than not he was gone, either to England, to New York City, or lecturing throughout the states.

Frank made fifteen trips across the Atlantic during the war. Obviously, this took determination, but it was also eased by British Intelligence. Frank was asked to act as a British presence among American Catholics, including the anti-British Irish with whom he had some reputation. In particular, he was to work to limit the influence of Father Coughlin, the isolationist radio priest.[5] Frank was apolitical; he believed that politicians and political parties were inherently dishonest. Nonetheless he was enormously patriotic. In this case his patriotism—never divided by other loyalties—helped him carry on his business during war. Later in the war when the Allies bombed Rome, the center of Catholicism, he supported the action with little hesitation.[6]

When Frank was at home, everyone was happy—Maisie, Min, and the children. Although Frank tried not to take lecture tours in the summer vacation, he was away much of the time during the rest of the year. The years in Torresdale were especially difficult for Wilfrid, and the summer of 1942 was particularly lonely. Friendless and desperately wanting to play baseball, the eleven-year-old frequently drafted Rosemary to pitch to him, and Maisie took her turn too. But he was miserable and later admitted to thoughts of suicide,[7] which no one seemed to have noticed. Maisie thought Wilfrid was merely lonely and temporarily antisocial. It would have been almost impossible for her to admit that anything was wrong. Nothing was supposed to be at odds in the family, and furthermore, she felt she could do little about any problem. It was better to work and long for Frank's return. "I feel a sort of impotence and discourage-

ment," she wrote. "My darling, come home and look after me—
and I after you. We're hopeless apart."[8] During the war years
these were constant themes in her correspondence.

During 1940 the war was uppermost in her mind. Frantically she sent clothing and cans of food to England. Concern for
the safety of friends and family on the other side of the Atlantic
and for Frank on his transatlantic crossings fed her anxiety.
The Blitz was in full force, and she received letters from England telling of the devastation; there were also the personal
reports brought back by Frank. The worst came during the last
days of the year. Frank spent the weekend of December 30th
with Christopher Dawson in Oxford. He returned to London to
find that a bomb had decimated Paternoster Row, which was
near the docks, the financial district, and historic St. Paul's Cathedral. What was once the Sheed & Ward office was now rub-
ble. The entire book stock and all accounts were destroyed.
Frank reported that where once there was an office, there was
now a hole. With his indomitable spirit, by the next day Frank
had leased space in Fleet Street and within two months Sheed &
Ward was functioning again.

It was in this context that Maisie, secure and safe in Torresdale, began to write *This Burning Heat*. The work opens with the
lines of Scripture: "Think not strange this burning heat which is
to try you, as if some new thing happened to you."[9] The book
was dedicated to her widowed sister, Tetta, who lived in Little
Crosby and wrote and lectured as President of the Union of
Catholic Mothers.

Above all, *This Burning Heat* was a source book, a compilation of documents written by ordinary English people about the
war and how they survived its havoc. Maisie prepared the book
to counter the widespread belief that war despiritualized a
nation. In these documents she showed the opposite: lives renewed in courage and humanity. Her informants varied, but
included many friends: Marigold Hunt and Edward Connor at
Sheed & Ward; Dorothy Collins, Chesterton's secretary; Molly
Walsh, a Guild member and Catholic Worker; Caryll Houselander; nuns; Grail members; and, of course, Frank. In this
chronicle of social history Maisie defended the notion that good

can come out of evil. She saw people raised to new levels of heroism and unity. She argued that life had been made simpler and more sober because of the war, and people had learned to appreciate and enjoy life. There had been a return to the land, always a sign of health to her, a gradual return to God, and a proliferation of acts of human kindness.

This Burning Heat was very much the work of a woman who had mixed patriotism with religion. For Maisie, the suffering of war came from the choice to die for the ideals of Christ. The war was a moral act and British participation in it was justified. While it produced destruction, it would ultimately produce good. *This Burning Heat* reflected Maisie's world view; she gave little treatment of the social and economic consequences of the war, was totally uncritical of British participation, and saw it as a moral good. Her view from Torresdale would change once she returned to England after the war.

After completing *This Burning Heat* Maisie began to lecture more extensively. As she moved around the United States she could gauge a growing appreciation by Americans of England's predicament. Her lecture tours also allowed her to experience new examples of human cooperation. In the Canadian Maritimes of Nova Scotia, New Brunswick, and Prince Edward Island, she discovered the cooperative movement that ensured the personal dignity and economic security of its members. The movement, begun in Antigonish by two priests, Fathers Coady and Tompkins, encouraged members to study, save, and cooperate.[10] Through such cooperation members survived the Depression and endured the war. This encounter reaffirmed Maisie's personalist philosophy and affirmed the role of the small group in protecting the dignity of the individual.

Lecturing became a way of life for Maisie. Through it she not only earned money (by the 1950s she was paid $200 a lecture, plus expenses), but kept in touch with old friends. Lecturing also generated book sales and allowed for the solicitation of manuscripts and the cultivation of authors. Together and separately, Frank and Maisie lectured all over the country at Catholic colleges, Newman Centers, Catholic high schools, parish events, and many of the Catholic bookstores that burgeoned during the 1930s and 1940s. After a lecture they would take questions. Through this exposure they gained an understanding of American Catholics. Sadly, they found them poorly educated in their faith.

Their lectures were booked by and advertised through Sheed & Ward's American office. Maisie's repertoire of lectures expanded gradually. By the 1960s she had three different categories of lectures—general, which included topics on the Intellectual Apostolate and Women in a Man-Made World; literary, which included lectures on Ruskin, Dickens, Browning, George Eliot, the Brontës, Chesterton; and figures in church history, including St. Paul, Ambrose, Augustine, and other church fathers.[11] Frank was the more prolific lecturer. He could be engaged to speak on any one of twenty religious or literary topics and continued to do large lecture tours for many years. His longest was a seventy-seven lecture tour in the space of only six weeks.

If one were fired up about religion and admired the English intellectual tradition, one could appreciate Maisie as a speaker. For American Catholics who had endured a lifetime of poor sermons with no intellectual content, she was a breath of fresh air. She was zealous, devout, confident, intelligent, committed, and articulate. As one who had practiced for hours in the company of hecklers on street corners, she knew how to gain her listeners' attention. There was no way that she could be defeated. As a lay woman, admittedly an intelligent one, there were no expectations of her. This worked in her favor, on the one hand, and contributed to a dismissive attitude on the other. When she was with Frank, she was part of the team of Sheed & Ward, a marital and business institution. But alone, who was she? Clearly, someone to be admired, but not necessarily someone to be followed. She could provoke, excite, and challenge, but because of who she was and the times she lived in she could not mobilize followers. It was acceptable for a woman to inspire others to carry out the works of mercy; both Dorothy Day and Catherine de Hueck successfully did that. But Maisie's work was to enliven belief through thought, disseminated by publishing, writing, lecturing, and preaching. Hers was an intellectual and

Maisie and Frank at an award ceremony, c. 1941.
Courtesy of Rosemary Sheed Middleton

theological mission. No other Catholic lay woman had taken up this task in the public arena. Maisie was above all a pathbreaker and "free lance"[12] who had removed herself from the constraints of tepid belief and gender stereotypes. She was both liberated and trapped, a woman moving in the totally uncharted waters of Catholic intellectual life.

Through her work with the Catholic Evidence Guild and Sheed & Ward, and through lecturing, Maisie urged Catholics to reflect on their faith. As she interacted increasingly with Catholics dedicated to the lay apostolate, she became aware of the immense responsibility to heal and bless and do God's work in the world.[13] The defensive apologetic tradition was giving way in her to a more activist, compassionate response to suffering in the world. But this new orientation was only seminal in the 1940s. The previous sources for her inspiration—her family and Frank—were augmented now by Dorothy Day, Catherine de Hueck, and Caryll Houselander, each of whom would influence her in the coming years. Maisie was moving in a direction in which Frank could not go. In this arena she was on her own.

The exploration of the social and ethical implications of Christianity was already a dimension of Sheed & Ward publications. While the apologetics of Belloc and Chesterton dominated in the early days, French Catholic thought as expressed by George Bernaros, Charles Péguy, François Mauriac, and Jacques Maritain, published beginning in the 1930s, was full of intensity and an awareness of the unity, beauty, and drama of Catholic belief. Implicit in the French Catholic reaction against secularism and materialism was a radical critique of society and a desire to return to the roots of Christianity, a desire that necessarily had ethical and social implications. Influenced by this literature, Maisie would be led after the war to study the priest-worker movement in France, a movement that attempted to revive religion among French workers.

An even more powerful challenge to her apologetic tradition came through her friendships with Dorothy Day, Catherine de Hueck and Caryll Houselander. In each she encountered a woman who was engaged with the suffering of ordinary people. From each she learned a new vision of the meaning of the doctrine of the Mystical Body. Sheed & Ward published the works of all three, as well as works by their associates, Peter Maurin in the case of Day, and Eddie Doherty, the husband of Baroness de Hueck.

Dorothy Day and Peter Maurin began the Catholic Worker movement in 1933. Day, a journalist, Marxist, and convert to Catholicism, was responsible for developing the houses of hospitality that became the trademark of that movement. In 1939 Sheed & Ward published Day's *House of Hospitality*. In many ways Maisie and Day shared a world view. They believed in living simply and in sharing with the poor. They were both devoted Catholics. Maisie contributed financially to Day's causes and frequently visited Catholic Worker houses on her tours. There were many personal connections as well between Sheed & Ward and the Catholic Worker movement, although sometimes members felt themselves in friendly opposition. Frank was fonder of Peter Maurin than he was of Day. There is no doubt that Maisie admired her enormously and considered Day more moral than herself. "I am ashamed of my own limping life compared with yours," she wrote.[14] Obviously one of the appeals of Day to Maisie was her selfless effort on the part of the poor, work that followed from Day's understanding of the Mystical Body.

Maisie and Frank did not agree with Day on every issue; there was tension between them, especially over Day's pacifism. Frank's argument to Day was that she could not morally be rigid on the question of war and that such rigidity would only hurt the Catholic Worker's effort for the poor. "Whether you are right or I am right about war," he wrote,

> it is at least a matter on which the Church has not pronounced. Catholics as such are free to hold a pretty wide variety of views. Therefore, however convinced you may be of your view, you must surely hold it as your personal view of Christ's mind. Surely it is at least questionable that you should weaken the whole Catholic Worker movement by insistence upon your own personal view as against views that you can hardly deny the right of your fellow-Catholics in the movement to hold. . . . [B]ut I should certainly

feel it a duty to respect the liberty of their consciences on a matter where the Church allows liberty. And I should not make their cooperation in the great work in the service of the poor impossible, or at least difficult or distasteful.[15]

Maisie, who could not be a pacifist because the war involved England, agreed with Frank. Years later, however, her position would soften as she confronted American involvement in Vietnam.

As described earlier, one of Frank's responsibilities during the war was to keep tabs on Catholics in America, most of whom were of Irish, German, or Italian origin and sympathetic initially to the Axis powers. He had been told by the British Ministry of Information that if the Sheeds lived in the U.S. he would always be guaranteed transportation to England for business if he reported back to them on sentiments among the Catholic population. This included pacifist sentiment. In a report probably meant for British Intelligence he described

> the extreme pacifists of the Catholic Worker sort who hold that war is always evil because it is against the teaching of Christ: Dorothy Day, [who is] the leader of this group, has quite a fantastic influence over hundreds of thousands of Catholics. She is a friend of mine. I wrote out for her a twenty page discussion of her position, arguing that it was based on a misinterpretation of the Sermon on the Mount. She is very uneasy as a result & is avoiding discussion but she has very strongly modified her anti-war stand in the Catholic Worker. She may of course break out again but I am keeping after her.[16]

Day's pacifist stance was only a manifestation of what Maisie considered a rigidity in her friend's spirituality. Because she admired Day so much, she was perplexed by what she saw as a harshness expressed in some of her writing. This may have been a result of the influence of a radical retreat master, Father Hugo, who led Day to a more ascetical and austere spirituality.[17] Maisie was not ascetical or perfectionistic. Her optimism never allowed her to be captured by an unbalanced notion of redemptive suffering. Toward the end of the war, Maisie, who had begun a correspondence with Houselander, discussed Day's spirituality with her. Houselander, eager to impress Ward, responded with a long diagnosis of what was wrong with Day. The very psychologically astute Houselander argued that Day's rigidity derived from her failure to understand the doctrine of the Mystical Body. What was necessary was a variety of spiritual responses; the ascetical, the way of perfection, was only one way. Houselander saw a nervous tension in Day and a sense of scruple about sin. She argued that self-denial could not produce joy, only love could.[18]

In spite of the differences between them, Ward and Day remained lifelong friends. Day's constancy and her dedication to the poor were themes Maisie would wrestle with for the rest of her life. In her late seventies Maisie said, "I'm passionately devoted to the Catholic Worker. I think [Dorothy Day is] one of the greatest women in the world, a tremendous person. [The Catholic Worker] is the beginning of the most essential reform that the Church really needs. I haven't the courage to practice [poverty] like Dorothy Day does."[19]

During the war years the doctrine of the Mystical Body was widely discussed in Catholic circles. Maisie's reflection on this doctrine was furthered through her relationship with another Sheed & Ward author, Baroness Catherine de Hueck. The colorful Baroness, a Russian refugee, began Friendship House in Toronto in 1930. Established in New York some years later, Friendship House's purpose was to extend to people of color the Christian hospitality implied in the doctrine of the Mystical Body. This was to be done through breadlines and clothing rooms.

Friendship House became another extension of the lay apostolate where dedicated Catholics, mostly young and female, ministered to the needs of the destitute minorities of the cities. Growing up around Friendship House was a supportive group called the "Outer Circle," which gave assistance and attempted to deepen the bonds and connections across race lines. In New York, the "Outer Circle" used the Sheed's apartment for discussions on Sunday evenings. Eager Catholics, both black and white, attended. These meetings served as a forum, much like the Guild, to provide an opportunity for people to reflect on their lives and to form the "Catholic mind." The Guild method was resurrected—someone would make a presentation and others would heckle. The meetings ranged from small to large; sometimes up to 125 people were stuffed in the apartment. Sheed & Ward types, Catholic Worker volunteers, Friendship House people, friends and friends of friends, blacks and whites, gathered to explore the faith and have great fun together.

Although the Baroness founded the movement, she was usually not in New York; to some, this seemed for the good. Maisie thought the Baroness arrogant.[20] Frank and Maisie admired her, but they did not see her as of the same calibre as Day, who might be rigid but was never arrogant. Frank's judgment was harsher. "I once remarked that Kate [sic] had less self-knowledge than anyone I ever met. . . . The result is she can indulge an absolutely catastrophic ego with the maximum of innocence. The trouble with that [is] sooner or later (I don't know whether it's happened to her yet—if it hasn't it will) such people get into a situation where they can only carry on by *conscious* deception."[21]

Despite the limits of the flamboyant Baroness, she created a movement that attracted ardent Catholics who gave themselves to others in service. Because Friendship House had a specific interracial character, it fostered understanding across race lines. Through their association with it, Maisie and Frank came even to accept interracial marriage,[22] no mean feat in the 1940s. For them, all people were members of the Mystical Body. It was this new understanding of the Mystical Body as operative in the world that slowly began to transform Maisie's intellectual understanding of faith.

The final personal influence of the war years was that of Caryll Houselander, a spiritual writer whom Maisie met first in print in the *Grail Magazine*. Maisie was taken with Houselander's ideas and began a correspondence with her. In 1941, the same year that Maisie produced *This Burning Heat*, Houselander published *This War is The Passion* with Sheed & Ward. They had become friends, even before they met in person in 1946.

The dominant religious preoccupation of Houselander was the doctrine of the Mystical Body and its meaning in war-torn

England. In her correspondence with Ward, the younger Houselander took on the role of a spiritual friend who gave advice and counsel. From the start Caryll recognized that she and Maisie were very different in orientation. "The difference between most Catholic writers and myself," she wrote, "is that they start with the idea of preserving the good in people. They have personal traditions which lead them to thinking goodness is something already there but I who have a very dark background start with the idea of everyone being in ruins and getting back to goodness. I don't expect to find people good but I expect to find Christ wounded in them and that is what I do find."[23] Houselander admitted that she was a neurotic who had a tendency to asceticism and scrupulosity. She rejoiced that Ward did not have the same tendencies to perfectionism. "The only way through one's limitations is love," she wrote,

> a kind of creative life-giving energy which flows out and gives life to all the world. I am certain that sanity can't be in people who deny themselves either joy or suffering, feasting or fasting. By sanity I don't mean grey mediocrity which is so universally admired. I mean extremes which do not unbalance one because they balance one another. All this hard spirit of Puritanism seems too grey to me. I am conscious of a kind of continual disintegration or corrupting in myself, and of depending absolutely on sacramental grace.[24]

Although their relationship would develop intensely in the postwar years, in its early stages Houselander's message was already clear: what was needed was a love that spilled out to the suffering world. From Houselander in England and from friends in the United States Maisie heard again and again the notion that faith manifested itself in love. It was a message that steadied her through the war and through her son's illness.

During the first years at Torresdale Maisie's major undertaking was the Chesterton biography, which was published in 1943. She had done considerable work on it before she left England but had stopped to take on other projects. In 1941 Elizabeth Ada Chesterton, the wife of Cecil Chesterton, Gilbert's brother, published *The Chestertons*. Maisie saw it as a vicious and inaccurate biography and found new determination to move forward on her own interpretation of her old friend's life. This would not be the last time that anger catapulted Maisie into action; her biographies of Houselander and Browning drew from the same emotion. Although she was removed from some of her sources, the University of Notre Dame made the full run of *G. K.'s Weekly* available to her. Frank, on his many trips to England, interviewed people who had known G. K. and sought out source material for her.

Maisie came to her work with a theory of biography that she inherited from her father and which she helped preserve in his posthumous book *Last Lectures* (1918). Father and daughter shared the view that the biographer must examine all facts and then select from among them to show the whole person. The aim was to make one's subject known to posterity as that subject had been known by contemporaries and friends. Both were also convinced that one could only write biography if one admired one's subject. They wanted an accurate but sympathetic portrait, and that demanded both advocacy and judgement. They sought to explore "the springs of life," the sources of human motivation. With Belloc, Maisie argued that "a man is his mind." As a biographer she focused on her subject's intellectual development, particularly the early years. In researching her biography of Chesterton she read, at the suggestion of Christopher Dawson, all of Chesterton's books in chronological order so as to see the development of his mind.

Maisie shared many convictions with Chesterton. He was a devout Catholic, a convert who was declared Defender of the Faith by Pius XI in 1936. He was totally English in his manner and sensibilities, a patriot of the first order, and a Distributist. Like Maisie he loved Dickens and Browning, and he wrote books on both of them. He was an eternal optimist who saw the contradictions in life but always pointed toward the good. Maisie regarded him as a great creative force in English letters and a model of the life of charity. She believed it was impossible to admire Chesterton too much.

In reviewing Maisie's biography of Chesterton, Graham Greene wrote: "Mrs. Ward is too fond of her subject and too close to it to reduce her material into a portrait for strangers."[25]

Clearly, Maisie's enthusiasm for her subject blinded her and made her almost incapable of seeing any limitation in someone she loved. Since she had not been trained to be critical, her love went unchecked. Her "passion for documents" led her to include every scrap of information she uncovered. The result was not only an overlong book but one with too many digressions. Finally, she was never completely able to detach herself from the apologetic tradition in which she was schooled. There was an air of defensiveness about the book, as if she were defending a client against slanderous claims. And, of course, she was doing just that. From the very beginning of the book she took on the charges against G. K. and his wife made by Mrs. Cecil Chesterton (Elizabeth Ada) in *The Chestertons*.

What Maisie achieved in thoroughness, she missed in interpretation. Throughout the biography there is only one theme, that of admiration. She did not attempt a critique of Chesterton's literary achievement, nor did she undertake any psychological interpretation of this lovable but eccentric man. By modern biographical standards her work was hagiography. It attempted no interpretation other than to defend him against the charges of his sister-in-law. His supposed innocence and fear of sexuality, his glorification of wine, his complex psychological makeup went unexplored. These limitations were traceable directly to Wilfrid Ward's theory of biography, which held that

> the primary duty of fidelity to fact which forbids the biographer from being content with a surface picture, and makes it imperative to present those traits which indicate the whole man, makes it also unlawful to go still deeper; for these depths are in the case of a real human being matter only for conjecture.[26]

Maisie avoided any such conjecture. She was either incapable of this more complex exploration of personality or unwilling to undertake it. It is insufficient to claim that her writing was unobjective. She would admit to this, but from her point of view the purpose of biography was to understand a subject, and understanding presupposed love and admiration. When she did not love someone, as in the case of Hilaire Belloc, she could not

write a biography of him.[27] All of her biographical subjects—
her family, Chesterton, Newman, Houselander, and Browning
—were deeply admired by her. While her writing about them
captured something essential, it was one-dimensional and did
not explore the complexity of human personality.

Everything about the Chesterton biography was massive.
Maisie reviewed Chesterton's one hundred volumes and hun-
dreds of his articles and lectures, and she interviewed many
people who knew and revered him. As the first Chesterton biography based on unpublished materials, her work would be an
important source for all subsequent biographers. The almost
universal acclaim of the book was also a significant indication of
popular admiration for her subject. The reception was so positive that her book was reissued in paperback by Penguin. In
response, Maisie would take up the writing of a sequel, *Return to
Chesterton*.

Most of the Chesterton biography was written while the
Sheeds were in Torresdale. Frank continued to travel during
much of this time. In the fall of 1942 he waited in London to
meet Leo, who was returning from Japan. The Pope had or-
dered the exit of all British and American missionaries. The
hoped-for reunion never happened. Six days before he was
due to arrive in England, Leo died on board ship and was buried at sea. Although the cause of death was listed as encephalitis,
Leo may have also suffered from injuries sustained in a Japanese prison.[28] Maisie grieved the loss of her luminous, ardent
brother. His passing brought the war home to her in a personal
way and ensured her sympathies with the Japanese Christians
he left behind.

By the summer of 1943 the Chesterton biography was complete. Maisie and Frank finished editing the manuscript in a
hotel in New York City. They then traveled together to San
Francisco, where Frank continued on alone for a four-month
trip to Australia. On his return Maisie met him in Los Angeles,
stopping first in New Orleans. While Frank was away, she
moved the family to New York. After three years in Torresdale,
it was time to leave. The Darlingtons wanted to sell Birdwood,
and there was increasingly more reason to live in the city. Although all their Philadelphia friends argued against living on

Manhattan's less desirable west side, they rented an inexpensive apartment on Riverside Drive, near Columbia University. Wilfrid continued as a boarder at Delbarton, and Rosemary transferred to a Sacred Heart school on 91st Street, where she proved to be an excellent student in spite of her extremely poor eyesight. Both Rosemary and Wilfrid enjoyed the city; they could ride the subway anywhere and have their pick of friends. There were movie theaters and endless opportunities for Wilfrid to play baseball, which he did, hours on end. He was, at last, a supremely happy thirteen-year-old.

The Sheed's apartment was an easy subway ride to the office on University Place. Frank was relieved of the long train trip into the city, and Maisie had access to the Columbia and Union Theological Seminary libraries and the Cloisters, the legendary New York museum of medieval art. Corpus Christi Church, which served the Columbia University community, was nearby, staffed by the liberal priest, Father George Ford.

In spite of the war, the Sheeds were all much happier in New York City than in Torresdale. Maisie had finished the Chesterton biography. The financial outlook for Sheed & Ward was good, even with the major theft of company assets by a disturbed company employee and the loss of the young poet, Robert Lowell, as editor;[29] expectations for continued success were high. With the expansion of Catholic colleges and seminaries, book orders were pouring in. This kept the small Sheed & Ward staff of about fifteen people very busy. *This Publishing Business*, the original company newsletter, was replaced by *Sheed & Ward's Own Trumpet*, a six-to-ten-page tabloid edited and mostly written by Marigold Hunt. Its purpose was to sell books and to convey the exciting, caring, and humorous ethos that dominated the Sheed & Ward office. This spirit was best reflected on the *Trumpet*'s back page, which announced marriages between Sheedwardians, births, and other social events. Wood block illustrations by Jean Charlot dotted its pages. Although its masthead listed its cost as "priceless," 150,000 copies of *The Trumpet* were distributed gratis each month.

Since Maisie was now living in New York, she could easily drop into the office. However, her presence was often intimidating to the staff. She combined a toughness, forthrightness, and singlemindedness that frightened many. Since she felt no need to impress or win anyone over, she engaged in few social pleasantries. She seemed aloof and invulnerable. She was about business. Some found her bossy and demanding, others remote and disengaged. She abhorred stupidity and said so. Although not uncaring or unappreciative of others' efforts, she was a taskmaster, and most of the staff, while they admired her, were just as happy if she were not around. If she had been a man, these characteristics might not have been so readily criticized.

Maisie was big-minded. She was never bitter, did not hold grudges, and never gossiped. Only Frank knew what she really thought about people. Although she usually looked severe, when she smiled she could be totally disarming. She was capable of being very loving, tender, and fully attentive to those who were family, friends, or committed to her ideals. In fact, in that circle she was almost incapable of seeing any wrong. Her enthusiasm and dedication gave her a lopsided view of her intimates. She could not accept the fact that someone she loved could really be bad.

In the second half of 1944 the Sheeds seemed to be in their prime. Frank was as busy as ever. The previous year he had published his translation of Augustine's *Confessions* and was planning what would be his most famous book, *Theology and Sanity*. Maisie was about to begin work on her book on the rosary. Wilfrid was still boarding with the Benedictines and enjoying summers in New York City, grateful to be out of Torresdale. Rosemary graduated from high school at sixteen and spent the summer at the Pius X Music Summer School at Manhattanville College. There was discussion of whether she might attend this college, run by Sacred Heart nuns, in the fall, but she rejected the suggestion. Although Wilfrid would be carefully prepared to enter an English university, Rosemary had not been educated for this purpose. Both Frank and Maisie shared the widely-accepted English opinion that university education prepared one for employment. Since Rosemary was headed for marriage, not a job, there was no point in applying to university. But there was more beneath the surface. Maisie lamented having been denied university education herself. Yet Frank had always said with pride that no woman in his family went to college. Whatever the underlying mix of attitudes, Maisie and Frank presented a united front. Rosemary was neither encouraged nor dissuaded from attending university. Rather, Frank's idea was that she should work as a translator for Sheed & Ward.[30] Her skills were needed there. But her long-term future would be in matrimony, regardless of her intellectual potential. One of the most compelling reasons to return to England after the war was to provide Rosemary the right social environment so that she could meet someone "on her scale"; New York was not the place to provide such opportunity.[31] It was ironic, at least, that forty years later Maisie offered her daughter the same alternative she received: a social season in lieu of a university education.

In order to celebrate Rosemary's graduation from secondary school, Maisie took her to Canada in the fall. Maisie was to lecture first in Montreal and then in Calgary and Vancouver. Frank, who had returned from Australia for the summer, had now left for London. Min stayed in the New York apartment to look after Wilfrid on the weekends when he returned from Delbarton.

The graduation trip had its problems from the start. In Montreal, Maisie got pneumonia. This was particularly threatening because she had only one functioning lung. When she and Rosemary arrived on the West Coast, they were stunned to learn that Wilfrid had been diagnosed with polio and was in the Morristown hospital. Since he was in an isolation ward and could not be visited, they continued on with part of the tour. As they returned home, both Maisie and Rosemary were ill with an influenza infection. Finally, alone and frightened, Maisie moved Wilfrid to St. Vincent Hospital in New York City. He was brought home and set up in a bed in the living room. A physiotherapist was employed to visit three times a week, and Rosemary was trained to assist with the rehabilitative exercises on alternate days.

In hopes of a cure, Maisie tried everything. She was sure she needed to pray more for Wilfrid. She wrote to Frank: "All this suffering so early, must be fashioning him for something unusual. But it's hard to bear."[32] Every string was pulled to get Wilfrid into the Warm Springs, Georgia treatment facility in 1945. But after six weeks Wilfrid was lonely and begged to leave.[33] His parents assented. Maisie was jubilant to have him home and wrote Frank she was willing to spend all her royalties from the Chesterton book on his recovery.[34]

Wilfrid was in bed for many months. Although Min and sometimes Maisie helped, Rosemary carried out most of the laborious tasks of caring for him. After the autumn of 1945 Wilfrid was out of bed and in a wheel chair. He moved on to a brace with two crutches, then to two canes, and then to one. It was a long, trying haul, but by the end of 1945 life was somewhat normal, although he would always use a brace and never play sports again. Maisie and Frank were eternally optimistic about his recovery.

Both Maisie and Frank had ways of coping and blocking out their sorrow. Frank, as always, traveled and immersed himself in business. A letter to Maisie shows both his grief over Wilfrid's illness and his ability to move on to other matters.[35] "I am in a kind of daze over Wilfrid," he wrote,

> finding it extraordinarily hard to concentrate on anything. Whatever other subject I'm talking of, I'm thinking of that grand little boy. If only he had got it 4 days sooner, so that we might have been together.
>
> The sales here [London] verge on the fantastic. . . . The problem, however, as in America, is where the new books are coming from. I'd like to see some established authors appearing. [O]bviously, the Continent is our hope: there's no sign of a new author of the first rank here.[36]

Maisie, for her part, threw herself into writing her book on the rosary, doing much of the research for it in the libraries of Union Theological Seminary and Manhattanville College. Frank later said she put more of herself into this book than any other.[37] The effort was evident: There was a sense in which the subject matter was totally internalized, as if it were written after long meditation.

The Splendor of the Rosary was a truly collaborative effort. Suggested by John Walker, it was dedicated to Kathryn Conroy, a Sheed & Ward manager, who Maisie said "forced me to write it." Chesterton prepared Maisie for this work by his love of Mary and his belief in her accessibility to all people. Caryll Houselander lived through each of the mysteries with Maisie. This not only deepened their friendship but gave them a common prayer during the war years. Maisie also "collaborated" with the fourteenth-century Dominican artist, Fra Angelico. This was her second book to focus on Dominican spirituality, the first being her study of the people's preacher, San Bernardino. She referred frequently to Julian of Norwich, the English mystic, to whom she would return in subsequent years. The book ends with a quote from Robert Browning, an old love who would remain one of Maisie's favorite poets to the end of her life.

The most remarkable aspect of the book was that it brought together art, prayer, scripture, and theology. Maisie explored a specific Fra Angelico painting for each of the fifteen mysteries connected with Mary's life. She then quoted the appropriate scripture passage, added her own theological reflections on the mystery, and ended with a brief prayer/poem by Houselander. In this way, each of the five Joyful, Sorrowful, and Glorious mysteries was explored from four angles—the artistic, scriptural, theological, and prayerful. What was unique was Maisie's insistence that theology be linked to art, the Gospel, and prayer, thereby enriching each of them.

The Splendor of the Rosary very much reflected Maisie's interests. She included a chapter on the history of the rosary, a biography of Fra Angelico, a theology of the rosary, and commentary on the use of the rosary by the Catholic Evidence Guild. She saw the rosary not so much as a pious devotion but as a vehicle through which prayer led to mystery. She countered the argument that the rosary was a prayer for simple people that should not be complicated by theology. Theology was, she said, a telling of God's love. When one prayed into the rosary, one could grasp its theological meaning. Theology provided a knowledge accessible to both the most ordinary and the most sophisticated person.

One of Maisie's explicit assumptions was that beauty, knowledge, and love all intersect with each other. In the paintings of Fra Angelico she saw realized her conviction that knowledge and love of God are intertwined. This realization permeates every page. As Frank wrote, "The whole book is practically a meditation on the instructed heart, or in her preferred phrase, 'Love made wise by knowledge.' "[38]

The Splendor of the Rosary appeared in 1945 as the war in Europe abated. Both Frank and Maisie had been great patriots in the European war. Frank had worked for British Intelligence, and both of them were adamantly anti-pacifist. But the United States' bombing of Japan was a different matter. Frank and Maisie had an emotional tie to Japan through Leo's work with Japanese Christians. The destruction of Hiroshima was bad enough, but the bombing of Nagasaki, which included the oldest Christian settlement in Japan, was appalling. The widely-accepted arguments that the bombing saved American lives and brought the war to a swift end did not have convincing power for them. Their belief was that if an amoral society had destructive nuclear technology, it would always be used. Frank wrote to Maisie:

> This atomic bomb is a pleasant discovery: the human race really can blow itself off the face of the earth now. Perhaps *that's* how the Holy Ghost is going to renew the earth's face—scrape the human beings off it.[39]

* * *

> Why in the name of heaven did the Americans have to hit Nagasaki with the Atomic Bomb? Hiroshima was bad enough: but they might have waited a little longer before doing it again. I suppose if you have a thing as destructive as that, you are all the time itching to use it . . . , so much destructive power at the hands of a humanity with no moral principles. The mere using of such a weapon at this stage of the war is an indication that there are no moral principles left at all.[40]

With the war over, the Sheeds now had to reconsider where to live. Frank and Maisie deliberated for some time and concluded that a return to England was the best decision for the entire family.[41] Maisie had ambivalent feelings about a return; she had come to love much about the United States. Of course she was eager to see family and friends after many years, but America seemed a second home. However, she had already begun work on a new book on John Henry Newman, and it would be easier to proceed with research in England than in the United States. Rosemary, who considered herself English, was very eager to return. Maisie believed that in order for her daughter to meet the "right people," she needed a London social season.

Wilfrid was adamant that he did not want to go back, but Frank gave him a heart-to-heart talk, insisting that he must return for his education. Maisie and Frank considered American Catholic universities inferior, and for professional reasons they could not send their son to a secular ivy-league institution. Although his parents allowed Wilfrid the fullest latitude in his career choices, they were adamant that he must go to Oxford. Since they were both concerned over the woefully inadequate education he had received in the United States, they insisted that he enroll in an English secondary school, thus ensuring entry into one of the Oxford colleges. There was no better place to prepare for Oxford, at least in Frank's mind, than the Benedictine school at Downside. Since Wilfrid's Latin was terrible, Frank, who was a master teacher, became his tutor whenever time was available in the next few years.

The decision to return to England had different consequences for family members. Rosemary and Wilfrid would live there year round, but Frank and Maisie would spend six months in the states. Global travel was now a permanent part of their lives. They left for England in 1946, Maisie's first trip by airplane. Her exhilaration and eagerness soon waned when she encountered a devastated homeland and contemporaries exhausted by long years of war. The England she had known was no more.

EIGHT

England Revisited

✳ A RETURN TO ENGLAND AFTER SIX YEARS meant reunion with family and friends and an end to Maisie's guilt over having lived in America, safe and secure, while England endured war. Now, at least, she could work and make use of the good the war had unleashed in Britain.

The Sheeds arrived in England in April 1946. Since housing was scarce, they lived for three months with Dorothy Collins. Wilfrid went straight to the Benedictine school at Downside. But Maisie, Frank, Rosemary, and Tetta's daughter, Hester, crowded into Dorothy's place at Beaconsfield. Rationing was still enforced and day-to-day life was difficult. Maisie had a startling introduction to postwar living conditions when she trudged all over London looking for a home. Not only had the war destroyed many houses, but six years of neglect had badly deteriorated many others. There seemed no immediate prospect of the Sheeds getting their own home, when Maisie found a flat in Kensington. They moved in by summer and stayed for the next eight years. Oakwood Court would be a place of great hospitality and warmth for the family and the many friends and relatives who visited.

It did not take Maisie long to realize that her expectations of a revitalized England were illusory. The war had done immense physical and psychic damage to the nation. The environment was decayed, and people looked tired and aged. Bureaucracy was pervasive and oppressive. English society was in a state of exhaustion. Maisie could not comprehend the discouragement, bitterness, and lack of concern she saw everywhere. England had given up, and she was sure that the cause of its malady was not material or psychological but spiritual. Unwilling to accept defeat, she set out to find new sources of vitality.

In an effort to "do something," she sold Chestnuts to the Catholic diocese of Surrey and with royalties from the Chesterton biography bought Gosse's Farm in Essex. Like Chesterton, Maisie felt great sympathy for the Polish people, who, she believed, had been betrayed by England in the war. She hired a Polish manager to run the farm, and when he proved incompetent she brought on another one, who worked out successfully. The farm provided both the opportunity to give employment to Polish refugees in England and to reaffirm the Distributist philosophy at a time when she saw increasing bureaucracy crushing individual initiative.

Since farming would never be enough to sustain Maisie, she sought other forms of renewal. In late 1946 she went to France to visit her mother's old friend, Lady Ashbourne, who was dying. While in Paris she met Henri Perrin, one of the first priest-workers. Captivated by this movement, she traveled to France frequently during the next several years to search out priest-worker communities.

Maisie's most important personal inspiration during the postwar years was her friendship with Caryll Houselander. Frank had met Houselander several times on his return trips to England, but Maisie knew her only through the correspondence and cooperation on the rosary book, which had made them fast friends. Maisie's anticipation of their meeting must have been great; in Caryll she knew she had a kindred spirit. But when Maisie finally met her at a dinner party arranged the first night of the Sheeds' return to England, she was startled. Houselander's physical appearance—the thick glasses, the fringe of red hair, and especially the dead-white face—was bewildering to her.[1] Nonetheless, Houselander was a source of energy, a vibrant, creative writer and person who gave herself for others. It was her intellectuality and spiritual depth that appealed to Maisie. Although Maisie credited Newman, Chesterton, and Browning as the most important intellectual forces in her early life, and Christopher Dawson at midlife, during the postwar period, Houselander was clearly the dominant force. Maisie never described Houselander in these terms. However, one cannot read Maisie's biography and the edited letters of Houselander without realizing this friend's great influence on her.[2]

Houselander was a unique and sometimes difficult woman. She was totally unconventional in appearance and behavior. Inspired and dedicated, she was also quick-tongued and liable to easy judgment of others. Unlike the secure, optimistic Maisie, Houselander had known material poverty and psychological and social rejection. She was a self-proclaimed neurotic who learned to live with her psychological limitation and use it in service of others.

Houselander's theology and spirituality aroused a deep response in Maisie. Houselander's religious belief had been influenced by a series of visions, much like the "showings" of Julian of Norwich. She saw these visions in pragmatic terms: it was only through them, she claimed, that she could learn the fullest meaning of the doctrine of the Mystical Body. For her, Christians cooperated with God and were the means by which God's love entered the world. Conversely, she equated the suffering of Christ with the suffering of the world and vice versa. To enter into human suffering was to enter the passion of Christ. Houselander's elaboration of this aspect of the doctrine of the Mystical Body was articulated in her book, *This War is the Passion*. The corollary of her view on suffering was that Christians brought Christ's love into the world. To love Christ was to love one's fellow humans. Houselander wrote: "Our fidelity to One, Is to fall in love, With the whole world."[3] For her admirers, the self-styled "Caryllinati," there was one vocation for all Christians: to be Christ in the world. By healing and consoling, one continued Christ's work.

Maisie first learned of the importance of the doctrine of the Mystical Body[4] from Hugh Benson; it was now elaborated by Houselander. Because of Maisie's own recent suffering—through the war, with Wilfrid's polio, the death of Leo, and later in 1949 the mental breakdown of Tetta—she was open to this new understanding.

Houselander's vocation was specifically to serve those with severe mental problems. Although she had no formal training, her psychological acuity and extraordinary perception brought her to the attention of Dr. Eric Strauss, psychologist, neurologist, and president of the psychiatric section of the Royal Society of Medicine, who asked her to take on some of his clients. Houselander's aspiration was to give these patients hope that they too might have some place in the body of Christ. Her work with the mentally ill prepared her to write *Guilt* (1951), in which she maintained that happiness and even sanity begin when one knows God. The first step in healing was to allow oneself to be loved by God. "The beginning of integrity is not effort but surrender," she wrote, "it is simply the opening of the heart to receive that for which the heart is longing. The healing of mankind begins whenever any man ceases to resist the love of God."[5]

Maisie was enormously impressed with *Guilt*.[6] Although she could never be called a neurotic, she was driven by a powerful sense of duty and loyalty. This is evident in her relationships with her family, her enormous sense of responsibility to others, and her longtime commitment to institutions. This sense of duty, grounded in both her religious and social understanding, was burdensome. Houselander's mystical theology gave Maisie a new starting point. Through it, the conscientious Maisie came to appreciate more fully the mystical tradition and the power of love, rather than duty, as the greatest Christian motivation.

Houselander's theology helped Maisie think about problems she had with Dorothy Day and the Catholic Worker movement. In her correspondence with Maisie, Houselander offered her advice about Catholic Workers. In 1948 she wrote to another friend, Lucille Hasley:

> You get papers from them [The Catholic Worker], in which practically every article is a very vital grouse about injustice, and a few boosting up the worker as such. But what is lacking in these papers is any articles that seem likely to make Christ more real to the worker himself in his own life, as if the only consideration is his just grievance, and the duty, shared by him with all men, to try to remedy it. What is absent is the suggestion of his being in unity with Our Lord in *suffering* injustice, or any real understanding of

work itself. Also it seems to be presumed that the rich man (a) doesn't work at all, (b) doesn't suffer any injustice at all. I could start pages on the superficial side of this, but don't want to get away from the heart of it—namely, that in the Mystical Body we are all one, and we do all experience the passion in a thousand secret ways and we share—if we want to or not—others' lives and responsibilities.[7]

Houselander believed that the spirituality of the Catholic Worker was one of asceticism and detachment, and she argued against it. She began from the mystical assumption that one needed first to allow oneself to be loved by God. From that choice, a whole new way of being followed. Love led to the moral response, not vice versa. This new way of understanding the human relationship with God would very gradually shift Maisie's line of vision.

Houselander's odd physical appearance, her unorthodox behavior, and her brief liaison with the British spy, Sidney Reilly, ensured that she had detractors.[8] However, many others were inspired by her. Her books were published by Sheed & Ward and sold well. Ronald Knox was so impressed with her work that he urged her to establish a school of spiritual writing. But it was Maisie who would preserve Houselander's memory. After Houselander died of breast cancer in 1954, Maisie wrote her biography, subtitling it *That Divine Eccentric*, the name given her by Dr. Strauss. Subsequently, Maisie edited a volume of Houselander's letters, evidences of what she called House-lander's "acts of compassion." These letters showed her for what she was: a neurotic and an oddity, but one in whom the love of God had broken through, healed, and set free. For Maisie, Houselander was no saint, but a friend who understood suffering intimately and who worked to console those who needed healing.

Friendship with Houselander sustained Maisie during the postwar years when life was hard and all of England seemed exhausted. In an effort to counter apathy, Maisie threw herself into Guild work and the writing of the Newman biography, a subject that returned her to her past.

Decades earlier Wilfrid Ward had written the definitive work on John Henry Newman, but at Newman's own request Ward did not focus on the Cardinal's early life before he became a Catholic. Maisie felt that this was a grave omission and decided to examine the young Newman, the Anglican, who had been allotted only seventy-five pages in her father's biography.

In undertaking a study of the young Newman, Maisie continued the English Catholic tradition of biographical accounts of living faith. *The Wilfrid Wards and the Transition* and *Gilbert Keith Chesterton* were in this same genre. A study of Newman's life followed logically from her and her father's work, but the choice of Newman was more than logical. For Maisie, Newman was not only the most important English Catholic of the nineteenth century, he also had more influence on the present than any of his contemporaries.[9] Through his writing and preaching the foundations of Catholic thought were transmitted to the present. As with her studies of San Bernadino and Maturin, Maisie was again exploring the life and work of a great preacher.

In *Young Mr. Newman* Maisie sought the "springs of life" of a man she admired immensely. She believed it was her best book.[10] On the face of it, this estimate is difficult to understand. The book seems ponderous, seldom rising above the documentary evidence. But it was the evidence, the sheer weight of it, that gave her enjoyment. As she said, she "had a passion for documents" and nowhere is that passion more evident than in this book. She steeped herself in the background of nineteenth-century Oxford, read the published sources and biographies of Edward Pusey, John Keble, Dr. Tait, Dr. Arnold of Rugby, James and Richard Froude, and pored over unpublished material. At the Birmingham Oratory where Newman's voluminous and meticulously organized papers were kept, she met resistance. Since 1885 only she and her father had requested use of Newman's early letters and notes, yet she was denied access because of the restrictions of monastic enclosure. As she wrote, my "sex is a *great* drawback."[11] To get around this restriction Frank was sent to sort through the documents and bring them to her. Father Henry Tristram, to whom she dedicated the book, lent her his own copies of many unpublished letters. The mere fact of resistance spurred her on.

In *Young Mr. Newman,* as in *Gilbert Keith Chesterton,* Maisie traced the development of a mind. In both cases she dealt with intellectual men who were also immensely spiritual. The defining moment in both lives was a conversion to Catholicism. Of the two, Newman was the more towering figure. Both his intellectual and spiritual genius were unparalleled. It was in the interconnection between these two qualities that Maisie saw his particular achievement. "Newman's genius," she wrote, "found its scope in a unique vocation—at once spiritual and intellectual—of drawing the world nearer to God not by prayer but by thought. His was perhaps the greatest theological vocation since St. Thomas."[12]

Young Mr. Newman was about personal development; it traced "the development of *this* child into *that* man." Her intent was to show how John Henry, the child and boy, became the Newman of Oriel, Newman the cleric, and finally Newman the convert. The book covers the forty-four years before his entrance into the Catholic church.

Because her aim was to show the slow and difficult decision to convert, she was forced to confront the suffering in Newman's life. She entered into this and carefully documented its manifestations. She traced the tensions in his life and what he had to give up to convert. She explored the development of his mind during his early family life and at the university, as well as the influence of evangelical and clerical life and of Anglican friends, particularly Keble and Froude. She created the tension of great decision and showed the loss and suffering it created. Hers was the tentative Newman, the man under trial before the security and peace of conversion came to him. Given a treasure trove of documents, Maisie mapped what she considered the greatest decision of the greatest mind in modern Catholic history: Newman's assent to the Church of Rome. She made her portrait a study in heroism. It is no wonder she loved the book.

Christopher Dawson and E. I. Watkin read the Newman manuscript, as did her old friend Walter Moberly. She had high expectations that the book, building on the work of her father, would sell many copies; it did not. She was disappointed and filled with self-doubt.

The postwar weariness of English life fed a restlessness in Maisie. She kept on with her many projects—Gosse's Farm, the Guild, and a robust family life at Oakwood Court. There, at the big wooden table extended with leaves, many were fed from the parcels sent every week from the farm. C.E.G. members, family, writers, and friends from America, Australia, Europe and all over England gathered at the Sheeds. Rosemary, now working as a translator for Sheed & Ward, was in charge of domestic life. She was an excellent cook who oversaw the kitchen now that Min was very old. In the midst of all the comings and goings, Maisie and Frank wrote and carried on business.

In 1947 Frank published *Theology and Sanity*, his most well-received book. None of his subsequent writing would match its popularity. It established him as a well-known Catholic lay theologian. Maisie wrote, but she also looked for new commitments. Now, as at other times in her life, her pattern was not to replace one engagement with another, not to jettison anything, but to add commitment on commitment.

After the Newman biography was finished, Frank urged Maisie to write a book on Fatima and the Marian apparitions. His estimate was that there had been no adequate treatment of this subject.[13] Instead, Maisie threw herself into exploring the priest-worker movement which she had discovered earlier.[14] Her experience with the Catholic Worker and Friendship House in America prepared her to understand the importance of this movement. Priest-workers confronted a rapidly changing world and shaped it along human and Christian lines. As a rival to Communism, this movement melded a concern for material and spiritual needs. This emphasis led Maisie to rethink the relationship between religion and politics, which she had radically separated, at least in part because of the Guild's insistence on the primacy of religious doctrine over political application.

The priest-worker movement emerged during the war both in France and Germany.[15] One of its most articulate spokesmen was the Jesuit Henri Perrin, who went to Germany during the war to minister to deported French youth. Unlike most of his colleagues, Perrin survived and returned to France where he published *Journal d'un prêtre-ouvrier en Allemagne* (1945). This book was translated into English by Rosemary as *Priest-Workman in Germany* and published by Sheed & Ward in 1947. Priest-workers were also associated with the ministry of Abbé Godin, who established a mission in Paris after the war to evangelize the proletariat. Through this work he became friends with anti-clerics, communists, and atheists. In 1943 he wrote, with Yvan Daniel, *France, Pays de Mission?* which sold 100,000 copies and impressed Cardinal Suhard, Archbishop of Paris. *France, Pays de Mission?* was a handbook on how to reach the proletariat, who had been written off by the French church. It considered the practical problems of the poor and the difficulties in missonizing among them. Maisie translated this book, adding a biographical section on Abbé Godin and a summary of the impact of his work in France. In 1949 it was published under the title *France Pagan? The Mission of Abbé Godin.*[16]

As the chaplain of the Young Christian Workers, Godin was above all an evangelist. Since French workers were alienated from the church, he advocated that priests learn new modes of thinking and a new language to win them over. He rejected the negative, combative, and superficial aspects of proselytizing evangelization and urged that the evangelist should not merely bear witness to the truth but show it. This could be done best through the small Christian community that radiated faith. In these communities, the work of evangelization was carried out by priests and laity who lived with the poor, worked with them in the most difficult jobs, and helped them reflect on the conditions of their impoverishment. These communities focused not on doctrine but on the ordinary lives of the poor and forgotten. Entering into the material lives of the poor was the prerequisite for sharing their spiritual lives; this was the method for genuine evangelization.

Maisie was electrified by these ideas. She visited priest-worker communities, listened to their discussions and assisted at mass with them in their small, humble rooms. There she experienced a vibrancy like that of the early church. Here was

Catholicism at its best—vital, reflective, communal, lived out among the poor, and witnessing to the faith. She saw the priest-worker communities as models of contemporary religion. They represented what she called "the new French Revolution."[17]

The impact of Abbé Godin's thinking on Maisie was profound in several ways. He believed that the most immediate tragedy for the worker was a terrible loss of marital ideals, exacerbated by the conditions under which couples were forced to live. Godin's themes of marriage and housing would soon become major ones in Maisie's life. Godin also advocated voluntary poverty, believing that religious life and ostentation were antithetical. This inspired Maisie, who always tried to live as modestly as possible. Except for air travel, which was necessary because of her work, and eating out, which she usually did in the cheapest places, Maisie spent almost nothing on herself. What she saved she gave to those in need. Godin also suggested a new vehicle for living a Christian life—the small, dedicated community. While Maisie never lived in one herself, she wrote and supported such communities for the rest of her life. Her final autobiography is structured around dedicated communities that she encountered throughout the world.

By the early 1950s the knotty problem of the relationship between the political and the spiritual divided the priest-worker movement. Priest-workers were increasingly engaged in political activity. Some became labor union leaders or joined the Communists. Because their work was demanding and exhausting, they had little free time for prayer or evangelization. They became remote from their principal commitment to reclaim the proletariat for the church. Since much of their political activity was liberal or radical, the French cardinals moved to hem them in. Priest-workers were told to ally themselves directly with a parish and were restricted in the number of hours of manual labor they could perform. Of the hundred priest-workmen, seventy-two refused to accept these restrictions. Some left the church and continued to work among the poor. Some became communists, and others joined the ranks of the white-collar bourgeois. In 1954 Rome called a halt to the movement. Maisie,

their staunch supporter, was startled. It was at this moment that
the manuscript of the dissident seventy-two priest-workers, *The
Worker Priests*, arrived at Sheed & Ward. She read it and realized
she could not support them. However much she believed that
the situation between the priests and Rome might have been
resolved otherwise,[18] she agreed that Christianity demanded
"the primacy of the spiritual."[19] Because the dissident priest-
workers no longer held the spiritual as primary, Maisie reluctantly withdrew her support. *The Worker Priests* never appeared
on the Sheed & Ward list.

It was in the person of Henri Perrin that Maisie saw the
movement disintegrate. Both she and Frank liked Perrin when
they first met him after the war and agreed to publish his book.
He was for them "a towering personality." But as he became
more engaged in politics, they came to see his work with the
poor as obsessive and leading to spiritual starvation. When
Maisie attended one of his masses, she realized that he spoke
only of politics. Perrin rejected the church's constraints on him.
When he died subsequently in a motorcycle accident, Maisie saw
his life as summarizing a tragic element in the priest-worker
movement. While religious dedication had drawn theses priests
to serve the poor, many had come to reject the spiritual for a
political commitment.

Although Pius XII restricted the priest-worker movement
in 1954 and halted it in 1959, its impact was extensive. Through
it the church confronted the unjust conditions of the working
poor and used their lives as a basis for theological reflection.
Rather than derive theology from doctrine, priest-workers
saw life experience as a source of theological reflection. In
the movement, Christians—cleric and lay—came to understand
their responsibilities not merely in terms of charity but in terms
of justice. For them the Christian community was the vehicle for
evangelization. The priest-worker movement provided the the-
oretical and practical elements necessary for a paradigm shift in
the understanding of what it meant to be a Christian. Maisie
understood the movement as the living out of the doctrine of
the Mystical Body. In 1950 she wrote that Christians were called

to leave no one solitary in the world and to create a world in which "souls" could flourish.[20] A few years later, in a brief religious autobiography, she wrote:

> Slowly we realized our immense responsibility, God, becoming incarnate, worked through a human nature. He used that nature to heal and to bless, he gave pardon through his human lips, He gave Himself with His human hands. In that human nature He suffered and died for the world. When, at the Ascension, that human nature left the earth, God incarnate continued to act, through a multitude of human beings. We, his Church, are the Incarnation continued. Layman as well as priest must be the channel of Christ's redeeming power. . . .[21]

Although Maisie spent much of the late 1940s engaged with the priest-worker movement, she remained a prolific writer, publishing *Young Mr. Newman* in 1948, *Return to Chesterton* in 1952, and translating *France Pagan?* in 1949. But writing was never enough for her. She threw herself into the C.E.G., hoping to rejuvenate it. Always on the lookout for able young Guild leaders, she found one in the remarkable Cecily Hastings, a dedicated Catholic and a charismatic speaker.[22] After finishing her education at Oxford, Hastings went to the United States in 1945 to work for the British Consular Service. There she met the Sheeds and joined their circle in New York, where, like many others, she discovered the power of theology in their living room. When she returned to London after the war she joined the C.E.G. and worked for Sheed & Ward. She became one of the Guild's best speakers, and was elected "Master," the first woman to hold that position. Maisie had high hopes for Cecily's leadership but lamented the fact that she was a woman, knowing full well the limitations that implied.[23]

Busy with the Guild in England, priest-workers in France, and a myriad of writing projects, Maisie also needed to give time to her family. Wilfrid had left Downside at the end of 1947 since it was too difficult for him to negotiate the physical environment of the school, particularly in winter. This was no loss for Wilfrid; he hated the place with its "world-weary aesthetism" and "languor."[24] He returned to America to be tutored by Frank

Maisie lecturing for the
Catholic Evidence Guild.
*Courtesy of
Rosemary Sheed Middleton*

Maisie in the 1940s (?).
*Courtesy of
Rosemary Sheed Middleton*

and to do physical therapy. In 1949–50 he took some college courses in New York City in hopes of being better prepared for Oxford. Maisie worried about Wilfrid continually, particularly his tendency to hold people in contempt.[25] Yet she and Frank adored him and constantly idealized his abilities. They all had some relief from each other when he spent the summer of 1949 with Clare and Henry Luce in Connecticut. Wilfrid learned to drive there, and at the end of the summer Clare Luce presented him with an Oldsmobile. No one was quite sure how Wilfrid got invited to this dream vacation, Mrs. Luce, a recent convert, had just lost her daughter and Wilfrid somehow filled the gap. As he later reminisced, he was the "resident smart kid who knew theology." When the summer was over "the resident smart kid" had to return home to quite different circumstances.[26] By the following year, in the fall of 1950, he enrolled in Lincoln College, Oxford. Maisie and Frank were jubilant and grateful.

Rosemary, on the other hand, had not yet met the English man who was supposed to appear, although she had an active social life. Maisie, like Min, wanted Rosemary to move in the right circles, but she was too busy to do much to arrange this. Rosemary worked at Sheed & Ward as a translator, was active in the Guild (although she hated platform speaking), and traveled back and forth to America several times. When she was twenty-one, she thought seriously about entering the Carmelites. She discussed this with people on both sides of the Atlantic, but finally decided against it. Maisie and Frank were relieved. Although they would have loved to have had a son who was a priest, they opposed the convent for a daughter. They thought most nuns were poorly educated and their lives were too narrow. They wanted more for Rosemary, who, if she entered the convent, would be cut off from them.

Other parts of the family presented more difficult dilemmas for Maisie. Her brother Herbert had severe alcohol and money problems. He had begun drinking when he was a soldier in Mesopotamia and continued after his return to England, except for periods when he would go on the wagon. His drinking was particularly dangerous given that he was a diabetic.[27] Tetta had other problems. After her marriage to Francis Blundell, much her senior, she moved to Crosby, her husband's ancestral home. The boredom of her life there brought out her mental fragility, which worsened with age. When Francis died of a heart attack in 1936, many concluded that Tetta's poor mental health had contributed to his stress. The death of their youngest child, his favorite son, also probably hastened Francis' death. During the war the widowed Tetta functioned well. She worked for the Union of Catholic Mothers, wrote, and organized family life for her remaining two children. But in 1949 Nick, always strangely underdeveloped, contracted polio and died within three weeks. Tetta's daughter, Hester, married a few weeks later. Soon after, Tetta suffered a severe mental collapse and went to live in a home run by the Dominican Tertiaries. During this difficult period Maisie sought the help of Houselander to try to understand her sister. Gradually Tetta improved, and several years later she joined the community of Dominican Tertiaries permanently, where she became a leader and wrote on Christian spirituality.

Throughout these family crises, Maisie and Frank traveled extensively. In 1949 Maisie was in America for three months, then Paris, and spent all of June in Italy with Wilfrid, finishing up with a trip to Lourdes with him where she prayed for his cure. Frank traveled back and forth across the Atlantic as usual and also visited Ireland with Rosemary. In the summer of 1950, Maisie, Frank and Rosemary saw Switzerland together, where Maisie continued to read in scripture and the lives of the saints. In 1950 she also finished writing *Return to Chesterton,* which appeared two years later.[28]

The earlier publication of the Chesterton biography produced a flood of letters and new material. In response, Maisie planned to enlarge the book, but she realized that the new material added fresh perspective. As a lover of documents, she decided to weave them into a story that she entitled *Return to Chesterton.* In it readers discover Chesterton as seen by his barber, his secretaries, the artist who painted him, the taxi men who transported him, and many who knew him as children. Maisie used the occasion of a new book to correct some of her errors and to fill the gaps that were left in her earlier work. In its introduction she reiterates again her view of biography. The work of the biographer was not to "read the riddle of the subject's character" but to tell "the story of a life . . . to get the documents into order and proportion, to tell the story truthfully. . . . [The biographer's job] is to draw the man so that he is recognized by friend and foe as the man they knew: he cannot hope to pierce the abysmal depths of personality."[29]

Although she never tried to pierce Chesterton's depths, *Return to Chesterton* clarified what she thought was his importance for the violent modern world. In such times the only appropriate spirituality seemed to be that of asceticism and total renunciation of the world. Chesterton, however, reasserted the importance of mystical spirituality at the heart of Christianity. As such he was a religious genius who offered a new direction to his contemporaries. *Return to Chesterton* completed Maisie's obligation to preserve the memory of her mentor but it also indicated her new interest in sanctity and holiness, subjects she would continue to explore for the next several years.

In 1950 she published four small books in a series called *Saints in Pictures,* "a tribute to the strength and beauty of sanctity." Her brief sketches of Francis of Assisi, Jerome, Anthony of Egypt, and Catherine of Siena contain biographical information and color and monochrome plates of the saint by various artists. Although slight in content, these sketches indicate the importance of the saints in Maisie's developing theology. For her they were continual reminders of God's love living on in time.[30] Each was diverse; each responded to the particular needs of a historical periood.

When Maisie finished the Chesterton manuscript, she began to read frantically for her next biography. She hoped to write the second half of Newman's life to supplement her father's two-volume study. As she read the documentary materials at the London Oratory she became fascinated by Newman's opponents and their motives. Slowly she grew more sympathetic with them and realized that any biography she might write could well contradict her father's interpretation. "In a way, it will be too funny if I reverse Papa's reversal of his father!!" she wrote Frank.[31] Maisie could never write a biography of someone with whom she was not in complete sympathy; neither could this loyal daughter reverse her father's most important work. In the end, she decided not to traverse the second half of Newman's life. And no other subject for a biography emerged, at least at the moment.

There was a pause in her writing, and when she published again in 1953, the subject was one completely removed from anything she had done previously. The years in America, the friendship with Houselander, and the experience of the priest-workers had changed her. At age sixty-three, she was ready to cut a path through completely new terrain.

NINE

"Chaos, Shot Through with the Brightest Delights"

✻ IN SPITE OF MAISIE'S DESCRIPTION of her life as "chaos," it was not exactly that. Rather, it was excessively full—with manuscripts, lectures, writing, preaching, and dealing with visitors, house guests, and all those who somehow made their way to her. Sometimes her life was so busy that it felt like chaos. Her "brightest delights" were travel, the people she met, the success of Sheed & Ward, the coming of age of Rosemary and Wilfrid, and her new areas of research—the New Testament and the early church fathers. Life was so full that she asked, "How did we get like this?"[1] The explanation was that the needs were many, the times exciting, and she was open to new possibilities. Unlike so many who close down as they age, Maisie remained responsive and full of energy.

For twenty-five years Sheed & Ward had been fueling the Catholic intellectual revival by reprinting Catholic classics and encouraging new Catholic writers. The company was at the apex of its success in the mid-1950s. But while publishing, writing, and lecturing were quite enough for Frank, they were not enough for Maisie. She plunged into new areas of study and was impelled simultaneously to respond to the homeless, in her words, "to harbour the harbourless." For her, Catholic thought had to be integrated with action, lest it be nothing at all.

In 1951 her new direction was not yet clear. What *was* clear was that Maisie and Frank were well-regarded Catholics. In June of that year they jointly received the Leo XIII Medal awarded annually by the Sheil School of Social Studies in Chicago. Previous recipients included Cardinal Stritch, archbishop of Chicago, and Jacques Maritain. The Sheeds were presented

141

the award by Bishop Bernard Sheil in acknowledgment of their outstanding work with the C.E.G., their achievements as writers and lecturers, their contribution as cofounders and partners of Sheed & Ward, their exemplary family life, and their devotion to the difficult responsibilities of the Catholic laity in the modern world. Frank, in accepting the award for both of them, said he did not "know how Pope Leo XIII feels that an old buzzard like me should get this medal, but I know he must be very pleased to know that it is also being given to my deserving wife."[2]

This joint award spoke of the reality of their lives; as Maisie never would have been who she was without Frank, so he never would have been who he was without her. Both of them knew this and knew that their marriage was based on love and common goals. But from the early 1950s on, Maisie would move along a new course.

The year 1951 had begun auspiciously, even before the joint award in June. After both traveled independently to America, the Sheeds returned to England in mid-March, only to leave again in April for a clandestine trip to Paris in celebration of their twenty-fifth wedding anniversary. Of course, they never took a trip exclusively for pleasure; it was always combined with business. This time the trip to Paris was followed by one to the Belgium office of Sheed & Ward, which had opened after the war under the direction of Louise Wijnhausen, a convert who had previously operated a publishing house in Bruges. Although Wijnhausen continued on with Sheed & Ward for many years, the Belgium branch existed for only a short time. Sheed & Ward would remain an Anglo-American firm, although there were efforts made in the 1960s to open a branch in Australia as well.

Frequent trips were normal for the Sheeds. With the children grown, Maisie undertook even more extensive travel during the 1950's. Especially when she was in America, this meant lecturing and Guild work. She was at her height in the early 1950s when, after twenty-five years experience and completely in her element, she lectured at lunchtime on Wall Street in New York City on the outdoor C.E.G. platform.

Back home in England, Min, who was now in her eighties, was increasingly enfeebled. Bone fractures, incontinency, and mild dementia all afflicted her. Ironically, Rosemary, who had had such a difficult relationship with Min, was the caregiver. Like so much in the Sheed household, this responsibility was expected but not discussed. It was a difficult labor for Rosemary, and Maisie knew it. She wrote to Frank, "Poor Rosemary in tears cannot face being left with grandmother. She'll cheer up presently, I think, and Wilfrid is a tower of strength."[3] The truth was that although Min adored Wilfrid, he could be of little help since he was at Oxford. After more than a year of illness Min died in July 1953. The passing of his mother, the woman who adored him, must have been difficult for Frank. From then on he carried in his wallet a picture of Min in her casket.

A hopeful event for Rosemary was her engagement to Neil Middleton, a bright former communist who had converted to Catholicism. The fact that both he and Rosemary were active in the C.E.G. seemed to Rosemary's parents a good basis for a marriage. Since Min died nine months before the wedding, Frank and Maisie never had to decide who would care for her once Rosemary left.

A fire in the New York office about late 1952 forced a disruptive relocation to a new office on Broadway. Sheed & Ward prospered nonetheless. Increasingly, it operated like a real business and made a profit. Louise Wijnhausen, now with the New York firm, was a tough businesswoman who brought some order to the operation. David Reeves helped find a new editor, Philip Scharper. Marigold Hunt faithfully edited *The Trumpet* and supervised advertising. For help with professional and personal chores, what Frank and Maisie wanted and needed was the likes of a Dorothy Collins, Chesterton's secretary, who had devotedly managed his life. Fortunately, such women kept turning up on both sides of the Atlantic to keep their tumultuous lives in order.

Since business was good, there was pressure on Maisie to read manuscripts, but given the demands of her own writing and other new commitments, she longed to be free of publishing.[4] However, Frank was not about to give it up. He said he would rather be conductor of an orchestra than first violin.[5] The truth was that Frank's personality was a big one. He needed to be center stage, and since his stage was now global, he was not ready to bow out.

As a prolific author, Maisie's style was to be writing one book and reading for another. During the early 1950s she spent considerable time reading New Testament materials, but her writing and editing project was *Be Not Solicitous.* The origins of this book went back several years to her relationship with *Integrity* magazine and the Marycrest community in Nyack, New York.[6]

Integrity began in 1946 with the Sheed & Ward mailing list. Its birth reflected a new vigor among Catholic laity, although its roots were in the English Catholicism of the 1930s. *Integrity* offered an alternative both to conservative, devotional Catholicism and to secularism. It advocated the need for community, the integration of work and prayer, a return to a traditional relationship between men and women, and an emphasis on sexuality for procreation. Under the early leadership of Ed Willock and Carol Jackson, *Integrity* advocated a spirituality of self-abnegation. A few years later, under Dorothy Dohen, it supported a more balanced theology. Although it lasted only a decade, *Integrity* represented a lay point of view independent of ecclesiastical control or influence.

By 1948 there was a growing interest among *Integrity* staff members to create a Christian family community. For many months a group of heads of household met to fashion a constitution for a rural community. By 1949 fourteen families signed on, paying $600 each for a sixty-three-acre site near Nyack, New York. Each family was given an acre of land and the rest was held in common. Most families of the Marycrest community were supported by one wage earner each and had between six and twelve children per family. They were dedicated to living a self-sufficient, primitive Christianity. Only gradually were the families able to clear the land, make roads, install water, and build homes. The pace was slowed by the community's unwillingness to use modern machinery. Their attempt to live countercultural lives and to trust in God created, at least initially, a camaraderie that attracted many others. Maisie Ward was immediately supportive. Here was a group of serious lay Catholics attempting to live out the principles of Christianity and Distributism. She backed up her commitment with money. In the early 1950s she lent two families $4,000 each to build houses at Marycrest. But as community members became divided and squabbled over principles and practices, Maisie became disillusioned. By 1956 she was fed up with the experiment and felt that her money could have been used better by some other project.[7] Although Marycrest ultimately disintegrated,[8] in the early 1950s it was a witness to lay, Christian community. Male domination and female subordination marred the experiment, but Maisie learned from this and brought its lessons to bear in her subsequent work in housing in Britain.

Maisie's interest in lay Christian communities was stimulated not only by Marycrest in America, but by the Taena community in Gloucestershire, England. Begun in 1949 by George Ineson and three others, this community, consisting mostly of converts was empowered by the doctrine of the Mystical Body. Members followed the Benedictine rule, shared a prayer life, and held land in common. Maisie was intrigued by this group, and she was determined to get a book out of them.[9] In 1956 Sheed & Ward published Ineson's *Community Journal,* the story of his life in Taena.[10] Like Marycrest, Taena was a precursor of the small lay communities Maisie encountered in the last years of her life.

Maisie's commitment to Marycrest and Taena was nurtured by her earlier friendship with Abbé Godin, who had introduced her to the needs of Christian families in France. By the late 1940s much of the Catholic lay apostolate was focused on vitalizing spirituality through family life. In the fall of 1949 Maisie attended an international meeting in Northamptonshire on the modern problems of the apostolate. In her description of the meeting she noted how greatly lay involvement had changed since Catholic Action had begun. Increasingly independent of clerical control, the lay apostolate meant integral Catholicism in which a profound spiritual life was tied to the liturgy and intense Catholic home life.[11]

This link between lay spirituality and Catholic family life was at the heart of *Be Not Solicitous: Sidelights on the Providence of God and the Catholic Family* (1953).[12] Maisie edited this compilation of fourteen articles, some of which had appeared previously in *Integrity*. The married couples who wrote them, including Maisie's old friends, Molly and Bob Walsh of the English Catholic Worker movement and Ed and Dorothy Willock of Marycrest, all attested to the experience of the providence of God in their family lives. Their stories, lessons of faith and courage lived out in the face of financial and psychological strains, provided the raw material for a theology of the laity.

The underlying assumption of *Be Not Solicitous* was that the Catholic ideal of marriage could reintroduce a spiritual principle into the center of human life. That ideal entailed trust in God and affirmation of a traditional view of the family with the father as head and the mother as helpmate. It was in the family that a man discovered his mission in life and a woman her vocation to perfection through suffering. This ideal, portrayed in high relief in *Be Not Solicitous*, was also widely shared by the burgeoning family movements such as the Cana Conference, the Catholic Rural Life Movement, and the Christian Family Movement.

In "Plea for the Family," her introductory chapter to the book, Maisie portrayed the family as a natural structure, a counter to the paternalistic state, a means for personal and societal rehabilitation, and a witness to the providence of God. It was in fact a plea for the family and an effort to find ways to strengthen it. Availability of housing, maternal and elderly care, and responsiveness and empathy by the church and clergy were all needed. However, her pragmatic introduction which emphasized what needed to be done to support families was in sharp contrast to the subsequent articles, which emphasized abandonment to God's will. While Maisie was impressed by the courage of those who created very large families, she was also clear that procreation for procreation's sake was not what was called for.[13] A husband's first duty was to his wife and existing children, who should not be jeopardized. While she was eager to find ways to support large families, she cautioned against criticizing small ones. There might be reasons—illness, late marriage, poverty —to explain them. Maisie's own late marriage and several miscarriages must have made her sympathetic to this reasoning.

Be Not Solicitous carried with it all the Catholic contradictions about women; Maisie was not free of these herself. She assumed that a woman's vocation was within the family, but her own life was always a public one. Her suggestion in "Plea for the Family" that women care for each other's children was in the very least ironic, given her own inability to care for her young children. But this disjunction between belief and practice was not limited to Maisie. As the lay Catholic movement expanded, women took up significant leadership roles, while at the same time avoiding a reevaluation of their subordinate role in Catholicism or the larger society. Maisie was no exception. She advocated an ideal "balance" between family and public life. But she believed that the problem of women was so immensely personal that she could not give a general suggestion to improve their lives. In a speech given in the mid-1950s, however, she urged women to develop their minds. As a God-given gift, the mind was supposed to serve one's spiritual growth; therefore, it needed to be cultivated. She also realized how difficult it was to be both a private and public woman. "But it is a difficult balance, you see, I have been violently attacked by the home people who say I'm allowing too much and on the other hand by the business women who say I'm not allowing enough. . . . It is a difficult balance, but if it can be done it is a most triumphant success."[14]

It is questionable whether Maisie ever established this balance herself. She was a public person who defended family life. By temperament, training, and choice she was incapable of being a traditional wife and mother. It was other women—Min, Rosemary, and a succession of unmarried women—who made Maisie's private life possible. In this regard she operated like a man, and like one she defended the traditional role of women. She could not or did not take on this contradiction in her own life; to do so meant that she would have to take it on in Catholicism as well. Given the culture of Catholicism in the 1950s,[15] it was impossible to conceive of any Catholic woman doing this. The only alternative was to find some way to escape the restrictions. Women such as Dorothy Day and the Baroness de Hueck were able to do so by adopting a radical life-style.[16] In the United States, Maisie's alternative was provided by class and national difference. Her lineage gave her a status that insulated her from the expectations for ordinary Catholic women. The fact that she was a foreigner protected her as well.

It was only in the 1970s that Catholic women began to re-evaluate their traditionally defined role. The integration of Catholics into mainstream American society and the increase in status of the laity preceded the more specific redefinition of the role of the Catholic woman. In the era in which this redefinition took place, Maisie was very old, and feminism had never been her cause. Instead, in her last twenty-five years, when her contemporaries narrowed their perspectives, Maisie widened hers by taking up the work of "harbouring the harbourless," a work that would dominate much of the rest of her life.

Maisie's most important work during 1953 and 1954 was the reading and exegesis of scripture. Scripture studies by Catholic scholars had recently emerged from the doldrums of the Modernist period and the field was now burgeoning, particularly in France. Maisie's intent was to digest the new scholarship, synthesize its insights, and make it available to Guild members and other educated Catholics whose understanding of scripture was limited. She was encouraged in this work by Father Alexander Jones of Upholland College. This was an immense project. She often felt "very out of her depth" and wished she had persevered with a second biography of Newman.[17] Nevertheless, she continued to study the New Testament and in mid-1954 was spurred on by a trip to Jerusalem, where she connected her voluminous reading with her experience of the historical sites of the Holy Land.

Life was very full. In part this fullness resulted from personal and public achievement. Sheed & Ward was more financially successful than it had ever been.[18] Maisie and Frank enjoyed growing reputations in Catholic circles and the attendant honors. Maisie won the Cardinal Newman Award and Frank received an honorary degree from St. John's University, both in 1953. And then there was family achievement.

Rosemary Sheed and Neil Middleton were married during Easter Week in 1954. Father Bevan, an Oratorian and old friend of the family, officiated at the full dialogue mass. A series of parties were held at Oakwood Court preceding the wedding, and a breakfast followed. When the couple returned from their honeymoon, they moved into a small flat at the new Sheed & Ward offices on Maiden Lane. The following year they moved to Ilgar, a large house near Wickford in Essex.

Wilfrid Sheed graduated from Oxford in 1954. Never a diligent student, he received Third Class Honors. The lack of academic distinction made no difference, at least to his parents. By going to Oxford he had realized their dream and probably that of his grandparents as well. He was now off to Australia to spend a year in his father's old haunts.

Maisie and Frank's first trip around the world in the summer of 1954 served almost as a turning point in their lives. They went first to San Francisco, then on to Hawaii, Canton, Fiji, and Auckland. In August they were in Sydney; Frank had not visited the place for ten years. They lectured and, as usual, Maisie continued her research while traveling from place to place. The return trip took them through Calcutta, Karachi, Beirut, Damascus, Jerusalem, and Athens. They returned to London in October in time to visit with Houselander, who had been ill and who died in 1954 shortly after their return.

Although 1953 and 1954 may have seemed typical busy years, important changes had taken place in the Sheeds' lives and in their close relationships: the deaths of Min, of old friend Hilaire Belloc, and of Caryll Houselander; Rosemary's marriage and Wilfrid's graduation. In late 1954, following the Australian trip, the Sheeds also moved out of Oakwood Court, their home of eight years. It had housed many people besides the Sheed family, some of whom, like the Australians Niall Brennan and his wife, stayed six months or even longer. But now the hospitality and warmth of Oakwood Court was over. It was indeed the end of an era for the family.

Foremost in Maisie's mind was the writing of her book, *They Saw His Glory: An Introduction to the Gospels and Acts.* Soon after her return from the round-the-world trip, in early 1955, she spent a month in Father Jones's scripture library at Upholland College. Her feelings about this project were acutely divided. She had established herself as an authority on the nineteenth century, but now she was working in a much earlier period. She tested her ideas about the Gospels on the outdoor speaking platform. In this sense she was working from her strength, since lecturing was her forte. What she talked out and explored with the crowd was then committed to paper. Her purpose in both speaking and writing about scripture was to bring to Guild members what they were not likely to acquire themselves—a synthesis of the best research on the New Testament. This daily reading and reflection deepened her in new ways. She began to internalize the scripture as never before. Several years after Maisie gave a lecture on this research at St. Mary's College in Indiana, its president, Sister Madeleva, commented:

> Almost inevitably the theologian is a scripture scholar and the scripture scholar is a theologian. Of Maisie Ward this is gloriously true. While sensibly refraining from identifying her with any of her capacities and activities as her best, we all are quick to recognize in her studies of the New Testament the rich and lasting fruit of her apostolate of the Word. I think of *They Saw His Glory* as the best and most profound of her writing in the areas of spirituality. No one, I believe, will differ with me.

> Some years ago Maisie Sheed lectured at our college on the reading of the New Testament. With her sense of impact and immediacy she focused at once on the Gospel of Saint Mark. For a moment I was disappointed. Saint Mark is not my favorite evangelist. But in a breath I was caught up in the chronicle of Saint Peter in this quick-moving duality under one inspired pen, one instrument of the Holy Spirit. That was the high hour of my life with Maisie Ward, unforgettable, luminous, to be compared with very few hours of my life.[19]

Throughout all of 1955 Maisie continued to work on her book. After Rosemary and Neil moved to Ilgar, she and Frank occupied the small flat they vacated on the top floor of the Sheed & Ward building on Maiden Lane. The place was convenient—one floor up from the office and in a lively section of London. Corpus Christi church was a few doors down and Rule's restaurant nearby. The flat had a bedroom and a large main room with space for dining at one end. It was always cluttered with manuscripts and books. Since neither Maisie nor Frank cleaned much, and house cleaners were not available in an office building, the place was often messy. When the Sheeds were away, their quarters were lent to others, adding to the disarray. Rosemary had always managed domestic life for Maisie and Frank, and with her departure they were at a loss. Fortunately, the vacuum was filled by Erika Fallaux, a young Austrian woman. Erika was what they were looking for: their own "Dorothy Collins," someone who could order both their domestic and professional lives. She began as a Sheed & Ward translator and became a secretary to Frank. She joined the Guild and served as Maisie and Frank's "adopted daughter."[20] Living around the corner from them, Erika was able and willing to shop, cook, entertain, run errands, and dedicate herself to their well-being. As a young woman without family in England, the Sheeds' companionship meant a great deal to her. Frank's ability to pay attention and make associates feel special ensured her devotion. To show appreciation for Erika's dedication they gave her the premium from a life insurance policy, established a deed of trust for her, and spent handsomely on her wedding.[21]

The great excitement of the year, the birth of a son—Simon Francis Wilfrid—to Rosemary and Neil in November 1955 became a tragedy nine weeks later, when he died of capillary bronchitis. This firstborn grandson was buried in a grave next to his grandmother Min. Through this sorrow Maisie worked on *They Saw His Glory* and began reading in the lives of the early saints. Again, she tested her ideas on the crowd, deepening her understanding of these holy men as she lectured.

In December, Frank received word that he would be honored by the University of Lille with a Doctorate of Theology. He was the first lay person to receive such an honor. December produced another surprise as well. Wilfrid, who had returned from Australia, was reintroduced to an old friend. Although Maisie was always on the lookout for nice Catholic girls for her son, Wilfrid was perfectly capable of attracting them himself. He found one in the most unlikely place—the eightieth birthday party for the Sheeds' old friend, Grace Smith from Torresdale.

At this gathering Wilfrid encountered Missie Darlington, his parents' godchild and one of his first American friends. One would not have expected anything to come of their meeting since Missie was about to enter the Carmelites—yet within a short time they were engaged.

The sadness of Simon's sudden and unexpected death and the joy of Frank's award and Wilfrid's impending marriage mingled on the surface of Maisie's emotional life, seemingly prompting no great change. But on a deeper level, that life was shifting. Her years of studying scripture and the lives of the saints were leading her in a new direction. Since her return to England after the war Maisie had become increasingly aware of the importance of housing as a prerequisite for a human and Christian life. Her work with the French priest-workers and with her friend Molly Walsh of the Catholic Worker movement had confirmed this need even more. In *Be Not Solicitous* she spoke of the importance of housing for Christian family life. But it was not until she was confronted directly with this need that she responded.

Once when she was at Ilgars visiting Rosemary, she encountered a woman she called "Mrs. Smith," who had read *Be Not Solicitous* and come to her for help.[22] The woman was about to be thrown out of Council housing because of the birth of her seventh child. Maisie offered to give the Smiths a bit of her farmland, but she quickly realized that given the couple's highly emotional orientation and their inexperience, such a gift would not be helpful. When Maisie was unable to help them, they condemned her as uncharitable. The condemnation stung. How was one to keep compassion alive, to have patience and to help? Although the context was different, the dilemma was the one she faced constantly on the outdoor platform. How to remain open while you were heckled and condemned? It was years of experience as a Guild speaker that gave her a willingness to be empathetic, to not walk away, to remain in dialogue. That deeply ingrained behavior helped her to a creative solution.

The confrontation with Mrs. Smith hurt, but it also revealed her most admirable attribute. Tough-skinned, intellectual and sophisticated, Maisie nonetheless allowed herself to be vulnerable and open to those in need. When she realized the parameters of the needs of the poor, she wept for an entire night. Within a few months she founded the Catholic Housing Aid Society.

Maisie's responsiveness forced her to change. Her old age was characterized by a psychological flexibility that complemented her inherited conservatism. From her youth she was incapable either of rebelling against the past or rejecting it, yet she never became rigid and fixed. As she moved in new ways, she dragged with her all her prior commitments, all her former loyalties and friendships. She became more inclusive and, finally, global in her affections.

These psychological qualities of loyalty and vulnerability were linked to a particular way of understanding reality, that of Christian humanism. Following in the tradition of Chesterton and Dawson, Maisie saw no contradiction between the humanist tradition and theological orthodoxy. Rejecting the dualism of neo-orthodox Protestant theologian, Karl Barth, she stressed that the Incarnation had restored human nature to its original integrity. She not only viewed creation as good, but human creative action as a means by which one could teach about God.[23] This world view gave benediction to the creative life. At this point in time, to be creative for Maisie was to respond to the Mrs. Smiths of the world. She had helped rebuild Christian thought through Sheed & Ward, now she wanted to rebuild the social order. She was almost sixty-seven and raring to go.

TEN

Hitting Her Stride

✻ INSTEAD OF QUIETLY MOVING INTO venerable old age, Maisie hit her stride in her late sixties. She wrote, she lectured, she organized, and she continued to travel extensively. In 1956 she went to America in March; by May she was back in England, and during the summer she went to France and Spain. By fall she was in America again, and at Christmas she returned to England. Such was her pace. Maisie had always been active and engaged, but now her energies went in new directions.

For eight years she read, researched, and wrote *They Saw His Glory: An Introduction to the Gospels and Acts*. In doing this she left the well-known world of nineteenth-century biography and plunged into the burgeoning literature on scripture. Research in a new field of scholarship might have been sufficient stimulation for a person, but not for Maisie, who did not dole out her energy in a controlled way. Confronted simultaneously with the dramatic need for housing in the postwar period, she acted, and with her longtime friend Molly Walsh began purchase houses for the poor. The sale of Gosse's Farm and subsequent royalties received from a Penguin edition of the Chesterton biography provided capital for this venture. In September 1956 Maisie, Molly, and a few friends founded the Catholic Housing Aid Society. Maisie was off on yet another project, eager and determined to convince others to lend support.

Her zeal for housing oriented her in a direction foreign to Frank. He would not dissuade her from action, but this was clearly her interest, not his. In some ways Maisie had been preparing for this moment for decades. It was she who bought the farms, supported the Marycrest and Taena communities,

backed the priest-workers, and argued for decent housing as
the prerequisite for good family life. Although eight years
Frank's senior, Maisie still had another round in life to go. They
would live it together, but it was she who was clearly breaking
new ground and filled with energy.

The year 1956 began gloriously for Frank when he received
the honorary doctorate from the University of Lille, but it
ended with an event that marked a serious deterioration in
health. At an outdoor Guild lecture in Hyde Park, Frank fell off
the platform and remained unconscious for forty-eight hours.
It was never determined what happened to him, but when he
regained consciousness, his hearing was affected and his timing
off. His life was slower after this incident, and he suffered from
periodic bouts with depression. His mind would never have
the same agility. Erika Fallaux was in the park when the fall
occurred. She got Frank to the hospital, called a priest, and
notified Maisie. In Maisie's mind, Erika saved Frank's life, and
she was forever grateful to her. At fifty-nine, the eternally optimistic Frank began to decline, just as Maisie fully came into her
own.

Maisie's prolific intellectual and social activity went on simultaneously with increasing business and familial complexity.
Wilfrid and Missie married in early 1957 at St. Thomas More's
in New York City, with Wilfrid's close boyhood friend, Father
Chris Kennedy, officiating. Although the parents hoped that
Wilfrid might ultimately take over the running of Sheed &
Ward, New York, it quickly became evident that he was a writer
above all. Philip Scharper soon became editor-and-chief in what
grew to be the more successful office of the Sheed & Ward
operation. Wilfrid worked first for Bishop Fulton Sheen and
the Society for the Propagation of the Faith and then joined
the staff of *Jubilee;* he also wrote for *Commonweal.* In London,
Neil and Rosemary became the heirs apparent of the firm, and
after about two years Neil became editorial director. When he
demanded changes that would strengthen the London office
vis-a-vis New York, the New York staff began to fear a take-
over. Differences of editorial opinion developed between Neil

and his father-in-law. Irrespective of these tensions, on the surface everything seemed normal and Sheed & Ward continued to flourish financially.

The firm grew and so did the Sheed family. Rosemary and Neil and Wilfrid and Missie were rapidly producing progeny. Between 1957 and 1960 five grandchildren were born. Rosemary and Neil had Mary Jo, Bridget, and Giles. Elizabeth and Frank were born to Missie and Wilfrid. Benet Middleton and Marion Sheed were added within the next few years. On whichever side of the Atlantic they found themselves, Maisie and Frank visited their growing family. They were always popping in on their way to somewhere else. Frank, the perfect grandfather, sang and carried on in his usual uproarious manner. Daunted by small children, Maisie was nonetheless devoted to her grandchildren, but she longed for them to get to the stage where she could take them seriously.

Maisie's disparate activity—familial, social and intellectual—did not debilitate her. Although she drove herself relentlessly, and her low blood pressure, collapsed lung, varicose-veined legs, and gnarled feet all made their demands, she tried to ignore these maladies. When she was extremely exhausted or nervous, liquor provided a lift. Maisie always drank, and in her old age she drank more. Despite the demands of life and myriad distractions she became increasingly focused. "It is my business," she wrote, "a) to pass on the Good News and b) to feed the hungry and harbour the harbourless, and in twenty-four hours to the day there is not time to accomplish the essential if one involved oneself in the inessential—even if it is in its own way important."[1] Maisie's expansive activity cohered with this vocational clarity.

In 1956 *They Saw His Glory* was published.[2] Its title, taken from John's Gospel—"The Word was made flesh and dwelt amongst us—and we saw His glory"—summarized Maisie's belief that scripture made Christ present among believers. She had frequently used scripture to teach Catholic doctrine on the street corner. But most Catholics were unfamiliar with the Bible and had no access to the scholarship that could help them understand it better. It was her intent in *They Saw His Glory* to digest the new biblical scholarship that had appeared since the 1940s and make it available to ordinary Catholics.

In working on this book Maisie frequently felt out of her depth; she longed to return to the safe waters of nineteenth-century biography. She sifted through linguistic, historical, and archaeological scholarship and immersed herself in the writings of Père Lagrange, the Dominican who founded the École Pratique d'Études Bibliques in Jerusalem and its organ, the *Revue Biblique*. It was through the scholarship of Lagrange and his followers that Maisie was able to revivify scripture and make it a means by which one could see "His Glory."

They Saw His Glory was a remarkable book that broke with the historical and biographical tradition of English Catholic thought.[3] Generally, English Catholics relied on translations of continental writers. In Maisie's book they got not translation but a digestion and popularization of French theological and philosophical scholarship. This was a significant achievement, made even more noteworthy because it was accomplished by a lay woman. In this regard Maisie had no rival in England or America.

Her purpose was not to prove the authenticity of texts or refute critics but to give the historical background and to set out the uniqueness of each gospel. She hoped to capture the person of Christ as transmitted in the words of those who knew and loved him. Her work was merely another aspect of her dedication to spreading the Good News. *They Saw His Glory* was well received. One reviewer claimed that it was "a real spiritual work of mercy."[4]

When she finished the manuscript for *They Saw His Glory*, Maisie began work on *Saints Who Made History*,[5] another new venture, this time in early church history. Like the former work, this book was also based on French scholarship, in this case that of the French patristic scholar Abbé Duchesnese. It was difficult work, and as before, she asked Christopher Dawson and E. I. Watkin to read the manuscript. Many experiences had prepared Maisie for writing this book. Her reading of Gibbon as a young girl gave her a wide sweep of history. The study of

Maisie on a donkey in Spain.
Courtesy of Rosemary Sheed Middleton

Maisie and Frank in
Auckland, New Zealand.
Courtesy of Rosemary Sheed Middleton

Newman, who had been brought to the Church of Rome by his study of the early church fathers, inspired her to study their lives. Her work on the series, *Saints in Pictures,* had kindled a love of the early church fathers, especially Jerome and Anthony. And her years on the outdoor speaker's platform taught her that next to scripture, the lives of the saints inspired people most of all.

Maisie believed that "to know the Faith we must study not only God but men too."[6] The history of humankind in relation to God was church history, and the way to uncover its dynamism was through a study of those who made it. As she described *Saints Who Made History,* it was not a "Church history but a handful of portraits to illuminate it."[7] What she portrayed was not the creation of a system of ideas, but a "living organism" that developed through the martyrs, theologians, bishops, and hermits who each shaped it by their own limited lives responding to historical circumstances. *Saints Who Made History* was a revisionist narrative that showed how the human/divine society called the church emerged from human fallibility and mistakes. As such it was vastly different from the church history Maisie had learned as a youth, in which scandal and human struggle were erased from the story.

The research and writing of *They Saw His Glory* and *Saints Who Made History* dominated the last years of the 1950s. Two of Maisie's earlier books—*The Splendor of the Rosary* and *G. K. Chesterton*—were reissued.[8] Royalties from the latter came at just the right time. Every bit of money she could get her hands on was plowed back into her latest housing project. Writing and housing were her two passions; they were not disparate activities but different expressions of belief.

The postwar housing situation in Britain was critical.[9] A million and a half homes had been destroyed in the war and another quarter of a million were severely damaged. No new construction had taken place and repairs on existing houses had been delayed. An increasing birthrate and an expanding immigrant population put additional pressure on limited housing options. Directly after the war the government estimated that there was a need for three to four million new homes—but given a weak economy, only one million had been built after six years. The housing situation remained serious, particularly in urban areas.

Maisie was initially introduced to the housing problem when she returned to England after the war and began looking for a family home. The French priest-workers had also alerted her to the need for housing. Her old friend Molly Walsh told her of many tragic cases of the homeless she encountered in the Catholic Worker movement. Maisie's research also contributed to her attentiveness. Her study of the lives of the early saints showed how they responded to the immense social needs of the decaying Roman empire. Her reading of manuscripts on Lamennais and Mary Ward confirmed this point too.[10] In Maisie's case experience and scholarship conspired to move her to respond.

What drove her was not merely charity toward the less fortunate but a new theological understanding that insisted on engagement in and for a suffering world. "God has made us citizens of earth also," she wrote in *Be Not Solicitous,* [and] "has given us the task of building the earthly city as well as preparing for the heavenly."[11] It was her childlike openness to the needs of others that propelled her into responding to the housing crisis. Once begun, she worked in the only way she knew how —by driving herself, sometimes almost beyond capacity, and by bullying, demanding, and harassing those from whom she wanted support. Obsessed with the housing question, no argument dissuaded her. Since it was evident that she did not operate out of self-interest, her friends and fellow Catholics either submitted to her demands for time or money, or evaded her. If one could not or would not join up with her cause, one became invisible to her.

While it is true that Maisie was ahead of her times by responding to the critical need for housing in postwar Britain, she was no organizer or strategist. Untrained and unsystematic in approach, she was an amateur who was incapable of analyzing the causes or finding solutions to a national housing problem. Her deep-seated fear of bureaucracy colored all of her responses. While her contribution was essential and noteworthy, it was also limited.

In 1956, in response to the need for housing particularly among Irish Catholics, Maisie and Molly joined with Anthony G. Cockerill, an accountant, Edward (Ted) W. Wade, a property agent, and Lance Thwaytes, a solicitor, to form the Catholic Housing Aid Society—CHAS.[12] The approach of the new society evolved slowly. The original plan was to buy a large house to be rented at a low rate to two families. That rent plus donations would be used to buy a second house. But limited resources and the urgent need for flats led CHAS to purchase houses on mortgage. The idea was that couples would gradually repay the loans from CHAS both through their earnings and by renting flats in their house to other couples. In its first two years CHAS bought homes for families to rent, provided loans for home purchase and repairs, guaranteed loans, and offered financial and legal advice.

Besides these services, some of CHAS's individual members, including Maisie, purchased houses to provide rentals for couples until these families could save enough to become homeowners. Beginning in 1957 Maisie bought houses in Croydon and Lewisham.[13] Each was divided into several flats. Part of the weekly rent was put into a savings account for the renter, establishing a fund that might serve as a deposit for the purchase of a house. In this way, persons were being housed while also being taught to save. Maisie continued to retain these homes until 1970, when they were given to Rosemary.

Confronting enormous need, CHAS's response was limited, yet in about six months after its founding it had helped fourteen families purchase houses. By October 1958, an additional thirty-four couples had been helped. Many others were served through advice and counseling.[14]

Initially, it was Maisie's name that sustained CHAS. She did the fund-raising, begging money from friends, soliciting it in newspapers, giving talks in churches, and persuading prominent Catholics to lend their support, time, and talent to the organization. Most of CHAS's money came from Catholic sources, and Maisie took it on herself to chide Catholics if they did not respond. When parishes refused to support CHAS because they needed money for Catholic schools, for example, Maisie argued that even the best school was of little use if children were sent home to horrible housing conditions.[15] She stated unequivocally in *Be Not Solicitous* that housing was the prerequisite to maintaining the Catholic family. And to ensure the Catholic family she would do almost anything, even beg from and pester wealthy friends for money.

Originally, CHAS was housed in the Sheed's Maiden Lane flat, but within a year of its founding the daily administration of the program was taken over by Ted Wade and moved to his office. By the late 1950s the myriad functions of CHAS were separated. CHAS continued as a registered charity, helping families through advice and loans, but the actual management of properties was taken over by a new entity, the Catholic Housing Association—CHA. CHA later became the Family Housing Association Limited, one of Britain's leading housing associations.[16]

The vision and creation of CHAS belonged to Maisie and Molly, but the organization grew dynamically in the early 1960s when Father Eamonn Casey, who had been working among Irish immigrants in Slough, became CHAS's director. By 1962 CHAS had an office and a salaried secretary. Its twenty volunteer solicitors had helped almost two hundred families.[17] Maisie remained on as Chairman of CHAS until 1964, when she became honorary president. It had been her intent from the beginning to hand the organization over to others; it just took many years to accomplish this task.[18]

Fearful of large bureaucracy and government organization, Maisie invested her hope in the voluntary association. She believed it could bring attention to a problem, take risks, and begin new ventures that government could not. Although CHAS remained a small voluntary alliance, it did have a multiplier effect, spinning off local CHAS groups in a variety of cities and stimulating interest in housing. Maisie, aware of the immensity of the housing problem and the puniness of CHAS's efforts, was often tempted to give up. She did not, nor did she relinquish her belief that the best work was done personally through small groups.[19]

Aware of the magnitude of change in her lifetime and her own aging, Maisie began to think in terms of an autobiography. In 1955, for the first time, she kept a journal for several months and she read the Wilfrid Ward family history again. In the next few years she also wrote a first draft of the autobiography that would later become *Unfinished Business*. Her old friend Christopher Dawson, at Harvard University from 1958 to 1962, while introducing Maisie to a public audience, encouraged her to write a memoir. His reasoning was the obvious: The history of English Catholicism was inseparable from that of the Ward family, beginning with W. G. Ward through Wilfrid Ward to Maisie. "I hope," he said, "that perhaps some day in the future she will crown this long series of works by writing her own memoirs and giving a personal impression of that age of new beginnings in Catholic intellectual and spiritual action that followed the first world war and to which we all owe so much."[20] In fact, Maisie already had begun those memoirs, and she would ask Dawson to read her manuscript. For the present she set the manuscript aside and began work on other projects—an introduction and epilogue to Mary Oliver's biography of Mary Ward and an article on Father William Maturin. Both pieces helped her revisit her own past.

Maisie was taken with Mary Oliver's manuscript when she first considered it for publication by Sheed & Ward. It was no wonder. Its subject, Mary Ward, had been an inspiration for her in her earlier life and the person she portrayed in *The English Way*. But much had changed in the estimate of Mary Ward since Maisie had written that chapter in 1933. At two World Congresses on the Lay Apostolate, one in 1951 and the other in 1957,[21] Pius XII had lauded Mary Ward as "that incomparable woman," one to be held out as a model for Catholic women to emulate. In her introduction and epilogue to Oliver's biography, Maisie described Mary Ward as a leader of the lay apostolate and a woman who had known "the long loneliness." Maisie explored the reasons for Mary Ward's failures, attributing them in part to overextension of energy and resources and the propensity, common among English women, to speak too bluntly and therefore to alienate. Ironically, Maisie herself was often found guilty of these same defects. Despite such liabilities,

Maisie saw Mary Ward as an extraordinary woman of the seventeenth century and called on her readers to pray that this valiant English woman be canonized within their lifetimes.[22]

Her revisiting of Mary Ward forced Maisie to rethink pieces of her own life. Another project on Father Maturin caused her to do likewise. As preacher and revered family friend, Maturin had influenced Maisie's early years. In a 1960 article, she portrayed him as a forerunner of the new spirituality.[23] Like Newman, Maturin was also a convert who had been nurtured on scripture and liturgy, and hence escaped the negative post-Reformation Catholic spirituality that afflicted Maisie's generation. In his sermons Maturin redefined theology and offered a psychology of religion. Rejecting beliefs in self-denial, he admonished his hearers to find God within themselves. By reviewing Maturin's life, Maisie saw the vast changes in spiritual understanding that had occurred during her own lifetime.

Through these cursory returns to Mary Ward and Father Maturin, Maisie not only reviewed her personal past and clarified elements of her autobiography, but she discovered the roots of the activist and life-affirming spirituality that was burgeoning in the late 1950s. This spirituality, growing for decades, was pushed to the foreground when in early 1959 Pope John XXIII called for a council to bring the church into the modern world.

Although John XXIII's plea for *aggiornamento* would mean the end of Tridentine Catholicism, this was not threatening to Maisie; she had been working in this direction for thirty years. Liturgical renewal, renewed consciousness among the laity, and a redefining of the church as the "People of God" were areas in which she had labored to bring about change. Although she would have her disagreements with the huge innovations brought by Vatican II, the paradigm shift it called for had already taken place in her.

At the beginning of the Second Vatican Council, expectations for renewal were high among many lay people. During the 1950s, two world congresses of the laity that had been held in Rome. Some twenty lay persons were invited to attend the first session of the Second Vatican Council.[24] During its early months, Maisie felt it was impossible to evaluate the Council's implications. "Of all Unfinished Business in the Universal Church, affecting also my own life, the Second Vatican Council looms largest—too large and too close to be written of here."[25] Nonetheless, it was clear to her that Sheed & Ward had helped prepare for this great event. The major theologians of the Council—Hans Kung, F. X. Durrwell, Hans Urs von Balthasar, Karl Rahner, and Edward Schillebeeckx—were all published by their firm.[26] In fact, on the eve of the Council Sheed & Ward published Kung's *Council, Reform and Reunion,* from the German text, *Konzil und Wiedervereingegung,* selected by Maisie and translated by Cecily Hastings.

If Maisie were reluctant to speculate on the impact of the Council, she was well aware that it was an important transition in the life of the church and that she was, in mind and spirit, at the center of the change. "I have felt strongly of late," she wrote,

> that we are, with our new beginnings, back in some sort to the days when the Church was young in her new found freedom, when in the social field she was feeling her way, taking on responsibilities which the state had hitherto held . . . that we are back in the days when theology and the implications of scripture were being worked out. . . .[27]

She continued,

> [T]he most heartening element of all in the new vitality is the degree to which the laity have their part in it. . . . In my lifetime I have heard the stirring call to Catholic Action by Pius XI, have witnessed the immense share borne by laymen in the intellectual apostolate, have received from my Bishop authority to teach theology on the street corner, sharing as my warrant tells me in the Church's commission, "Go ye and teach all nations."[28]

The change in religious understanding between the First and Second Vatican Councils was immense. In her late sixties, Maisie began to consider this shift. During her youth, piety was equivalent to mortification; one was urged to be detached in friendships and to love a person only in God. Maisie came to see this so-called piety as self-centered and turned away from the world and the suffering of one's fellows. Through the years this unreal spirituality faded, and she found spiritual vitality in ordinary life. "I realized more and more," she wrote, "that God who had made the order of nature meant it not to be abolished but consecrated and widened by the order of grace. In the family there may be irritations, but we *like* as well as loving [sic]. And while it is easy to love in general terms a world remote from us, the effort to like the neighbour whom we are obliged to help is an essential element in Christian love. If vitality is to be there it must be in a framework of reality."[29] Ordinary life with all its limitations was the framework of reality of which she spoke.

As Maisie's theology and spirituality changed, so too did her attitude toward ordinary life. She began to think of the world as the theater in which God operates and one for which she had responsibility. The avenues for expression of that responsibility became wider. As a Christian she had always believed that one must help one's neighbor through individual acts of charity. But for most of her life Maisie was uninterested in civic society, believing that religion itself was the appropriate means to ameliorate the world. Gradually, she became more aware of the complexity of social reality. Even her rabid antibureaucratic tendency was curbed. It took her many years, but she finally could appreciate the national health care system. (She was impressed both with the excellent care all the Sheeds received when they came down with pneumonia in 1952 and with Rosemary's prenatal care when pregnant with Simon.) As she became more keenly aware of the complexities—economic, social, and psychological—of the housing question, she saw that individual effort, even small collective efforts like CHAS, were incapable of meeting vast social needs. Voluntary effort could recognize a problem and bring it to public attention, but it must then be turned over to the local or central government.

Maisie was never a political person. The deep conservatism of the Ward family ensured that she would always be leery of government. And Frank's almost irrational distrust of all politicians hemmed in her response. But three decades of Catholic thought had moved her from an insularity and suspicion of the world to a belief that economic, political, and social power could be a force for good in the world. Before the decade was out, the C.E.G. stalwart who had maintained a rigid separation between religion and politics would become a public supporter of Eugene McCarthy, the Catholic contender for the presidency of the United States.[30]

Although to outsiders the Second Vatican Council appeared to radically modify Catholic life and practice, in fact the transformation had been going on throughout the century and accelerating since the 1930s. Maisie Ward exemplified that transformation. For her, the Council was a culmination of what she had worked for. Her recommendation to wary contemporaries was "to give it a chance." She saw the Council's changes in liturgy as a revolution that returned the church to the energy, vitality, and dedication of the early Christian community.[31]

At this moment of rejuvenation of the church, the Sheeds were at the pinnacle of achievement. The Catholic Booksellers bestowed the Campion Award on Maisie and Frank in 1960.[32] But although confident of her personal success, Maisie was concerned about what the future might hold. She did not fear the changes brought on by the Council, but she was anxious about the growing chasm between the life of the mind and the heart. She continued to believe that as much as religion needed a vigorous intellectual life, so did intellectual life need the contribution of religion to keep it supple and vital. Her fear was that compartmentalization and specialization of religious knowledge weakened both mind and heart. Increasingly, she worried that Christianity was becoming an irrelevance to human thought.[33] She knew that she must find a way to reaffirm her Christian humanism. Biography and autobiography would provide the means.

ELEVEN

"A Rest Is Needed"

✳ MAISIE WAS DEEPLY MIRED in the particulars of
the Guild, CHAS, and new books, but she needed a rest. Slowly
she would extricate herself, but there was too much before her
to let up any time soon. She wanted to finish the autobiography
started several years before as well as a biography of Caryll
Houselander. Then there was Sheed & Ward. Frank and she
needed to gradually withdraw from decades of publishing. As
if this were not enough, the dramatic pace of change in the
church brought on by the Vatican Council also demanded her
attention. The Sheeds watched as the institution they loved
above all others opened itself to the modern world, setting itself
on a course of seemingly irrevocable transformation.

Although Maisie knew a break was long overdue, she gave
no indication of slowing down. She and Frank continued to
travel to Europe, America, and around the world. On one trip
to Australia in 1962 they stopped in the Philippines, where
Frank received an honorary doctorate from the Philippine Women's University. Maisie received an award as well, a "Citation
for Dedicated and Useful Womanhood" for her "role as illustrious daughter and wife and in recognition for service to God,
home and community." The award's wording showed in part
that there was growing recognition that Maisie was making her
own contribution, independent of being Wilfrid Ward's daughter and Frank Sheed's wife.

Life also contained anxieties. Maisie was acutely concerned
about the Guild. Forty-five years ago she had seen it as a dynamic movement; now it was clear that its potential had not
been realized. Although Guild classes were always full, few of

169

the participants emerged as speakers. Many serious Guild members became priests, and others withdrew for a variety of reasons. The decline of the Guild was symbolized for her in the death of the last of its important leaders, Father Martindale. She reminisced about the three priests who had been most influential in Guild history: the Dutch scholar, Dr. Arendzen; Father Bevan of the Oratory; and Father Martindale. To her mind each was a precursor of Vatican II. Their passing symbolized the end of an epoch.[1] Of course, the Guild still had excellent lay speakers such as Cecily Hastings, who lectured throughout America, and some clerics who might give leadership. Maisie was particularly encouraged by Father Charles Davis, professor of dogma at the ecclesiastical college at Ware, editor of *The Clergy Review,* and author of a compelling book on liturgy and doctrine.

The Guild did make a contribution during a crucial time in the church's development. In fact, probably its most important work was to sponsor a fifteen-month theology course immediately following the opening of the first session of the Vatican Council. Several well-known theologians made presentations, and sessions were well attended month after month. But as much as Maisie believed in the Guild and was indebted to it for her own theological training, she knew that it had no widespread influence on contemporary religious life. This perplexed and worried her, but she had no solution to the problem. She merely kept up her part as best she could.

Her work with CHAS was another matter. The need for housing increased yearly. Maisie was both overwhelmed by what had to be done and humbled by CHAS's feeble attempts in the face of the demand—but her belief that Christian efforts must always be personal allowed few options.[2] The stress took its toll on CHAS members; one casualty was Molly Walsh, who suffered a debilitating nervous breakdown. Some people thought that Maisie's entrance into the housing arena would kill her. On the contrary, she worked harder than ever before, raising funds and garnering support. Only after eight years did she become less involved, as CHAS's honorary president.

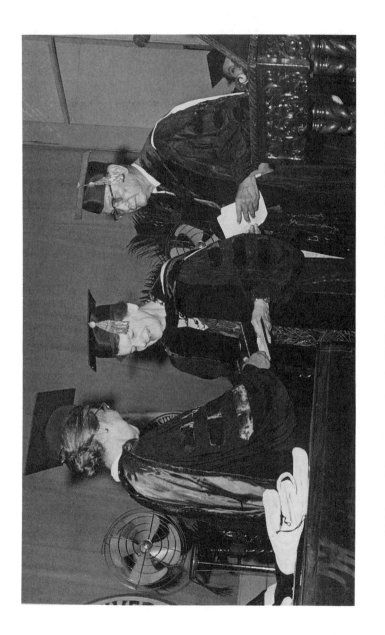

Maisie receiving an award at the Philippine Women's University in Manila, 1962.
Courtesy of Rosemary Sheed Middleton

Her own private efforts to house the needy continued in two of her own houses. She employed Gabrielle Murray, a woman from Lewisham, to collect rents from tenants and to do secretarial work at Sheed & Ward. Maisie continued to bind her friends and employees with double commitments. As it was unthinkable for her to let go of any of her own commitments, it was unthinkable that others would either. It was unacceptable to quit, and Maisie told them so in no uncertain terms. Her success in continuing her multiple responsibilities in part rested on her tenacious hold on those who worked for her and in part on her relentless search for others she could enlist in her cause.

It was these commitments and her scheduled writing that kept her from responding extensively to the developments of the Vatican Council. Although she traveled to Rome with Frank during the Council,[3] she maintained a wait-and-see attitude while it was in session. She was supportive of the Council's writings on the liturgy, however. On the eve of the Council she described the mass as the communal meal of the Christian people and the "breaking-through into earth of heaven's worship."[4] In this time of enormous theological reawakening and the dangers associated with it, she saw the liturgy as offering pastoral help. She urged readers to give the new changes a chance.[5] She lamented the loss of the Latin mass, but she recognized that the innovations made the mass more accessible to believers. If liturgical change was about anything, it was about bridging the gulf between priest and lay person. From her days in the little chapel at Horley, Maisie supported an enlivened congregation in dialogue with the celebrant. She believed that the dialogue mass could create a relationship much like that in the early church where all people participated in the act of worship.

Maisie had been influenced not only by the views of Charles Davis on doctrine and liturgy, but those of Brian Wicker as well. In his book *Culture and Liturgy*, published by Sheed & Ward in 1963, Wicker argued that the task of the Christian is not to be an apologist for the church but to mediate to the world the truths and values contained in the liturgy itself.[6] What was needed was to transmit doctrinal values through one's own personality. It was just such ideas that galvanized Maisie and helped her move beyond an apologetic orientation toward her Catholic faith.

The documents of the Vatican Council showed clearly that belief, nurtured in liturgy, expressed itself in lived commitment. Through her own life experience, Maisie understood how the church had come to this insight. Once the defensiveness of Catholicism ended, the great treasures of Catholic thought and theology were rediscovered. This intellectual revival led naturally to applied theology. As she saw it, this revival, which reached back to Newman, found its realization in the priest-worker movement and in myriad social commitments.[7] The connection between belief and action she found in her own life was now confirmed by the documents of the Vatican Council.

Although she felt vindicated, she was fully aware that the great reforming energy unleashed by the Council was a double-edged sword. While the new vitality might return the church to its early dynamism, it might also destroy it. She feared that empowerment of the laity could backfire if adherents did not really love the church. Might criticism of the church fuel a critique of the very doctrines she had preached for decades? To her mind, the point of the conciliar changes was to revitalize, not weaken the church,[8] but it was not yet clear which direction these changes might take.

Initially, Frank refused to concede that the "new theology," which spread through C.E.G. and was published by Sheed & Ward under the auspices of Scharper and Middleton, would change the church. "I feel all sympathy with you over what you call the unsettling effects of the bright new theologians," he wrote a friend. "I can only tell you that they don't unsettle me. The really big ones give me nothing but solid nourishment, but the little ones are the trouble."[9] While the Council appeared to support his belief in the accessibility of the sacraments and empowerment of the laity, he worried that biblical criticism might lead believers to attack the very veracity of scripture itself. As his son saw it, Frank envisioned "the new critics as mainly a bunch of smart alecks nibbling like mice on a piano . . . at the very foundation of the Faith. If one began, like them, throwing out bits and pieces of the Gospels on scientific grounds, who was to say that some new and shinier research method wouldn't soon throw out the rest?"[10]

Frank's denial that real chaos was emerging could not be sustained indefinitely. A year after the Council he wrote:

> I remember a conversation we had just before I left San Antonio. Twenty things have come my way since to confirm my view that chaos is staring us in the face—from the priest in Australia who in the pulpit took a rosary apart and flung pieces into the congregation with the remark 'That's the end of that nonsense,' to the priest who in the cafeteria of a Catholic university shouted out 'I wish the pope would keep his fucking hands off things.'[11]

In 1962 Frank published *To Know Christ Jesus,* which traced the development of the person of Jesus through the Gospels. His intent was pastoral, to have Jesus come alive to his readers through scripture stories. *Is It the Same Church?* (1968), published after the Council, was Frank's attempt to deal with a church that had undergone profound change.[12] Although he tried to console the confused by arguing that the pre-conciliar church was not so different from the post-conciliar one, he acknowledged that the church of the future might be smaller and less vital and that the Vatican Council might be a sunset, not a sunrise. Finally, he had confronted the fact that the church he loved was in disarray.

The Second Vatican Council was an event prepared for by decades of work by and for the laity. During the late 1950s the newly-released religious energy expressed itself in a variety of ways, not least of which was a steady expansion of religious publishing. Sheed & Ward, especially in America, was thriving. With its financial assets increasing on a yearly basis, the decision was made to diversify ownership of the company. Throughout the firm's history the Sheeds had controlled 95 percent of the stock in the New York company while Clare Booth Luce owned the remainder. Now Frank was eager to pass on control to others. He had given himself to publishing for thirty-six years. With the daily decisions being made by Philip Scharper in the New York office and Neil Middleton in London, in 1962 it seemed appropriate to pass on control of the firm. The plan was to have Frank and Wilfrid retain 25 percent of the stock and to reinvest profits from the sale in a diverse portfolio that would bring Frank and Maisie a yearly income. Although the Sheeds did not completely dissociate themselves from Sheed & Ward, during the middle years of the 1960s their influence was considerably limited. They continued to offer their manuscripts for publication and to extend their invaluable contacts to the company, but most of the time their involvement was restricted.

The transfer of control was not without its problems. Increasingly, in both England and America, Sheed & Ward took new publishing directions that Frank did not like. Middleton and Scharper were highly critical of authoritarian and absolutist tendencies in the church, and they encouraged publications of the same point of view. Neil did not like the Sheed & Ward backlist, and though he originally promoted Frank's books, especially *Theology and Sanity,* his support faded. He broke with ecclesiastical censorship and stirred up office and family relationships when he ended the historic subordination of the poorer London office to the wealthier New York one.

Neil also irritated Frank by his publication of the *Slant* journal and of books treating the relationship between Catholicism and social analysis. The Slant Group, begun in 1958 among Catholic Cambridge undergraduates, espoused a radical Christianity linked to socialist principles.[13] Like the Distributists forty years earlier, the Slant Group was allied with the Dominicans and called for religious commitment with social, political, and economic implications. Short-lived and small in number, the Slant Group had influence far beyond what might have been imagined. Since Sheed & Ward published *Slant* and its associated books, its radical agenda was linked to the company. This was particularly hard for Frank to bear, given his conviction that social and political issues should be kept separate from religion. As an old Distributist, Maisie, on the other hand, was more open to this kind of exploration.

In the New York office there was less tension. Frank thought Scharper was a good editor, but he did not always agree with his editorial policy. According to Frank, Wilfrid, too, was concerned about Scharper's control. Even before the transfer Frank wrote to Maisie:

Philip . . . not only wants my letting him publish more or less what he wants . . . but my warm approval of his choices. . . . P[hilip] asked W[ilfrid] what he thought of the Spring and Fall lists. W. named some of the books that he did not much admire. P. defended them all, & this was [what] hit Wilfrid, not only their quality but on the press reaction: such & such a paper had praised this or that book. (What W. hadn't grasped was that none of these books had had good sales). Anyhow it seemed to him that this was an editorial approach new in S & W and one that he would find it very hard to work with. He foresaw endless conflicts. . . . [H]e couldn't see P. as the sole or decisive mind in the firm.[14]

Of course, Scharper had his own quarrels with Frank and Wilfrid, especially since he did not always agree that Wilfrid's writing was of the highest quality.[15] But when Frank bowed out of the New York firm in 1962, Scharper took control.

Although there were strains between New York and London and between Frank, Middleton, and Scharper, the late 1950s and early 1960s were heady times at Sheed & Ward. As in the 1920s and 1930s, when the firm stimulated a Catholic intellectual revival with publication of some of the greatest Catholic writers, so now the best Catholic theological writing appeared with the Sheed & Ward imprint. Hans Kung, Edward Schillebeeckx, Hans von Balthasar, Karl Rahner, Charles Davis, and Hubert van Zeller came in on the European side. Dan and Sidney Callahan and Andrew Greeley were brought in by the American firm.

In America Sheed & Ward books sales remained strong during the Council, but they began to decline soon after it ended. There were fewer clerical and lay readers, and as the number of women religious dwindled, Sheed & Ward's largest readership disintegrated. Smaller enrollments in college religion courses meant fewer book orders as well. In England the decline in sales began earlier and became truly precipitous after 1965. By early 1967 Neil Middleton left Sheed & Ward, and the company was subsequently refinanced by a new editor, Martin Redfren. Sheed & Ward, New York, struggled through the late 1960s, until in 1970 Frank came out of retirement to try to save it.

The transition to the post-Vatican II church was difficult for Frank and Maisie. Both had spent their lives preaching the doctrines of the church, and now those very doctrines were being denounced by those who called themselves Catholics. But Maisie more than Frank could see the changes as opportunities for new growth. Since her principal interest was never doctrinal orthodoxy but lived belief, she found ways to continue to respond to the good she saw around her.

When Sheed & Ward was diversified in 1962, the Sheeds simultaneously established their legal residence in the United States. They settled in Newark, New Jersey to be near Wilfrid and Missie, who lived in Leonia. Leaving New York also meant that they avoided the higher state taxes there. For the next several years they would live in the Carlton, a residential hotel which was in easy reach of the Newark Public Library and its excellent collection of material on Robert Browning. Maisie was already planning her next major project—a biography of her most-loved poet.

At this stage in their lives Frank and Maisie had both discretionary time and money. Their living expenses were always low, and when they were out of the United States, which was three-fourths of the year, they stayed with friends or relatives. They were more comfortably off than in earlier times. Their income from lectures and royalties was about $20,000 per year, and this was supplemented by nontaxable stock dividends of about $6,000.[16] Their extensive travel was often paid by some institution granting them an award. The plan for these retirement years was to spend three to four months a year in America, England, and Australia, respectively. In order to comply with tax regulations they often went to England via Ireland; since their entry into England was not recorded when they crossed the Irish Sea, they could stay in England longer than allowed. Frank and Maisie had been global travelers long before it became fashionable; rather than cut back on travel as they aged, they augmented it.

While Maisie may have longed for a respite, there was none in sight in the early 1960s. In addition to Guild and housing commitments, she published three more books—her biography of Houselander (1962), her own autobiography (1964), begun several years before, and an edited volume of Houselander's letters (1965). She also wrote an article on John Henry Newman, which appeared in *The Clergy Review*.[17] Although she had definitely decided not to pursue a sequel to her Newman biography, this short piece summed up his importance for the twentieth century. She painted him as "one of the great Fathers of the Church," whose most significant contribution was intellectual—he rebuilt the foundation of Catholic thought through preaching and writing. Newman was "the Indicating Number" among his contemporaries, the only one to have a lasting influence on the future. She urged her readers to pray for his canonization and to remember that he would be made a saint because of, not in spite of, his intellectual contribution.[18]

If Newman was a peculiar type of "saint," Houselander was even more peculiar. But in both cases they pushed their contemporaries to a new understanding of sanctity. When Houselander died in 1954, Maisie became her literary executor. Four years later Sheed & Ward sent out a call for letters and information about her; an immense quantity of material poured in. The suspicion that some criticized Houselander adversely, and that some one else might write a biography of her, spurred Maisie on.[19] She stopped work on her own autobiography to finish *Caryll Houselander: That Divine Eccentric*.

This biography was Maisie's attempt to come to grips with the meaning of her friend's life. She struggled to make sense of Houselander's unorthodox life, admitting that it was immensely difficult to write her biography. The problem was not merely Houselander's eccentricities, visions, and general oddity, it was the immensity of the material, the diversity of opinion about her, and the obvious lack of historical perspective. She had to sort through completely conflicting views of Houselander's person and life and make sense of them herself. She was not totally successful. *That Divine Eccentric*—repetitious, diffuse, and too chatty—is not a well-written book.

Houselander's life was colorful. She grew up a sickly child consumed by a sense of guilt. She experienced a broken home, social ostracism, and an unsuccessful love affair with a Russian Jew, Sidney Reilly, a naturalized British citizen and a spy. Houselander worshiped him, and when their relationship ended, she experienced profound rejection. In response, she became increasingly ascetic and strange. Through several visions she came to believe in the Russian idea of Christ as a humble, suffering servant. She realized that it was impossible to be Christ's follower unless his poverty and humility were accepted as one's own. She began to work in London among the most despised—mental patients and lunatics. As Maisie said, Houselander loved them back to life. Although some argued that Houselander was starved for love, others claimed that she loved those who were spiritually lost. Like Dorothy Day, Houselander believed that the most important work was to create a force of love in the world strong enough to combat hate and fear. Houselander realized this belief through her work among the poor, her counseling, and her writing.

In spite of its diffuseness, *That Divine Eccentric* clarified the meaning of Houselander's life. As a neurotic, she was able to use her disability to assist those beyond the help of the medical profession. Her personal brokenness became the means through which she healed others. Maisie saw that Houselander lived out the belief that Christ dwelt in each person. Theologically, hers was a life which had internalized the doctrine of the Mystical Body.

Maisie created a sympathetic portrait of Houselander. She saw her as having a great capacity for love and generosity, a strong desire for God, a strange psychological power, extrasensory perception, and considerable artistic talent. A strange and broken personality, she was nonetheless transformed by God. But the complexities of her personality were never fully explored by Maisie. Nor did Maisie deal with Houselander's critical attacks on Catherine de Hueck, Dorothy Day, or the Grail. Maisie excluded from her book some of the most salacious accustions against Houselander that came to her attention. She interpreted her as loving, perceptive, and immensely creative, but left her judgmentalism and quick tongue unexplained. Her portrait was not fully convincing.

There was much in Caryll Houselander that Maisie loved. She admired her intensity and her commitment to voluntary poverty and nonworldliness. She shared her great love of the sacramental life of the church, especially the Eucharist, her attraction to the imagery and meaning of the doctrine of the Mystical Body, and her generosity and life-affirming qualities. Her positive attributes stand out clearly in *The Letters*, a volume Maisie edited after completing the biography. These letters of counsel and advice reveal Houselander's spiritual genius, independent of the complexities of her life.

Maisie was aware of the historical importance of Houselander's work. It was immensely popular among postwar Catholics because it both captured the suffering of the period and explained it in terms of religious doctrine. For Houselander, not only was Christ in every person, but every person's suffering could be understood as Christ's suffering and could be used by God. Conversely, as one eased the suffering of others, one eased Christ's suffering. This theological interpretation had profound resonance for a whole generation of Catholics.

While acknowledging the popularity of her work, Maisie was also aware of the prejudice against Houselander as a lay woman writing about theology. She suggested that one had to return to Julian of Norwich of the fourteenth century in order to find an English Catholic woman predecessor. In fact, Julian's work was a great inspiration to Houselander, and through her Maisie came to appreciate this early English mystic in new ways.[20]

After completing *That Divine Eccentric* and *The Letters*, Maisie returned to writing her own autobiography.[21] She had been thinking about it for a good part of a decade. What she crafted was the life of a twentieth-century Ward, rather than the story of her life with Frank. In a very real sense *Unfinished Business* was volume three of the Wilfrid Ward family history.

As the embarrassed son of peculiar parents, Wilfrid Sheed claims that he urged Maisie not to focus her autobiography on private family life[22] but that might have been Maisie's inclination in the first place. If autobiography were governed by her biographical standard, then it should emphasize the thoughts, ideas, and actions of a person. While she included familial aspects in the autobiography, what she attempted to capture was the public person, who was far more interesting than the private self. Although religious themes abound, *Unfinished Business* is not a pious rendering of a life. Rather, it is a lived realization of her favorite line from Kipling's "Boots": "There's no discharge in the war!"[23] Her premise is that life is high adventure that must be approached with vitality and verve. One keeps at it; there is no rest, no letting up, in short, no discharge.

Like so much of Maisie's writing, *Unfinished Business* is not tidy. Its organization is jarring; Maisie moves from a discussion of the most lofty ideas to minutiae, all in the space of one paragraph. Her focus is diffuse, reflecting not only the way she thought about a subject but the nature of her life itself. She was interested in many things simultaneously. She was always finishing one book and planning another. Her endless travel and speaking engagements diverted her, as did her commitments to the people she met and worked with. *Unfinished Business* captures this relentless activity and vitality. If she had been interested in ideas alone, the book might have been neater, more systematic and reflective. But ideas were important to her only in so far as they could be put into action. Whenever she saw that an idea could be carried out, she was galvanized. The result was continuous explosions of energy.

Because she was committed to the rightness of her idea-experiments, Maisie had a difficult time letting go of them, even when she wanted to move on to something else. Her involvement with farming and with the Guild are examples of this. When she found she could pass her work along to others, as with CHAS, she did so easily. But if there were no logical heir to her efforts, she persevered, unable to give up on an idea. The result was that after almost three-fourths of a century of living, she had a myriad of commitments. Convinced that there was no cessation to her work, she presents her life as "unfinished business." Her autobiography stands as an invitation for others to pick up the pieces.

Following the model of the Wilfrid Ward family history, Maisie's autobiography combines her own history with the great movements of Catholic intellectual life—the Modernist crisis, the Catholic Evidence Guild, the Catholic Worker movement, the lay apostolate, the priest-worker movement and Catholic publishing. While its plot is her life, its subplot is the coming to consciousness of Anglo-American Catholicism. *Unfinished Business* is that story in microcosm, a personal guide to Catholic history over the last century.

Maisie completed the first draft of her autobiography in the late 1950s. She revised, pared it down, and finally published it in 1964. Finishing it gave her permission to take the rest she had wanted for so long, especially since she had substantially disengaged from Sheed & Ward and from CHAS. But for Maisie a rest did not mean idleness, but rather diversion in some big writing project. At this point the big project was a biography of Robert Browning. In the conclusion of *Unfinished Business* she had written: "I have already taken refuge in the Browning love letters . . ., in the poetry I have lived with for sixty years and over. More than ever these days Browning is my poet. . . ."[24]

Maisie turned to Browning as an embodiment of what she called "Christian humanism," a belief that does not reject the glory of this world because of belief in another. The concluding paragraphs of her autobiography contain these lines from Browning:

> What is the buzzing in my ears?
> Now that I come to die,
> 'Do I view the world as a vale of tears?'
> Ah, reverend sir, not I![25]

Like Browning Maisie did not flee worldly engagements. "We need not lose the natural to gain the supernatural,"[26] she wrote. That was the summary of the philosophy she chronicled in *Unfinished Business*.

As she ended one book, she took up another. Browning's life provided yet another means to explore her philosophy of Christian humanism. Driven by love and enthusiasm, the seventy-five-year-old Maisie plunged into this new work. It would give its own kind of rest.

TWELVE

"A Refuge in Browning"

✳ IN THE MID-1960S, MAISIE FOUND REFUGE in her Browning project and relief in new social commitments. Refuge and relief were needed, given her concern for the Guild, her family, and the church.

The Guild was in the doldrums as never before. With no new leadership emerging, its future was bleak. Family problems were also particularly pressing. Maisie's brother Herbert died in 1965, ending their relationship that had grown distant over the years. Although it was little known in the family, and Maisie certainly did not discuss it, Herbert had been plagued by alcoholism, erratic behavior, and financial problems of his own making. His death was depressing. Of her own family only Tetta remained, and although improved in health she remained psychologically fragile.

Maisie's greatest concern was for her children. Both Rosemary's and Wilfrid's marriages were fraying. Wilfrid and Missie separated in 1967 and were officially divorced four years later. Since Maisie idolized Wilfrid and firmly believed that it was a wife's duty to keep a marriage together, she acted coolly toward Missie after the separation, although both she and Frank continued to see her and their grandchildren. The disintegration of Rosemary and Neil's marriage was more complex because Neil was entangled in the family business. Sheed & Ward of London was in very bad financial shape by the mid-1960s. Neil wanted out of it and out of the church. He left Sheed & Ward in 1967 and went to Penguin as a political editor. Maisie seemed to genuinely like her son-in-law, but the relationship between Neil and Frank had been difficult for some time. In the mid-1960s, as Frank became more critical of Neil's management of the company, Rosemary sided with her husband against her parents. There was obvious strain on everyone. As far as the marriage was concerned, Maisie was probably ignorant of the other interpersonal stresses on her daughter and son-in-law's relationship. Rosemary waited for Neil to leave, which he finally did in 1973.[1]

For Maisie, Christian marriage was a sacrament; to watch it disintegrate within her own family was almost unbearable. The breakup of her children's marriages meant as well that their ties to the church would be threatened. The unthinkable had now happened. Wilfrid, trying not to hurt his parents, allowed them to believe what they wanted about his relationship to the church. What Frank wanted was an annulment of his son's marriage, and he set to work immediately to secure one. Rosemary was more forthright with her mother. She told Maisie that she could no longer believe in the church and was nonpracticing. Maisie said she would pray for her. But as nothing before in her life, the end of her children's marriages caused Maisie enormous pain. She wept openly in front of friends. Ironically, one of the reasons she undertook writing the Browning biography in the first place was to explore the meaning of Christian marriage. She now explored that "ideal" marriage as she watched her children's crumble before her.

Since youth Maisie had loved the poetry of Browning and shared that love with her mother and Chesterton. Although she cherished Chesterton's brief biography of Browning, she felt it did not adequately treat the great love story at the heart of his life, the theme that was of most interest to her. From her early days with the Guild, Maisie used Browning's words and ideas to lure the crowd to follow her logic. At age eighty, in front of a crowd of more than two hundred people in New York City's Times Square, she finished her career as a street preacher exploring Browning's search for belief. In writing this biography Maisie took up her first avowedly non-Catholic subject; but in her hands Browning became, at least in sentiment, a Catholic poet.

Maisie with her grandson Frank Sheed Jr.
Courtesy of Maria Darlington

One event that provoked her to write this book was the publication of Betty Miller's biography of Browning years earlier, in 1952. Miller's book infuriated Maisie and drove her to vindicate her hero. Her fury took a long time to be assuaged; she could not begin work on Browning until 1963. When she did, it became all-consuming; it took her six years of unstinting labor to complete the two volumes of *Robert Browning and His World*. The first volume, *The Private Face, 1812–1861*, appeared in 1967, the second, *Two Robert Brownings?*, in 1969.

Betty Miller's *Robert Browning: A Portrait*[2] was in Maisie's eyes the antithesis of biography. Brilliantly written in Stracheyesque style, Miller subjected Browning to a neo-Freudian interpretation. She portrayed him as a dependent personality who sought out Elizabeth—an older woman whose goodness and intellect he respected—to resolve his dependence. In line with this theory, his marriage was less than ideal and he was relieved when Elizabeth died. This interpretation was a mockery to Maisie and she determined, much as she had with her biography of Chesterton, to set the record straight.

This resolve to save Browning gave Maisie further reason to put aside, once and for all, the thought of writing a sequel to her *Young Mr Newman*, a project she had been toying with for many years.[3] She had great love for both men, but in the end, she gave herself to Browning. In a speech she delivered probably in the late 1950s, Maisie compared and contrasted what she called their "approach to reality."[4] Near contemporaries, Newman and Browning both understood unbelief and the difficulty of expressing truth. Both were highly sensitive poets—Browning a philosophic poet, Newman a poetic philosopher. One wrote in prose, one in verse. But their approach to supreme reality differed. Newman's was primary and direct, Browning's was indirect; he sought the infinite through the finite, the creations of God. Both men shared antipathy for Roman Catholicism. But where Newman ultimately came to see the church as the fulfillment of the truth he already possessed, Browning felt no need for organized religion or for public worship. His one sacrament was marriage, and it was that sacrament that transformed his life. Maisie painted Browning as the believer seeking the infinite. His poetry was shot through with a sense of the incarnation of the divine. Although Browning remained outside the Catholic fold, Maisie believed he was Catholic in sentiment. She quoted the poet himself as evidence for her conclusion:

> At the silver bell's shrill tinkling,
> Quick cold drops of terror sprinkling
> On the sudden pavement strewed
> With faces of the multitude.
> Earth breaks up, time drops away,
> In flows heaven, with its new day
> of endless life, when He who trod,
> Very man and very God,
> This earth in weakness, shame and pain,
> Dying the death whose signs remain
> Up yonder on the accursed tree,-
> Shall come again no more to be
> Of captivity the thrall,
> But the One God, All in All,
> King of kings, Lord of lords,
>
> As His servant John received the words,
> 'I died and live for evermore.'

Yet I was left outside the door.[5]

Like Browning, Maisie was a Victorian who was also a modern person. Biography allowed her to investigate themes they shared—the lifelong quest for God, the sacramental and transformative aspects of marriage, and an approach to God through the whole person. As Maisie saw it, Browning spent his life trying to pull the infinite into the finite. His was the philosophy of Christian humanism, which linked the natural and supernatural worlds. She amply illustrated this through his poetry.

For Maisie, Browning's life was a quest for God through the medium of nature and of human love. Love, she believed, was the key to understanding his theological and poetic vocabulary. No poet had studied the relationship between man and woman as Browning had; none had understood marital love as the manifestation of God's love. "And not only does Browning draw me," she wrote, "but he gives me a chance on what Christian marriage can be which I do think is needed for these days. . . ."[6]

Her own experience had taught her that human love was a glinting of divine love. Although never consciously acknowledged, the parallels between the Brownings' marriage and her own—an older woman saved from a suffocating family by a younger man—must have made Maisie more sympathetic toward her subject. His life also allowed her to deal with the epistemological problems of belief, a subject which interested her. She insisted, in the face of critics, that Browning did not reject rational intellect for irrational intuition. His apprehension of truth was not "the act of one faculty, heart or mind, but of the total human person."[7]

Maisie labored assiduously on the biography, doing research at the excellent Browning collections of the Newark Public Library and of Baylor University in Texas. It was fortunate that her ability to read rapidly, about a thousand words per minute, did not decline with age,[8] since she had to plough through more than six hundred sources in her research. She took her writing with her on her travels, producing chapter after chapter on the ground and in the air.

Her portrait of Browning was less hagiographic than might be expected. She took on some difficult questions presented by his life and answered them by building an argument from his poetry. She claimed, as she always had, that a biographer was not a judge and that one's subject ultimately remained mysterious. But Maisie failed to bring together the private and public worlds of Robert Browning. She took up the notion, advanced earlier by Henry James, that there were two Robert Brownings. Her solution was to argue that Browning had a simple character and a very complex intellect. However, in the end her Robert Browning remains opaque. Rather than reveal the man, her biography reveals her love of this poet and the questions he pursued.

Maisie's subject was an important one. Browning's writing was of lasting value itself and influenced the work of William Butler Yeats, Ezra Pound, and T. S. Eliot. The significance of her subject garnered the biography respectful reviews in England, the United States, and Australia. The *London Observer* listed it as a book of the year in 1969. The fact that it had nonreligious publishers—Holt, Rinehart and Winston in the U.S. and Cassel and Company in England—very likely helped its reception as well.

Writing the biography had been demanding, but it gave Maisie new contacts and interests. She became allied with the Browning Society and raised money to support Casa Guidi, the Brownings' home in Florence.[9] With the support of the Browning Institute she published in 1972 *The Tragi-Comedy of Pen Browning*, a postscript to the Browning biography.[10] The foreword by Robert Coles sets the tone of this little book. Maisie's interest in Pen, the curious and troubled son of Robert and Elizabeth, was purely psychological. Unlike her approach in the Robert Browning biography, Maisie made no attempt to use Pen's life to prove a point. Rather, she merely laid out his strange story—Pen's adoration of his mother; Robert's fixation on his son after Elizabeth's death; and Pen's own odd marriage. Pen's is the story of unwise love, of parental adulation and its consequences. Since Maisie never wrote a book without some purpose, one can only surmise that this interest in a parent-child relationship had some personal meaning for her.

Browning gave Maisie solace and respite from both familial stress and the religious chaos of the late 1960s. Not that refuge in Browning meant retreat! Maisie continued to travel and remain active. After his fall, Frank was not as mentally quick and agile as he once had been, but he loved to travel. Eight years younger than Maisie, he was continually on the go. Time limits on their stays in England meant yearly trips across the Atlantic and to Australia. Still, Maisie would have preferred to do less of this, as worldwide travel was taxing both physically and psychologically for her. In many ways she was living on the outer edges of her capacities. Her health gradually began to decline after an operation to remove gallstones in 1966 while in Australia. Old age and chronic health problems contributed to her exhaustion. For years her gnarled feet and fallen arches had impeded her walking long distances, and now this was exacerbated by retention of fluid in her legs. She was in her late seventies, and it was painful to haul herself up and down stairs. She also had diverticulitis, which meant that she had to watch what she ate. Her low blood pressure, which sometimes led to light-headedness, also contributed to her generalized fatigue. In order to give herself a boost, she drank more and began to put Scotch in her morning coffee. Daunting as her list of maladies was, she would not allow it to curtail her travel. In 1954 she included India as a stopover as she and Frank circled from New York to Australia and back to London. She visited India again in 1958 and in 1970. That country had a particular lure for her.

In the early 1940s, Maisie's cousin Muriel Neville had introduced her to Italian and Dutch priests and their self-help projects among Indian untouchables in Kerala and Madras.[11] As her work with CHAS abated in the mid-1960s, Maisie threw herself into this new effort. For almost a decade she begged money for this cause and sent thousands of pounds to India for the poor. She wrote articles about this work, extorted money at parties from well-heeled Catholics, and gave appeals in churches both in the United States and in England.[12] She often took up church collections herself and showed marked irritation at those who refused to contribute. At one point she tried to sell the Wilfrid Ward-Friedrich von Hügel correspondence in order to raise additional revenue.[13] On her eightieth birthday she asked that money be sent to India in lieu of gifts for her. With all her fundraising Maisie used the same tactics she had used in gaining support for her housing ventures; she bullied, challenged, pestered, and inspired. It was difficult not to respond.

Maisie's assumption in her support of the India projects was the same as it had been in her work for housing and her street preaching: begin where people are, with their needs. In this case it was the need for land, huts, and wells.

Maisie's funding went to three priests: Fathers Caironi and Zucol, who worked in Kerala, and Father Van der Valk in Andra Pradesh near Madras. All three lived and worked among the poor they helped organize. Like the French priest-workers before them, these men gave priority to the material needs of those they served, and like them they were criticized for not doing "priestly" work.

Since Maisie was convinced that the sharpest divisions in the world were not between nations or ideologies but between wealth and poverty, what she called this "new missionary" movement in India dealt with an important world problem. By serving the poor, these priests put human needs first. Maisie saw them as allied with the likes of Helder Camarra, bishop of Recife, Brazil, who proclaimed a "Church of the Poor." Like him they built up neither wealth nor power. She considered them the vanguard of a new church.[14]

Maisie continued her support of Indian untouchables for years. In 1970, after one of their trips to Australia, the Sheeds returned to England via India. They stopped in Madras where both Frank and Maisie lectured at Catholic colleges. They then traveled to Andra Pradesh to see Father Van der Valk and to visit the projects Maisie's money had underwritten. A banner with "Welcome Mrs. Sheed" greeted Maisie, and villagers performed fire dances for her. She was delighted by the warm welcome she received.[15]

Maisie was totally devoted to these Indian missionaries and might have overlooked the ineffectiveness of some of their work. Her commitment was understandable. She saw these new missionaries not as colonizers but as purveyors of a philosophy of self-help, something she had espoused all her life. By meeting material needs and sharing in the life of the poor, they pointed to Christian values. Increasingly, Maisie would be on the outlook for groups who, like them, did good in the midst of human suffering.

As Browning had provided her a refuge in difficult times, her work for Indian untouchables distracted her from the painful attacks on Catholic doctrine and practice in the late 1960s. These were difficult times for a woman who had given her life to the church. She was "heartsick" to learn in 1967 of the departure of Father Charles Davis from the church. He was the darling of the Guild and, in her mind, the best expounder of

Catholic doctrine in England. She had entertained high hopes for him as someone very much on her "wavelength," and a bastion between the extremes of right and left.[16]

Maisie had an opportunity to publicly discuss her views on contemporary Catholicism when she and Frank were interviewed by William F. Buckley, Jr. in 1969. During a session of *Firing Line,* Maisie candidly acknowledged the increasing skepticism and unbelief afflicting the church. She claimed that much Catholic belief was tentative and vulnerable because Catholics had not been taught to evaluate and discuss their faith. As Newman said, they were living on the intellect of a former age. They learned Thomas Aquinas by rote but never made belief their own. She claimed to have escaped this limitation herself because her parents discussed and challenged religion and taught her to do likewise. Her years of experience in the Guild also forced her to deal with questions about doctrine. She maintained that personal belief left unchallenged could crumble easily. But, she went on, there were larger historical currents that had contributed to the erosion of belief as well. The condemnation of Modernism and the fear it instilled ensured that most people never discussed their faith. Once questioning was allowed, unexamined belief disintegrated into skepticism or unbelief.[17]

Buckley's principal interest during the interview seemed to be scrutinizing Maisie's social commitments. She admitted to being politically left, while being center or right religiously. Buckley baited her: Can one oppose the church and still be a Catholic? Maisie responded that it was belief in Catholic doctrine and sacraments that made one a Catholic. In an effort to make the church more responsive to the needs of the poor, rebellion against church authority was sometimes necessary. The Gospel command to feed the hungry must be fulfilled even if it meant opposing church hierarchy. The greatest scandal of the church, she said, was the wealthy parish. When Buckley probed about her relationship with Dorothy Day she claimed Day was "one of the greatest women in the world, [a] tremendous person," and she only wished she had the courage to practice Catholic poverty as Day did.[18]

For forty years Maisie had worked through the Guild and Sheed & Ward to foster discussion of Catholic doctrine. Now that doctrine and the church she loved were under attack. As a woman who had given her life to "the intellectual apostolate," Maisie was confronted with finding another approach to renewal of the church. She found it in the new willingness of believers to live prophetically in a suffering world. Influenced by the theology of the "Church of the Poor," especially as articulated by Paul Gauthier, a priest-worker in Palestine, she began to seek out and chronicle the work of groups who lived out Christian values. The result of this search would be described in her final book, *To and Fro on the Earth* (1973).

As Maisie moved into her eighties, she allied herself more and more with those who challenged existing institutions. She backed Eugene McCarthy in the 1968 campaign for president of the United States and served with Women for McCarthy.[19] She visited the wives and children of conscientious objectors to the Vietnam war, and criticized the U.S. prison system as one which often broke its inmates.[20] She obliquely questioned the ability of celibate priests to appreciate the trials of marriage.[21] All the while she continued to promote the needs of untouchables in India and orphans in Peru and Mexico.[22]

For her own religious inspiration, Maisie turned to reading *The Showings* of Julian of Norwich and the work of contemporaries Dag Hammarskjöld and Teilhard de Chardin.[23] Although Julian had been one of the subjects of Maisie's 1933 book, *The English Way: Studies in English Sanctity,* it was Houselander who had shown her Julian's genius. Julian's spirituality was one in which God's love was found in microcosm—sustaining and loving natural things, like the little hazel nut. Hammarskjöld and de Chardin revealed a cosmic God working in the deeper and wider dimensions of human life. De Chardin had particular significance for Maisie. Like her, he too had been influenced during his student days by Father Hugh Benson, who had emphasized prayer and spirituality.

While these medieval and modern mystics might thrill her, and Browning's poetry provide her a haven, Maisie was never far removed from the demands of the mundane. Although she and Frank had withdrawn from active involvement in the business of Sheed & Ward, its disastrous financial affairs required some kind of response. For a variety of reasons, Philip Scharper left Sheed & Ward, and at the invitation of Miguel D'Escoto, a Maryknoll Father, began Orbis Books, a publishing company with a focus on the developing world. In 1970 Frank was persuaded to return to the chairmanship to try to save the company. At the very point at which he took over, a bank loan for $75,000 was recalled,[24] and he had to scramble to try to keep the company solvent. In order to ease the pressure in his life, the Sheeds decided to move to an apartment in Jersey City, New Jersey in 1971. Frank would have easy access by subway to New York City. For the next four years they lived in a cramped three-room apartment in an Italian and Polish area. Nearby were St. Aedan's Church and St. Peter's College, but the immediate neighborhood, without trees or flowers, had little beauty. It was a difficult place for Maisie to live. At age eighty-two, she had traveled a long distance from the lush landscape of the Isle of Wight to this decaying community in Jersey City.

"Hope in Near-hopelessness"

✻ FRANK HAD FOUND THE LITTLE APARTMENT on Tonnelle Avenue in Jersey City. He was delighted to have a place so convenient to New York. Maisie was less happy there, but ultimately, where she lived did not matter. The apartment itself was utilitarian. In keeping with the Sheeds' commitment to live modestly, there were no artifacts from global travels, nor books, except the Bible. The walls were unadorned except for some Chesterton cartoons. Two small couches with bolsters served as beds. Since neither Maisie nor Frank cooked, the modest kitchen was adequate for their needs. They usually dined out for one meal at an inexpensive restaurant. At home they ate simply, except for Maisie's one luxury of liquor. For them the apartment was adequate; others found it dreary and shabby.

Maisie usually attended the noon mass at St. Aedan's on Bergen Street, a short walk from the apartment. The fact that it was a very conservative parish did not disturb her. She went there for the sacraments. Once she and Frank got to know the St. Peter's College crowd—graduate students and liberal priests —they sometimes attended home masses with them. Although it meant climbing laboriously up long flights of stairs, Maisie loved those living-room eucharistic celebrations and the potluck dinners that followed.

When they did not walk—to mass, the stores, or restaurants—Frank and Maisie rode buses or subways. The priests at St. Peter's sometimes gave them lifts in their cars, as did some of the older female graduate students, especially Claire Dameo and Marie De Stena. Although Maisie was in her early eighties and Frank in his mid-seventies, they remained active. Frank wrote and went into New York City to deal with Sheed & Ward matters. Maisie also wrote. The Pen Browning book took her almost a year to finish, after which she worked on *To and Fro on the Earth*. What was important to them were ideas and people. No matter the diminishments of old age, they still had these.

Since travel facilitated reaching both, they kept it up, often to the state of exhaustion. Between 1972 and 1974 the Sheeds made three round-the-world trips. When they were in England, they always visited Tetta and her daughter Hester, who lived at Crosby Hall, a place Maisie loved. In 1973 Maisie recuperated at Crosby Hall after a minor operation for a growth which turned out to be nonmalignant, and in 1974, when she was very weak, she stayed at Crosby hoping to regain her strength. Although travel continued to be part of their lives, they clearly experienced a slowing down. This came at a time when public interest in their writing was diminishing. Thus, it must have seemed to them a particular honor when nearby St. Peter's College, a Jesuit institution, awarded them both honorary degrees in 1972. Ironically, Maisie continued to resent Jesuit education for what it had done to her brother Leo.

In 1973 Sheed & Ward was sold for $150,000 to Universal Press Syndicate, which was owned by Jim Andrews, a previous employee of Sheed & Ward, and John McMeel. Since the Sheeds' financial security was independent of the company, Frank's principal concern was to make sure that all the company's debts were paid and that investors were reimbursed. With Jim Andrews as the new editor-and-chief, Frank felt secure that the quality of imprints under the new ownership would be maintained.[1]

The faithful Sheed & Ward staff dispersed. Marigold Hunt, editor of *The Trumpet*, who had been with the company since before the war, was the last person out the door. For Frank's part, he was utterly relieved to be out from under a crushing weight. Finally, they were freed from what Frank called "the albatross around his neck."

After forty-five years, their lives were no longer entwined with Sheed & Ward. Neither Frank nor Maisie had regrets.

Their publishing house had met an immense need at a time when the church in England and America was expanding and changing. It had fueled Catholic intellectual life and made it possible to claim that one was a "thinking" Catholic, and could be one without benefit of clergy.[2] Without the nurture provided by their publications, English-speaking laity would have had a more difficult transition to the new church of Vatican II.[3]

Sheed & Ward clearly did what had to be done at a particular moment in history, and those associated with it did have fun. Conviviality and high adventure pervaded the Sheed & Ward operation. One never knew what would happen next in the firm, but whatever came it was dealt with lightheartedly and even with hilarity. "Hilarity" was a big word among Sheed & Ward types. Their cheerfulness was born of a certitude about faith and the rightness of their work. But the sense of being part of a special club, so characteristic of a minority church, began to wane by the early 1960s. Catholics became sophisticated and worldly believers and in the process, more skeptical, more critical, less willing to stick with their own kind, and definitely less filled with hilarity. It was the end of an extraordinary period in Anglo-American Catholicism to which Maisie and Frank had given their lives.

Frank might have looked back with some nostalgia, but Maisie did not. The only direction she could look was forward. But looking forward in the early 1970s was a dismal proposition. Everywhere she turned she found a sense of hopelessness and despair, "a despair wailing through literature and drama, smothered temporarily by drink or drugs but a despair from which suicide offers itself to many as the only exit."[4] The church she had always counted on to respond seemed mired in its own problems. "The Catholic Church of today," she wrote in 1973, "once so creative, seem[s] to have given up on the effort needed to meet a new situation with new ideas and techniques."[5]

As a woman who had spent most of her life researching and writing about the nineteenth century, Maisie was quick to compare that century with her own. If despair and hopelessness characterized the twentieth century, the Victorians offered an alternative. "They were trapped in their age as we are in the horrors of ours. The one thing we can learn from them is an unconquerable courage and an optimism which, often quenched, seems always to have arisen from its wet ashes. Convinced they could do everything, they did succeed in doing something."[6] As she pushed back further into history to the Middle Ages, another comparison confronted her. Although poor by modern standards, the medieval world was not "rudderless" or "hopeless" as was her own time. As usual, Maisie wanted her readers and hearers to confront this despair. Her final book, *To and Fro on the Earth,* was her response to this hopelessness.

In spite of her more than eighty years, Maisie continued to permit herself to be open to the currents influencing her contemporaries. In the first chapter of *To and Fro* she introduced the ideas of Hannah Arendt to confirm the seriousness of the malaise. "It is quite conceivable," Arendt wrote, "that the modern age—which began with such an unprecedented and promising outburst of human activity—may end in the deadliest, most sterile passivity history has ever known."[7]

Aware of the confusion and inability to diagnose the present malady, Maisie spoke from her own experience.

> I am groping . . . just as my friends are groping . . . for answers to the problems of a puzzled world. And the chief clue I have laid hold of I can only call personalism. . . . If these last years of my life have a theme running through them it would be that of hope dawning despite of, through, the well-warranted near-hopelessness. . . . Creation is at work everywhere—on a large scale occasionally, but more significantly in small scale achievements by the score, the hundreds, the thousands. All over the world I have found small groups who are building a new world in the shell of the old one that is crumbling around us.[8]

To and Fro on the Earth was Maisie's chronicle of a new world being born from within the old. Its title refers not only to her going to and fro, but to a line in the Book of Job in which God asks Satan if in traveling the earth he has considered Job. Maisie acknowledges that in her life she has considered Job, the symbol of human suffering. *To and Fro* is the story of how that suffering was being met by people of goodwill everywhere.

As ideologies and belief systems crumbled around her, Maisie fell back on what she knew to be true—humans must respond to suffering; good must be done. She was grateful, given her diminishing energy, that she could write this last book.

To and Fro is about contemporary life—its violence, ugliness, brutality and despair—and the people and groups who, using human creativity, face these realities head on. There is nothing pious or sentimental within its covers. In some ways it is her most critical book; both church and state are questioned. Although aging, Maisie was not oblivious to the hate and insensitivity of her times. She saw it firsthand in her travels and in her own neighborhood. She experienced street violence soon after moving to Jersey City when she was knocked to the ground by some young boys as she walking to St. Aedan's. None of them stopped to help her. Bleeding, blackened, and swollen, she learned personally about vulnerability.

The clear message of *To and Fro* is that human creativity is needed to build a new world. Maisie does not explore how one can be good in a world of evil but only asserts that good exists and that one must do it. While the book is in no sense a devotional one, there are places where she alludes to religious experience and its importance for the contemporary age. She laments that the world has become sterile, mechanical, and addicted to activity. Its frenzy needs the balance of mystical religion, yet the church had discarded its teaching of the mystical tradition. Even if mysticism is unclaimed, Maisie argued, "mystical religion remains, and with it the realization that help is given to our visible world through a continual personal contact with another—constant realization of God's presence."[9]

In her later years Maisie turned increasingly to that mystical tradition, especially to Julian of Norwich. She made no claims, however, to personal mystical experience. She notes with concern in *To and Fro* that her spirituality is different from that of the saints who move from service of neighbor to worship, solitude, and adoration. Her life had a different trajectory. Seeing suffering, she continued to respond. While she was aware that action and service could swamp prayer, she also saw, as Saint Theresa did, that service was a form of prayer.[10] Service and action were her prayer of choice.

To and Fro is Maisie's rendering of good overcoming evil. "Evil is large and loud, indeed raucous," she wrote:

> It destroys easily, quickly, on a vast scale—and always gets the front page.
>
> Good is quiet, slow perhaps, for to build takes longer than to destroy, but steadily, perpetually creative. Because it is personal it must be small in scale. Almost everything that grows large grows too large, ceases to do its work and dies of swollen heads and swollen purses. But all over the world small-scale groups that work at a thousand valuable things are coming into existence.[11]

Her book is a description of the work of these groups. Some, like the Catholic Worker, CHAS, and priests working among harajan had been part of her life for a very long time. Others were new—Fides House, Sursum Corda, the United Farm Workers in California, and the followers of Danilo Dolci in Sicily.[12] She highlighted the admirable work of Father Keogh, who brought the Alcoholic Anonymous' Twelve Step program to the mentally ill in Australia. She explored the Black Panthers and the movement of conscientious objectors opposing the Vietnam war. She examined efforts on the part of aborigines in Australia, prisoners in the United States, and orphans in Mexico and Peru. What united these disparate movements was their responsiveness to human need and commitment to remain small, to work with each person. What made this book more than a random sample of small communities doing good was Maisie's first-person narrative of their activities and her obvious commitment to them.

This interest was not new. Maisie's farms, the chapel community at Horley, and the Marycrest, Taena, and priest-worker communities were preludes to those she wrote about in *To and Fro*. While she always understood the importance of such groups, she was now more fully aware of their role in increasingly tumultuous times.

Maisie Ward
Courtesy of Maria Darlington

Maisie called *To and Fro* a "sequel" to an autobiography. It is not an autobiography in any ordinary sense of the word, and in tone, argument, organization, and style it is different from *Unfinished Business*. It is both a maddening and an extraordinary book. In many ways it is very poorly written—discursive, disorganized, digressive. Although Maisie enlisted the help of the unwitting Tom Cornell of the Catholic Worker movement as an editor, the book in its published form still needed work. It is dubious whether it would have ever been published if Sheed & Ward, in its last year of operation, had not brought it out. Yet for all of its faults, it is an amazing rendering of a life. There is no private or public life in it, no description of family, no coherent personal history. It is the story of Maisie's experience of good being done in the world through a variety of small communities. One wonders why she called it an autobiography, except that she wanted to ally herself with those who did good and lend her personal credibility to their work. This "life story" stands in sharp contrast to Frank's autobiography, *The Church and I*, which was published in 1974, one year after hers. Although much the more polished piece of writing, it presents him in terms of what he loves—the church. In *To and Fro* the church is barely mentioned except to be criticized.

To and Fro was Maisie's last book. It is the most powerful illustration of her unique ability to remain open to human need. The energy she summoned to write the book began to wane soon after she finished the manuscript. Her minor operation in 1973 weakened her, yet she and Frank kept on traveling, irrespective of her physical needs. After a trip to Australia in 1974 the Sheeds returned to England, where Maisie became increasingly more frail. They delayed their return to the United States until June. Within a few weeks of their return to Jersey City, Maisie was admitted to the St. Francis Community Health Center. She continued to need the assistance of a public health nurse during the next several months. Her last public event was the Doubleday reception for Frank's autobiography in New York City in the late fall. Thereafter, she had two minor strokes in close succession. Frank was at his wit's end to know what to do. Neither he nor Maisie were particularly informed about medicine. Confused and fearful, their situation worsened in early December when a fire broke out in the apartment building and the ailing Maisie, after having walked down five flights of stairs, was kept waiting for three hours before she was allowed to reenter her apartment.[13]

They were helped during these difficult months by friends from St. Peter's. When Frank was invited to France to give a paper on the revelations of the Sacred Heart to St. Margaret Mary Alacoque, he went reluctantly, knowing that Maisie was dying.[14] Marie De Stena, "their daughter in residence," stayed with Maisie. They spent some happy moments together. Marie read Maisie one of her favorite Kipling poems about Jane Austen's arrival in heaven and meeting there the man she loved.

Jane's Marriage

Jane went to paradise:
    that was only fair.
Good Sir Walter met her first,
    And led her up the stair.
Henry and Tobias,
    and Miguel of Spain,
Stood with Shakespeare at the top
    To welcome Jane—

Then the Three Archangels
    Offered out of hand,
Anything in Heaven's gift
    That she might command.
Azrael's eyes upon her,
    Raphael's wings above,
Michael's sword against her heart,
    Jane said: "Love."

Instantly the under-
    standing Seraphim
Laid their fingers on their lips
    And went to look for him.

Stole across the Zodiac,
Harnessed Charles's Wain,
and whispered round the Nebulae
"Who loved Jane?"

In a private limbo
Where none had thought to look,
Sat a Hampshire gentleman
Reading of a book.
It was called *Persuasion,* and it told the plain
Story of the love between
Him and Jane.

He heard the question
Circle Heaven through—
Closed the book and answered:
"I did—and do!"

Quietly but speedily
(As Captain Wentworth moved)
Entered into Paradise
The man Jane loved![15]

On January 4, 1975, Maisie's eighty-sixth birthday, a few friends from St. Peter's gathered with the Sheeds in their apartment for mass. Maisie read from the first letter of John, her favorite scripture: "Let no one deceive you; the man who acts in holiness is holy indeed, even as the Son is holy. . . . That is the way to see who are God's children. . . . No one whose actions are unholy belongs to God, nor anyone who fails to love his brother."[16]

Maisie's life had been one of great activity; she now felt useless. Her once strong voice was feeble, and because Frank was partially deaf she was not sure he could understand her. She desperately wanted to stay at home rather than go to the hospital, but that possibility waned as she became more debilitated, and Frank became more worried. Then her colon ruptured and she was in considerable pain. Finally, on a very cold January 11 Frank and Mary Jo Weaver, a graduate student friend who flew in from the Midwest to see Maisie, took her to City Hospital in New York. During the next several days Maisie was conscious but hooked up to monitors. When Frank visited they shared letters from the family and read, much as they always had. As her final reading materials, Maisie brought to the hospital Dickens' *Bleak House* and *Our Mutual Friend*, books she had read many times. The hospital chaplain, a Dominican, brought her communion daily. Wilfrid, who was in California, and Rosemary in England were in touch by telephone. Missie and the American grandchildren visited. When Maisie had been there over two weeks, after one particularly bad night, Frank arrived in the morning. It was as if both she and he were now ready for her to depart. She greeted the man she loved, and then died. It was the morning of January 28, the feast day of Thomas Aquinas, theologian and doctor of the church.

Frank and the young Jesuit priest from St. Peter's, Father Bill Scanlon, arranged for a wake the following day. No one seemed to sense the incongruity of Maisie laid out in the very upscale Frank Campbell's Funeral Home in New York City. The wake was an open casket presentation with Maisie dressed, not in a shroud as Frank first suggested, but in a Dominican habit given her by a young priest. Frank insisted that she would not have wanted to be buried in a dress that someone else could use. The offer of the habit seemed especially appropriate since she had long been allied to the Dominicans. During the wake, while mourners milled around in the adjacent room talking and drinking, Dorothy Day sat alone by the casket of her old friend.

Maisie's requiem mass was held on January 30, 1975 at the Dominican church, St. Vincent Ferrer, on Lexington Avenue. Its dim interior lit with flickering votive lights gave some reprieve from the cold January day. Cardinal Terrence Cooke and the pastor of St. Aedan's were co-celebrants. Twelve diocesan and order priests were also present. At Frank's insistence, Father Scanlon gave the homily, remembering Maisie's openness and greateartedness. There was no music at the service.

A touching moment in the otherwise stark mass occurred when Frank, filled with intense emotion, read from his translation of Augustine's *Confessions*. The scene was of Augustine and Monica conversing over things to come:

[S]he and I stood alone leaning in a window, which looked inwards to the garden. . . . There we talked together, she and I alone, in deep joy; and forgetting the things that were behind and looking forward to those that were before, we were discussing in the presence of Truth, which You are, what the eternal life of the saints could be like, which eye has not seen nor ear heard, nor has it entered into the heart of man. But with the mouth of our heart we panted for the high waters of Your fountain, the fountain of the life which is with You. . . .

And our conversation had brought us to this point, that any pleasure whatsoever of the bodily sense, in any brightness whatsoever of corporeal light, seemed to us not worthy of comparison with the pleasure of that eternal Light. . . . And while we were thus talking of His Wisdom and panting for it, with all the effort of our heart we did for one instant attain to touch it; then sighing, and leaving the first fruits of our spirit bound to it, we returned to the sound of our own tongue, in which a word has both beginning and ending.[17]

When the requiem mass was over, Frank, family, and friends drove back to Jersey City. Maisie was buried in a cemetery behind St. Peter's College, near housing projects and a major highway. As the surroundings of Tonnelle Avenue had not mattered in the end, neither did this final burial place, thousands of miles from England. What mattered were ideas and people, and those Maisie had with her to the end. She had fought the fight and only now had a discharge from the war.

A weary Frank left Jersey City with Wilfrid to spend some time with him at Sag Harbor. Later Frank returned to the apartment to sort through Maisie's belongings, calling in Tom Cornell to give him her clothes for distribution. A month later, back in London, he attended a memorial mass for Maisie at Corpus Christi Church on Maiden Lane, a place where she had spent many hours. The homily was given by Eamonn Casey, her CHAS collaborator and now Bishop of Kerry. The requiem was a prism of her life. The Duke of Norfolk was there, priests and the bishop and C.E.G types, along with family members, friends from CHAS, Sheed & Ward staff, authors, and those who knew

her as a platform speaker. Only Maisie could reach across these
social chasms, claiming each person as her own.

When the last of the crowd dispersed, there were only individual memories, one often contradicting the other—memories
of a Maisie Ward who was attentive yet distant, bloody-minded
yet sympathetic, convinced of the intellectual yet uncritical, absolutely singular, yet a lover of community. But the memory of
her shared by all was that of great humanity and a willingness
to stay open to human suffering. As a Ward she had extended
and broadened the family tradition; as Maisie, her legacy was *sui
generis.*

Epilogue

✳ As biographer, historian, publisher, lecturer, street preacher, and social activist, Maisie Ward was Vesuvius-like—erupting in many directions, dynamic because she was connected through subterranean routes to a vital center. Like a volcano she changed the religious landscape and left behind a rich lava soil from which new life and thought could grow. But the defining characteristics of Maisie Ward—her single-mindedness, her rock-ribbed confidence, her intellectual certitude—seem odd and strangely naive in the contemporary world where tentativeness prevails.

She is offered here not only as a reminder of a bygone generation, but as a symbol of what faith unfettered by doubt could do. She believed that "God mattered," that faith unlived was no faith at all. If one believed, one lived that belief and shared its empowering energy in service to others.

There was a tough-mindedness in Maisie Ward that unequivocally removes her from any claim to sanctity. Nor could one claim that she was immensely creative as a writer, even after twenty-nine books. She had one conviction—the Good News must be preached and lived. All of her activity can be subsumed under that mandate. There was nothing pious or cloying in her work. In its variety, its unity, and its global reach it was unparalleled in her time.

Her life achievement would be remarkable for a man; it was even more so for a woman, one who was hemmed in by familial, cultural, and religious restrictions. By her own definition she was not a feminine woman—she was too steely, too demanding, too unwilling to ingratiate. When that temperament is linked to enthusiasm—the desire to convince and win over—one has the making of an ideologue. And like an ideologue, Maisie saw the world whole. She believed in Truth and in the unity of mind and heart dedicated to a single, grand goal. She loved the community of believers and the gratification of shared ritual. She loved energy and conviction.

And like the true believer, she was unhindered and unnuanced by doubt. Such was her great strength and her great weakness. In judging and appreciating such personality one must evaluate the goal to which she gave herself and the means she used to realize it. In her case, the goal and its means are found in the living itself.

Notes

1. The Ties That Bind

1. Carolyn Heilbrun, *Writing a Woman's Life* (New York: Ballentine Books, 1988), p. 11.

2. See Maisie Ward's family history, *The Wilfrid Wards and the Transition*, vol. 1, *The Nineteenth Century*, vol. 2, *Insurrection versus Resurrection* (New York: Sheed & Ward, 1934, 1937); *Unfinished Business* (New York: Sheed & Ward, 1963); *To and Fro on the Earth: The Sequel to an Autobiography* (New York: Sheed & Ward, 1973). Hereafter volumes of the family history are cited by volume name.

3. Of William George's eight children, all except Bernard and Wilfrid had some mental fragility. Of Wilfrid's four surviving children, Maisie was the only one who had robust mental health as an adult. Tetta suffered from depression, Leo from some undiagnosed nervous disorder, and Herbert from alcoholism.

4. John Henry Newman, "Sermon X–'The Second Spring,' " *The Works of Cardinal Newman: Sermons Preached on Various Occasions*, vol. 25 (Westminster, Md.: Christian Classics, 1968), pp. 172–73.

5. *Unfinished Business*, p. 3.

6. "Reminiscences of Wilfrid Ward," as quoted in *The Nineteenth Century*, p. 35.

7. Ibid., pp. 77–78.

8. *Unfinished Business*, p. 3.

9. John Ruskin, *Essays and Letters Selected from the Writings of John Ruskin*, ed. Mrs. Louis G. Hufford (Boston: Ginn and Company, 1894), p. 87.

10. *Unfinished Business*, p. 3.

11. Maisie Ward to Josephine Ward, n.d. Letter in the possession of Rosemary Middleton.

12. *Unfinished Business*, p. 8.

13. Ibid.

14. Ibid., p. 19.

15. Josephine Ward, London, to Frank Sheed, Sydney, Easter Sunday, 1925, Sheed and Ward Family Papers (hereafter cited as CSWD 3/09, University of Notre Dame Archives (hereafter cited as UNDA). Although listed in the catalog of the Sheed and Ward Family Papers, this letter has been misplaced. James W. McLucas quotes the letter in "Frank Sheed Apologist" (doctoral dissertation, Pontifical University of St. Thomas, Rome, 1991), p. 43.

2. Through the Calm

1. *Unfinished Business*, p. 28.

2. Maisie Ward, *Insurrection versus Resurrection*, pp. 128–29.

3. See *Father Maturin: A Memoir with Selected Letters,* ed. Maisie Ward (London: Longmans, Green, and Co., 1920). See also Maisie Ward, "English Spiritual Writers—William Basil Maturin, 1847–1915," *The Clergy Review* 45, no. 2 (February 1960), pp. 65–77.

4. Modernism was a movement in the late nineteenth and early twentieth century which attempted to reconcile historical Christianity with modern science and philosophy. It had particular impact among Protestant scholars who attempted to apply modern critical methods to the Bible and the history of dogma. Modernism among Roman Catholics was specifically denounced as the "synthesis of all heresies" by Pius X in 1907. Catholic Modernists accepted the critical approach to the Bible, rejected the intellectualism of scholastic theology, and subordinated doctrine to practice. At their most radical, Catholic modernists tended to deny the authority of the church and the traditional Christian conception of God.

5. *Insurrection versus Resurrection,* p. 161. No cite given.

6. *The Dublin Review,* July 1916, as quoted in *Insurrection versus Ressurrection,* p. 364.

7. Charles Dickens, *Hard Times* (New York: Harper & Row, 1965), pp. 283–84.

8. In "Anti-Victorians Trapped in a Victorian Age," *Commonweal* 87 (23 February 1968), pp. 625–28, Ward discusses her favorite novels and quotes this paragraph from *Pride and Prejudice.*

9. Josephine Ward to Mary Howard, October 1899. Letter in the possession of Rosemary Middleton.

10. Bits of information on the Cambridge years are contained in *Unfinished Business,* in a letter from Sister Ursula, I.B.V.M., St. Mary's

School, Cambridge, Fall 1993, and in Letters of Maisie Ward, 1900–26, CSWD, 18/06.

11. *Unfinished Business,* p. 33.

12. Mary Ward is not a relative of the Wilfrid Wards.

13. Dorothy Day used this phrase as the title for her autobiography, *The Long Loneliness* (New York: Harper & Row, 1952).

14. See the introduction and epilogue in *Mary Ward, 1585–1645* by Mary Oliver (New York: Sheed & Ward, 1959), and "Mary Ward" in *The English Way: Studies in English Sanctity from St. Bede to Newman,* ed. Maisie Ward (New York: Sheed & Ward, 1933), pp. 242–67.

15. See Mary Jo Weaver, "Wilfrid Ward's Interpretation and Application of Newman," in *Newman and the Modernists,* ed. M. J. Weaver (Lanhan, Md: University Press of America, 1985).

16. *Unfinished Business,* p. 34.

17. Ibid.

18. Ibid.

3. "The Years the Locusts Have Eaten"

1. Maisie Ward, "Maisie Ward," in *Born Catholics,* assembled by F. J. Sheed (New York: Sheed & Ward, 1954), pp. 125–26.

2. *Unfinished Business,* p. 46.

3. See Wilfrid Ward, *Last Lectures by Wilfrid Ward* (London: Longmans, Green, and Co., 1918).

4. Mary Jo Weaver, "Wilfrid Ward's Interpretation and Application of Newman."

5. Wilfrid Ward as quoted in Maisie Ward's *Insurrection versus Resurrection,* p. 355. No cite given.

6. *Insurrection versus Resurrection,* pp. 187, 190–91.

7. See Maisie Ward, *S. Bernardino: The People's Preacher* (London: Herder, 1914).

8. *Unfinished Business,* p. 63.

9. Ibid., p. 73.

10. Ibid., p. 76. Maisie gives a slightly different account in her essay in *Born Catholics,* pp. 128–29.

11. At least some property, Egypt House and Northwood House on the Isle of Wight, was given to Wilfrid Ward and later passed on to his son Herbert. In 1929 Herbert Ward presented Northwood House and his twenty-seven acres to the town of Cowes. Egypt House remained in the Herbert Ward family and is now owned by John Ward.

Presumably some of Edmund's properties were also sold to endow his intended beneficiaries.

4. "A Future . . . Almost Too Bright to Look At"

1. Maisie quotes these lines from Josephine Ward's *Tudor Sunset* (London: Sheed & Ward, 1932) in *Insurrection versus Resurrection,* p. 535.

2. Father Cuthbert, ed., *God and the Supernatural: A Catholic Statement of the Christian Faith* (New York: Longmans, Green, and Co., 1920).

3. Frank Sheed to Maisie Ward, 14 March 1922. By the time he wrote this letter, Frank already believed he must get out of the Catholic Truth Society. He had promised more than he could deliver. Furthermore, he didn't think C.T.S. was spending money in the right way. He left finally by January 1923.

4. Frank Sheed to Maisie Ward, 22 April 1925. Letter in the possession of Rosemary Middleton. In this letter he reminisces about their courtship.

5. Wilfrid Sheed, *Frank and Maisie: A Memoir with Parents* (New York: Simon and Schuster, 1986), pp. 22–23.

6. Frank Sheed to Mary Sheed, 22 December 1920, CSWD 1/02.

7. Debra Campbell, "The Catholic Evidence Guild: Towards a History of the Laity," *Heythrop Journal* 30 (July 1987), pp. 306–24.

8. Maisie Ward, "The Church Missionary Inside England." TS (typescript) of a speech, CSWD 13/21. For Maisie Ward's contribution to the C.E.G., see Debra Campbell, "The Gleanings of a Laywoman's Ministry: Maisie Ward as Preacher, Publisher and Social Activist," *American Catholic Historical Society of Philadelphia* 98 (November/December 1987), pp. 21–28.

9. See Debra Campbell, "The Heyday of Catholic Action and the Lay Apostolate, 1929–59" in Jay Dolan et al., eds., *Transforming Parish Ministry: The Changing Roles of Catholic Clergy, Laity, and Women Religious* (New York: Crossroad, 1989), pp. 222–52; Joseph Chinnici, *Living Stones: The History and Structure of Catholic Spiritual Life in the United States* (New York: MacMillan, 1989); Jay Dolan, *The American Catholic Experience: A History from Colonial Times to the Present* (Notre Dame, Ind.: University of Notre Dame Press, 1992); James Terence Fisher, *The Catholic Counterculture in America, 1923–1962* (Chapel Hill: University of North Carolina Press, 1989).

10. CSWD 13/21.

11. *Unfinished Business,* p. 100. See also Debra Campbell, " 'I Can't Imagine Our Lady on An Outdoor Platform': Women in the Catholic Street Propaganda Movement," *U.S. Catholic Historian* 3, no.2 (Spring/Summer 1993), pp. 103–14.

12. Campbell, "The Catholic Evidence Guild."

13. Maisie Ward, TS (no title), CSWD 13/16.

14. Tom Burns, *The Use of Memory: Publishing and Further Pursuits* (London: Sheed & Ward, 1993), pp. 30–31.

15. Maisie Ward to Frank Sheed, 9 May 1921, CSWD 2/10.

16. Leo Ward to Josephine Ward, n.d. Letter in the possession of Rosemary Middleton. This letter indicates that Maisie had joined the third order by October 1921.

17. James J. McEnroe, "Maisie Ward: Her Theory and Art of Evangelization," doctoral dissertation, Dept. of Pastoral Theology, St. Michael's College, Toronto, 1986.

18. F. J. Sheed, *The Instructed Heart* (Huntington, Ind.: Our Sunday Visitor, 1979), p. 25.

19. Maisie Ward, "Notes, Manuscripts, Interview," p. 3, CSWD 13/18.

20. This is from Maisie's "Talk Concerning the Street-Corner Apostolate" as quoted by McEnroe, "Maisie Ward: Her Theory and Art of Evangelization," p. 5.

21. *The Catholic Evidence Training Outlines,* comp. Maisie Ward (London: Catholic Truth Society, 1925). F. J. Sheed was added as a compiler in *The Catholic Evidence Training Outlines* (New York: Sheed & Ward, 1934). Recently reissued by Servant Publishers, Ann Arbor, Mich., 1992.

22. F. J. Sheed, *The Church and I* (Garden City, N.Y.: Doubleday, 1974), pp. 55, 65.

23. Campbell, "The Catholic Evidence Guild," p. 319.

24. Maisie Ward to Frank Sheed, December 1921, CSWD 2/10.

25. Maisie Ward to Frank Sheed, 22 April 1921, CSWD 2/10.

26. Ibid.

27. Maisie Ward to Frank Sheed, 1920s, CSWD 2/04.

28. Frank Sheed on the train from New York to Washington, D.C. to Maisie Ward, London, 29 October 1924, CSWD 1/02.

29. Years earlier there had been the possibility of Walter Moberly, but nothing came of this. Frank was aware of Moberly and wrote to Maisie about him. See Frank Sheed to Maisie Ward, 31 December 1921. Letter in the possession of Rosemary Middleton.

30. *Unfinished Business,* p. 107.

31. Frank's principal concern seemed to be how to support Maisie. If they stayed in England he would have to wait to be admitted to the Bar. If they went to America, he would have to become a citizen and she would have to take his citizenship. The only logical thing to do was to return to Australia for at least a few years. See Frank Sheed to Maisie Ward, 11 February 1925 and 6 May 1925. Letters in possession of Rosemary Middleton.

32. See chapter 1, note 15.

33. Maisie Ward to Frank Sheed, 4 May 1925, CSWD 2/14.

34. Maisie Ward to Frank Sheed, 2 January 1926, CSWD 3/02.

35. Maisie Ward to Frank Sheed, 12 November, no year, CSWD 3/01.

36. Maisie Ward to Min Sheed, 28 April 1925. Letter in the possession of Rosemary Sheed.

37. Maisie Ward to Frank Sheed, no date, CSWD 2/04.

38. Maisie Ward to Frank Sheed, 9 April 1925, CSWD 2/14.

39. Maisie Ward to Frank Sheed, 16 April 1925, CSWD 2/14.

40. Maisie Ward to Frank Sheed, 5 April 1925, CSWD 2/14.

41. Maisie Ward to Frank Sheed, 15 April 1925, CSWD 2/14.

42. Ibid.

43. *Unfinished Business,* p. 112.

44. Frank Sheed to Maisie Ward, 26 May 1925, CSWD 1/02.

45. Frank Sheed to Maisie Ward, 4 December 1924. Letter in the possession of Rosemary Middleton.

46. Frank Sheed to Maisie Ward, 25 February 1925. Letter in the possession of Rosemary Middleton.

47. Frank Sheed to Maisie Ward, 1921. Letter in the possession of Rosemary Middleton. In this letter Frank confesses that he feels the social difference between them. He knew he was beneath her but also knew they were friends.

48. Frank Sheed to Maisie Ward, 18 December 1924 and 4 February 1925. Letters in the possession of Rosemary Middleton.

49. Ibid.

50. Maisie Ward to Frank Sheed, 14 June 1925, CSWD 3/01.

51. See letter from Frank Sheed to Maisie Ward, 27 January 1925. Letter in the possession of Rosemary Middleton.

52. Maisie Ward, "Speaking of Sex . . . And So Forth," *America* 124 (12 June 1971), pp. 613–15.

53. Wilfrid Sheed, *Frank and Maisie,* p. 58.

54. *Unfinished Business,* p. 103.

55. Maisie Ward to Frank Sheed, n.d., CSWD 2/13.

56. Maisie Ward to Frank Sheed, 30 December 1921, CSWD 2/10.

57. Maisie Ward to Frank Sheed, 12 November, no year, CSWD 3/01.

5. "The Blissful Catholic Summer of the Twenties"

1. The original shareholders were Josephine, Maisie, Herbert, Leo, Lady Anne Kerr, and Frank. Frank Sheed to Josephine Ward, 19 May 1926, CSWD 1/03.

2. Frank Sheed to Josephine Ward, 19 May 1926, CSWD 1/03.

3. Burns, *The Use of Memory*, p. 32.

4. F. J. Sheed, *Sidelights on the Catholic Revival* (New York: Sheed & Ward, 1940), p. 14.

5. Ibid., p. 157.

6. See Christina Dawson Scott, *A Historian and His World: A Life of Christopher Dawson* (New Brunswick, N.J.: Transaction Publishers, 1991).

7. *Unfinished Business*, p. 117.

8. Burns, *The Use of Memory*, pp. 23–55; Elizabeth Ward, *David Jones Mythmaker* (Manchester, England: University of Manchester, 1983), pp. 43–59; Robert Speaight, *The Property Basket: Recollections of a Divided Life* (London: Collins and Harvill Press, 1970), pp. 160–65.

9. Christopher Dawson, introduction to *Essays in Order* (London: Sheed & Ward, 1931), pp. v–vi.

10. Burns, *The Use of Memory*, p. 52.

11. *Unfinished Business*, p. 203.

12. Burns, *The Use of Memory*, p. 52.

13. *Unfinished Business*, p. 154.

14. Ibid., p. 120. Maisie quotes this jingle.

15. Ibid., p. 121.

16. These letters are the property of Maisie Ward's granddaughter, Mary Jo Middleton, London.

17. *Unfinished Business*, p. 142.

18. Ibid., p. 141.

19. Maisie Ward, "Life and Liturgy," n.d., CSWD, 15/04.

20. Ibid.

21. Frank Sheed to Maisie Ward, 4 November 1931, CSWD 1/03.

22. Ibid.

23. *Unfinished Business,* p. 154.

24. Burns, *The Use of Memory,* p. 53, quotes a similar appraisal from *The Manchester Guardian.*

6. A TRANSATLANTIC LIFE

1. Francis Talbot, "The Sheed and Ward Imprint," *America* 48, (4 March 1933), pp. 532–33.

2. Wilfrid Sheed, "Frank Sheed and Maisie Ward: Writers, Publishers and Parents," *New York Times Book Review,* 2 April 1972, pp. 2, 24.

3. Burns, *The Use of Memory,* p. 69.

4. Adrian Hastings, "Some Reflexions on the English Catholicism of the late 1930s," in *Bishops and Writers: Aspects of the Evolution of Modern English Catholicism,* ed. A. Hastings (Wheathampstead, England: Anthony Clarke, 1977), pp. 107–25; David Mathew, *Catholicism in England, 1535–1935; Portrait of a Minority: Its Culture and Tradition* (London: Eyre and Spottiswoode, 1936); Edward Norman, *Roman Catholicism in England: From the Elizabethan Settlement to the Second Vatican Council* (New York: Oxford University Press, 1985).

5. Frank Sheed to Maisie Ward, 28 June 1933, CSWD 001/03.

6. Ibid.

7. *Unfinished Business,* p. 305.

8. Letter from Maisie Ward to Father Bornman, 3 November 1969, CSWD 3/04.

9. *Insurrection versus Resurrection,* p. 495.

10. Ibid., p. 331.

11. *Unfinished Business,* pp. 117–19.

12. For a discussion of Dawson, see Scott, *A Historian and His World;* James Hitchcock, "Postmortem on a Rebirth: The Catholic Intellectual Renaissance," *American Scholar,* Spring 1980, pp. 211–25; Gerald J. Russello, "Christopher Dawson: Is There a Christian Culture?" *Commonweal* 123 (5 April 1996), pp. 19–20; E. Ward, *David Jones Mythmaker.*

13. *Unfinished Business,* pp. 171–72.

14. Gary MacEoin, "Sheed: Businessman-Theologian," *National Catholic Reporter,* 23 March 1973, p. 6.

15. In the U.S., until 1962 the Sheeds controlled 95 percent of all Sheed and Ward stock; Clare Booth Luce controlled the other 5 percent. In 1957 Philip Scharper became managing editor in New York.

In London, Neil Middleton, the Sheeds' son-in-law, became editorial director about 1957 and managing director in 1963. When he left in 1968, Martin Redfern, who had been editor, refinanced the company and became publisher.

16. Quoted by Wilfrid Sheed, "Frank Sheed and Maisie Ward: Writers, Publishers and Parents," p. 24.

17. For responses of English Catholics to Fascism, see Norman, *Roman Catholicism in England*; Speaight, *The Property Basket*; E. Ward, *David Jones Mythmaker*.

18. Speaight, *The Property Basket*, p. 164.

19. Maisie Ward, *The Oxford Groups* (London: Sheed & Ward, 1937).

20. Maisie Ward, "A Kingly People: How is the Church Democratic," *Catholic Digest* 2, no. 7 (May 1938), pp. 71–73.

21. Maisie Ward, "Waste Land at Horley! Is This Typical?" *The Weekly Review*, 2 November 1939, Sheed and Ward Family Papers: Printed Material (hereafter cited as PSWD) 1/08, UNDA.

22. Maisie Ward, *This Burning Heat* (New York: Sheed & Ward, 1941), pp. 3–23.

23. Vera Brittain, *Testament of Experience: An Autobiographical Story of the Years 1925–1950* (New York: Seaview Books, 1957), p. 229.

24. *New Catholic Encyclopedia* (New York: McGraw-Hill, 1967), s.v. "United States"; Debra Campbell, "The Heyday of Catholic Action and the Lay Apostolate, 1929–1959," pp. 222–52; Debra Campbell, "Reformers and Activists," in *American Catholic Women*, ed. Karen Kennelly (New York: MacMillan, 1989), pp. 152–81; William M. Halsey, *The Survival of American Innocence: Catholicism in an Era of Disillusionment, 1920–1940* (Notre Dame, Ind.: University of Notre Dame Press, 1980).

25. Patrick Carey, "American Religious Thought. An Historical Review," *U.S. Catholic Historian* 4, no. 2 (1985), pp. 123–42; Dolan, *The American Catholic Experience;* Philip Gleason, "In Search of Unity: American Catholic Thought, 1920–1960," *The Catholic Historical Review* 65, no. 2 (April 1979), pp. 185–205; Hitchcock, "Postmortem on a Rebirth: The Catholic Intellectual Renaissance"; F. J. Sheed, *Sidelights on the Catholic Revival.*

26. Dolores Elise Brien, "The Catholic Revival Revisited," *Commonweal* 106 (21 December 1979), pp. 714–16; Wilfred Sheed, *Frank and Maisie*, pp. 100–101; Garry Wills, *Bare Ruined Choirs: Doubt, Prophecy, and Radical Religion* (Garden City, N.Y.: Doubleday, 1972), p. 59.

27. Wilfrid Sheed, *Frank and Maisie*, p. 99.

7. "This Burning Heat"

1. Maisie Ward, *Gilbert Keith Chesterton* (New York: Sheed & Ward, 1943).

2. Maisie Ward, *The Splendor of the Rosary* (New York: Sheed & Ward, 1945).

3. Wilfrid Sheed, *Frank and Maisie,* pp. 125–35.

4. Maisie Ward to Frank Sheed, n.d., c. 1941, CSWD 2/08.

5. Wilfrid Sheed, *Frank and Maisie,* pp. 121–23.

6. Frank Sheed to Maisie Ward, 23 July 1943, CSWD 1/06.

7. Wilfrid Sheed, *Frank and Maisie,* p. 142.

8. Maisie Ward to Frank Sheed, c. 1941, CSWD 2/08.

9. 1 Peter 4.12.

10. See Father Leo R. Ward's *Nova Scotia: The Land of Co-operation* (New York: Sheed & Ward, 1942) for a description of this cooperative movement. This Father Leo Ward is not Maisie Ward's brother.

11. Flyer on Maisie Ward's lecture offerings, CSWD 12/01.

12. Campbell, "Reformers and Activists," p. 179. Campbell calls Ward and Dorothy Dohen "free-lance" female activists.

13. "Maisie Ward," in *Born Catholics,* pp. 123–44.

14. Maisie Sheed to Dorothy Day, 14 November 1943 or 1944. Series D-1, Box 22, Dorothy Day Catholic Worker Collection, Letters from Maisie Sheed to Dorothy Day (1943–1945), Marquette University Archives.

15. Frank Sheed to Dorothy Day, 24 October 1940, CSWD 1/05. Catholic Workers were being asked to leave the movement if they could not support the pacifist position.

16. McLucas, "Frank Sheed Apologist," p. 78. McLucas cites an undated, unaddressed, and unsigned first draft of a report among Frank's papers as CSWD 10/14. I have been unable to find this document, although its content has been confirmed in oral interviews with informants.

17. See Fisher's treatment of Dorothy Day in *The Catholic Counterculture in America, 1933–1962,* and Brigid O'Shea Merriman, *Searching For Christ: The Spirituality of Dorothy Day* (Notre Dame, Ind.: University of Notre Dame Press, 1994). In *The Long Loneliness: An Autobiography,* pp. 245–61, Day discusses the retreat movement's influence on her. She says that Maisie Ward first told her about a Lacouture retreat she attended in Montreal (Fr. Hugo followed in the Lacouture tradition). The Sheed and Ward Papers provide no evidence for this claim. How-

ever, Maisie did attend a retreat (no date given) and recorded notes in two notebooks. The retreat reflected the ascetical spirituality of a director who was very distinctive from Maisie's more life-affirming spirituality. The retreat notes were written during a war, presumably in early fall of 1939. Although Maisie could easily have gone to the Canadian retreat given by Abbé Saey as Day claims, that retreat was given in French. Maisie had good command of French, but the red and black retreat notebooks containing the retreat notes now in the possession of Rosemary Middleton are in English.

18. Caryll Houselander to Maisie Ward, 3 September 1944, CSWD 12/12; Caryll Houselander to Maisie Ward, 12 September 1944, CSWD 12/12; Caryll Houselander to Maisie Ward, 24 September 1944, CSWD 12/12.

19. "Ideas of God," interview with Mr. and Mrs. Sheed by William F. Buckley, Jr., *Firing Line*, TS 145, 1969 (St. Paul, Minn.: 3 Mim Press, Microfiche 5058, no. 2).

20. Maisie Ward to Frank Sheed, n.d., CSWD 2/06.

21. Frank Sheed to Maisie Ward, 15 February 1947, CSWD 1/07.

22. *Unfinished Business*, pp. 250–51.

23. Caryll Houselander to Maisie Ward, 7 July 1945, CSWD 12/12. See Moureen Coulter's " 'A Terrific Bond': The Spiritual Friendship of Caryll Houselander and Maisie Ward," *The Downside Review*, April 1989, pp. 106–18.

24. Caryll Houselander to Maisie Ward, 24 September 1944, CSWD 12/12.

25. Graham Greene, *Collected Essays* (London: Bodley Head, 1969), p. 135.

26. Wilfrid Ward, "On the Methods of Depicting Character in Fiction and Biography," *Last Lectures*, p. 167.

27. Belloc was always principally Josephine and Frank's friend, not Maisie's. Although she was grateful that she was not asked to write a biography of Belloc, she did include a chapter on him in *Unfinished Business*, pp. 308–20.

28. *Unfinished Business*, p. 240, and Wilfrid Sheed, *Frank and Maisie*, p. 46.

29. Lowell's public statement on pacifism in the early 1940s was clearly a contributing factor to his departure from Sheed & Ward.

30. Rosemary would go on to translate fifty books, most for Sheed & Ward.

31. Maisie Ward to Frank Sheed, n.d., CSWD 2/08.

32. Maisie Ward to Frank Sheed, n.d., CSWD 2/08.

33. Wilfrid Sheed, *Frank and Maisie,* pp. 154–56.

34. Maisie Ward to Frank Sheed, n.d., CSWD 2/09.

35. McLucas makes this point in his dissertation, "Frank Sheed Apologist," pp. 100–103.

36. Frank Sheed to Maisie Ward, 8 November 1944, CSWD 1/06.

37. F. J. Sheed, *The Instructed Heart,* p. 31.

38. Ibid., p. 32.

39. Frank Sheed to Maisie Ward, 7 August 1945, CSWD 1/06.

40. Frank Sheed to Maisie Ward, 9 August 1945, CSWD 1/06.

41. Frank Sheed to Maisie Ward, 8 December 1946. Letter in the possession of Rosemary Middleton.

8. England Revisited

1. Maisie Ward, *Caryll Houselander: That Divine Eccentric* (London: Sheed & Ward, 1962), pp. 121–22.

2. See *Caryll Houselander,* and *The Letters of Caryll Houselander: Her Spiritual Legacy,* ed. Maisie Ward (London: Sheed & Ward, 1965); Moureen Coulter, " 'A Mirror Set before the Face of God': Art and Mysticism in the Work of Caryll Houselander," *Studia Mystica,* Autumn 1990, pp. 83–95; Coulter, " 'A Terrific Bond': The Spiritual Friendship of Caryll Houselander and Maisie Ward"; Caryll Houselander, "Caryll Houselander," in *Born Catholics,* pp. 249–63.

3. Maisie Ward quotes these lines without giving a source in *Caryll Houselander,* p. 148.

4. Joseph J. Bluett's "Current Theology: The Mystical Body of Christ: 1890–1940," *Theological Studies* 3 (May 1942), pp. 261–89, is a compilation of periodical literature on the Mystical Body written in Latin, French, and English for this fifty-year period.

5. Caryll Houselander, *Guilt* (New York: Sheed & Ward, 1951), p. 279.

6. *Caryll Houselander,* pp. 273–81.

7. Caryll Houselander to Lucille Hasley, 27 May 1948. In *The Letters of Caryll Houselander,* pp. 225–26.

8. When Maisie wrote her biography of Houselander she received many letters regarding Houselander's unorthodox life. There were many people who had violently opposing views of her. See "Postscript," CSWD 15/04. One writer claimed that Houselander had not been cast off by her family and that she lived as a paid mistress for

some time. See CSWD 12/13. It is impossible to determine if these claims are credible. Maisie certainly did not deal with them in the biography.

9. Maisie Ward, "The Indicating Number," *The Clergy Review* 48, no. 3 (March 1963), pp. 139–53.

10. *Unfinished Business,* p. 260.

11. Maisie Ward to Frank Sheed, n.d., CSWD 2/08.

12. Maisie Ward, *Young Mr. Newman* (London: Sheed & Ward, 1948), p. 228.

13. Frank Sheed to Maisie Ward, 17 November 1947, CSWD 1/07.

14. For Maisie Ward's views on priest-workers, see *Unfinished Business,* pp. 270–97. For Frank Sheed's views, see *The Church and I,* pp. 269–75.

15. See *The New Catholic Encyclopedia,* s.v. "Worker-Priests"; David L. Edwards, ed., *Priests and Workers: An Anglo-French Discussion* (London: SCM Press, 1961); Henri Perrin, *The Priest-Workman in Germany,* trans. Rosemary Sheed (London: Sheed & Ward, 1947).

16. Maisie Ward, *France Pagan? The Mission of Abbé Godin* (New York: Sheed & Ward, 1949).

17. Maisie Ward, "The New French Revolution," *Books on Trial,* February 1950. In PSWD By and About Maisie Ward, UNDA.

18. Maisie Ward, CSWD 13/14. This untitled TS begins, "The bourgeoisie have had an unhappy fate. . . ."

19. *France Pagan?,* p. 294.

20. Maisie Ward, "The Climate of Christian Hope," *The Catholic Mind* 48 (September 1950), pp. 554–58.

21. "Maisie Ward," in *Born Catholics,* p. 141.

22. Cecily Hastings, "Cecily Hastings," in *Born Catholics,* pp. 161–84.

23. Maisie Ward to Frank Sheed, 9 April 1955, CSWD 3/03.

24. Wilfrid Sheed, *Frank and Maisie,* p. 176.

25. Maisie Ward to Frank Sheed, n.d., CSWD 2/09.

26. See Wilfrid Sheed, *Clare Booth Luce* (New York: E. P. Dutton, 1982).

27. Maisie Ward to Frank Sheed, 14 July 1949, and Frank Sheed to Maisie Ward, 9 October 1952, CSWD 27/09.

28. Maisie Ward, *Return to Chesterton* (New York: Sheed & Ward, 1952).

29. Ibid., pp. ix–x.

30. "Maisie Ward," in *Born Catholics,* pp. 136–41.

31. Maisie Ward to Frank Sheed, 3 March 1953, CSWD 27/09.

9. "Chaos, Shot Through with the Brightest Delights"

1. *Unfinished Business,* p. 339.

2. A. S., "The Personable Publishers," *Today,* October 1951. In PSWD 1, By and About Frank Sheed and Maisie Ward, UNDA.

3. Maisie Ward to Frank Sheed, n.d., CSWD 27/03.

4. Maisie Ward, "Journal," 1955, CSWD 13/19.

5. Ibid.

6. For information on Marycrest, see Campbell, "The Heyday of Catholic Action and the Lay Apostolate, 1929–59"; Fisher, *The Catholic Counterculture in America, 1933–1962;* and MacEoin, "Lay Movements in the United States Before Vatican II," *America,* 10 August 1991, pp. 61–65.

7. Maisie Ward to Frank Sheed, 3 September 1956, CSWD 3/04.

8. Marycrest ended as a community in 1976. However, a court case for division of the property had begun six years earlier.

9. Maisie Ward to Frank Sheed, 10 November 1954, CSWD 3/03.

10. George Ineson, *Community Journal* (New York: Sheed & Ward, 1956).

11. Maisie Ward, "Problems of the Apostolate," *Orate Fratres,* 24 December 1949, pp. 28–30.

12. "Plea for the Family," in *Be Not Solicitous: Sidelights on the Providence of God and the Catholic Family,* ed. Maisie Ward (New York: Sheed & Ward, 1953), pp. 3–54.

13. Ibid., p. 25. She quotes directly from a letter she received from Father Charles Davis, S.J.

14. Jane Mary Farley, "Maisie Ward Sheed Urges Women to Thought, Action," *Milwaukee Journal,* 28 February 1955. In PSWD 1/13, By and About Maisie Ward, UNDA.

15. See Campbell, "Reformers and Activists," and Gleason, "In Search of Unity: American Catholic Thought, 1920–1960."

16. Jeffrey M. Burns, "Catholic Laywomen in the Culture of American Catholicism in the 1950s," *U.S. Catholic Historian* 5, nos. 3 and 4 (Summer/Fall 1986), pp. 385–400.

17. Maisie Ward to Frank Sheed, 2 November 1953, CSWD 3/03.

18. Frank Sheed to Maisie Ward, 14 October 1955, CSWD 27/11.

19. Sister M. Madeleva, "Maisie Ward: A Shepherdess of Sheep," pp. 7–8, PSWD 1/12, By and About Maisie Ward, UNDA.

20. The Sheeds always referred to Erika in this way. See Connecticut Mutual Life Insurance Company policy in which she is referred to as a "daughter by adoption," CSWD 17/18.

21. See CSWD 17/07 and CSWD 17/18.

22. *Unfinished Business,* pp. 348–50.

23. Maisie Ward, "Restoring All Things," *Integrity* 7 (October 1952), pp. 14–24.

10. HITTING HER STRIDE

1. Letter from Maisie Ward to John V. Simcox, 30 December 1958, CSWD 3/04.

2. Maisie Ward, *They Saw His Glory: An Introduction to the Gospels and Acts* (New York: Sheed & Ward, 1956). *The Authenticity of the Gospels,* an abridged paperback edition, was published in the same year.

3. Ian Hislop, O.P., "A Century of Catholic Intellectual Life," *Blackfriars* 31, no. 366 (September 1950), pp. 412–15.

4. "Presenting the New Testament," a review of *They Saw His Glory: An Introduction to the Gospels and Acts,* in *The Dublin Review* 230 (1956), p. 261.

5. Maisie Ward, *Saints Who Made History: The First Five Centuries* (New York: Sheed & Ward, 1959). An English edition, *The Early Church Portrait Gallery,* was published in 1960.

6. *Saints Who Made History,* p. v.

7. Ibid., p. ix.

8. *The Splendor of the Rosary* was issued in 1957 in an abridged edition as *The Rosary,* and the biography of Chesterton was published by Penguin Books in 1958.

9. The following describe the post-war housing situation: John Howes, "History of the Catholic Housing Aid Society," unpublished manuscript, CHAS, London; Maisie Ward, "An Englishman's House," *Blackfriars* 43 (May 1962), pp. 204–13; Maisie Ward, "Report From England," *Jubilee* 9 (1962), pp. 2–5.

10. *Unfinished Business,* pp. 342–44.

11. *Be Not Solicitous,* p. 34.

12. Howes, "History."

13. Gabrielle Murray, "A Housing Tale from the Parish of St. Saviour's, Lewisham," unpublished manuscript.

14. Howes, "History."

15. Maisie Ward, "Postscript," p. 2, CSWD 15/04.

16. Howes, "History."

17. "An Englishman's House," p. 209.

18. Maisie Ward to Frank Sheed, 20 February 1956, CSWD 3/03.

19. "Postscript," p. 2. In 1996 CHAS celebrated its 40th anniversary as a small voluntary organization serving those with housing needs.

20. "Introduction to Maisie Sheed" by Christopher Dawson. TS in possession of Christina Dawson Scott, London, n.d., c. 1950.

21. Maisie attended this Second World Congress on the Lay Apostolate in Rome in 1957.

22. Introduction and epilogue in Oliver, *Mary Ward, 1585–1645,* pp. xi–xx and 215–22.

23. "English Spiritual Writers—William Basil Maturin 1847–1915," pp. 65–77.

24. Campbell, Debra, "The Laity in the Age of Aggiornamento, 1960–69" in Jay Dolan et al., *Transforming Parish Ministry,* p. 259.

25. *Unfinished Business,* p. 366.

26. Ibid.

27. "Postscript," p. 5.

28. Ibid., p. 9.

29. *Unfinished Business,* p. 345.

30. Maisie was listed as part of the Speakers Bureau for Women for McCarthy. She probably spoke only once or twice in this capacity. "Women for McCarthy" folder, Eugene McCarthy Collection, Georgetown University.

31. "Postscript," p. 11.

32. "Campion Award," Catholic Booksellers, CSWD 14.

33. "Postscript," pp. 15–16.

11. "A Rest Is Needed"

1. Untitled essay, CSWD 13/16.

2. "Postscript," p. 2, CSWD 15/04.

3. As a bookseller, Frank was in Rome for every session of the Council. See F. J. Sheed, *The Church and I,* p. 304.

4. Maisie Ward, "Changes in the Liturgy: Cri de Coeur," *Life of the Spirit,* October 1961, pp. 127–36.

5. Maisie Ward, "New Liturgy I: Give It A Chance," *America,* 122 (30 May 1970), pp. 589–91.

6. Brian Wicker, *Culture and Liturgy* (London: Sheed & Ward, 1963).

7. "Postscript," pp. 5–10.

8. "Postscript" and "Changes in the Liturgy."

9. Frank Sheed to Violet Fitzgerald, 6 April 1965, CSWD 1/14.

10. Wilfrid Sheed, *Frank and Maisie,* p. 249.

11. Frank Sheed to Bishop Stephen Leven, 8 August 1966, CSWD 1/14.

12. F. J. Sheed, *Is It the Same Church?* (London: Sheed & Ward, 1968).

13. See *The Slant Manifesto: Catholics and the Left* (London: Sheed & Ward, 1966) and Adrian Hastings, *A History of English Christianity, 1920–1990* (London: SCM Press, 1991), pp. 571–72.

14. Frank Sheed to Maisie Ward, 18 May 1961, CSWD 1/13.

15. Frank Sheed to Philip Scharper, 19 November 1963, CSWD 1/13.

16. The Sheeds' financial records, including IRS statements, are scattered throughout their personal papers. See particularly CSWD 17/11 and CSWD 16/20.

17. "The Indicating Number," pp. 139–53.

18. Although Maisie often argued against canonization of Newman lest it divest him of his humanness, in this 1963 article she urges her readers to pray for canonization. In her essays in Mary Oliver's 1959 biography of Mary Ward, she argues for Ward's canonization as well.

19. Maisie Ward, *To and Fro on the Earth,* p. 4 and CSWD 12/13.

20. The Sheed and Ward Papers contain a manuscript draft of Julian's writings probably done near the end of Maisie's life; CSWD 13/10.

21. Maisie wrote several pieces that ultimately were not included in the final version of *Unfinished Business.* She felt that she owed a great deal to Christopher Dawson and wanted to include a chapter on him, but found that she had none of his letters. She also wanted to include something on C. C. Martindale, but neither he nor Dawson appeared in the final text. Instead, she included a chapter on Belloc that she said Frank pushed her into writing. Letter of Maisie Ward to Christopher Dawson, n.d. Loaned by Christina Dawson Scott.

22. Wilfrid Sheed, *Frank and Maisie,* p. 260.

23. F. J. Sheed, *The Instructed Heart,* pp. 36–37.

24. *Unfinished Business,* p. 367.

25. Ibid. She quotes from Browning's "Confessions."

26. Ibid., p. 368.

12. "A Refuge in Browning"

1. Rosemary Middleton to Maisie Ward and Frank Sheed, n.d., CSWD 5/01. In this letter Rosemary explains to her parents, who had not heard from her in over a month, that Neil had left. There is no

documentary evidence to indicate that Maisie knew the causes of the demise of either of her children's marriages.

2. Betty Miller, *Robert Browning: A Portrait* (New York: Scribner, 1952).

3. *To and Fro on the Earth*, p. 5. Maisie explains that she did not have the same total sympathy for Newman that her father had, hence she was unwilling to take up the sequel.

4. See "Newman, Browning and Approach to Reality," CSWD 13/14.

5. Maisie quotes from Browning's "Christmas-Eve and Easter Day," in *Robert Browning and His World*, vol. 1, *The Private Face, 1812–1861* (New York: Holt, Rinehart & Winston, 1967), p. 179.

6. Maisie Ward to Frank Sheed, 14 October (no year), CSWD 2/09.

7. Maisie Ward, *Robert Browning and His World: The Private Face*, p. 188.

8. F. J. Sheed, *The Instructed Heart*, p. 28.

9. Maisie Ward, "Casa Guidi, To Be Lost or Saved," an essay based on a speech delivered to the 63rd Annual Luncheon of the New York Browning Society, 13 May 1970. Published subsequently in *The New York Times Book Review*, 31 May 1970.

10. *To and Fro on the Earth*, p. 6. Maisie explains that she had been asked to write an introduction for a volume of Browning's letters to Pen, which led to a biography of Robert and Elizabeth's son.

11. See chapter 7, note 14.

12. Maisie Ward, "The New Missionary Approach," CSWD 13/17 and "Changed World: Changed View?" *The Catholic Herald*, 21 October 1966.

13. Maisie Ward to John (no family name given), 7 August 1970, CSWD 12/01.

14. "The New Missionary Approach," CSWD 13/17.

15. *To and Fro on the Earth*, pp. 76–94.

16. "Ideas of God," p. 14.

17. Ibid.

18. Ibid., pp. 24–25.

19. Several years later Wilfrid Sheed, now a noted essayist, critic, and novelist, wrote a veiled attack on Eugene McCarthy in *People Will Always Be Kind* (New York: Farrar, Straus, and Giroux, 1973). This apparently saddened Maisie.

20. See *To and Fro on the Earth*, pp. 95–135.

21. Maisie Ward, "Speaking of Sex . . . and So Forth."

22. "Give the Children a Chance," CSWD 13/14.

23. See the untitled speech on Julian, Hammarskjöld, and de Chardin, CSWD 13/10. Also see "Dag Hammarskjöld and Teilhard de Chardin," *The Dublin Review* 242 (Fall 1968), pp. 203–15.

24. CSWD 16/20.

13. "Hope in Near-hopelessness"

1. The owners of Universal Press Syndicate were Jim Andrews and John McMeel, both of whom had great interest in Sheed & Ward and tried to keep its list together. In about 1977 the company was named Sheed, Andrews and McMeel. In 1982 the company was sold to the National Catholic Reporter, which still runs it.

2. This is the evaluation of Wilfrid Sheed in "What Frank & Maisie Did in America," *Commonweal* 112 (1 November 1985), p. 604.

3. For an evaluation of the achievement of Sheed & Ward, see Gary MacEoin, "Lay Movements in the United States Before Vatican II"; F. J. Sheed, "The Future of Religious Publishing," *Religious Book Guide,* July/August 1971, pp. 2–4, in PSWD 1/10, By and About Frank Sheed; Wilfrid Sheed, "Sheed and Ward Inc.," Catholic Imprints, PSWD 1/07, By and About Frank Sheed and Maisie Ward; Timothy Unsworth, "Catholic Publishing Dithers Between Business and Apostolate," *National Catholic Reporter,* 10 September 1993, pp. 25, 32–33.

4. *To and Fro on the Earth,* p. 7.

5. Ibid., p. 15. Although John Tracy Ellis comes to a different conclusion, he describes the same reality in "American Catholicism in 'An Uncertain, Anxious Time,'" *Commonweal* 98 (27 April 1973), pp. 177–84.

6. "Anti-Victorians Trapped in a Victorian Age."

7. Hannah Arendt in Maisie Ward's *To and Fro on the Earth,* p. 10. Maisie quotes from Arendt's *The Human Condition* (Chicago: University of Chicago Press, 1958), pp. 294–95.

8. *To and Fro on the Earth,* p. 11.

9. Ibid., p. 174.

10. See "Notes for Report," CSWD 13/17, pp. 136–39.

11. *To and Fro on the Earth,* p. 175.

12. Maisie described many Christian communities in this book. Fides House and Sursum Corda were both in Washington, D.C. Cesar Chavez organized migrant farm workers in California, and Danilo Dolci worked with the poor in Sicily.

13. Frank Sheed to Paula Bowes, 17 December 1974. Letters in the possession of Paula Bowes, Monrovia, Md.

14. Frank's paper, with a short biographical study on Maisie, was published subsequently as *The Instructed Heart.*

15. Rudyard Kipling, "Jane's Marriage," *Rudyard Kipling's Verse Inclusive Edition, 1885–1926* (Garden City, N.Y.: Doubleday, Page & Co., 1927), pp. 703–04.

16. 1 John 3. 7–10 is the liturgical reading for January 4th.

17. *Confessions of St. Augustine,* trans. F. J. Sheed (New York: Sheed & Ward, 1943), pp. 199–200. There is no written documentation on how much of this selection Frank read during the service.

Bibliography

INTERVIEWS

The following persons graciously agreed to be interviewed either in person, by phone, or letter. I am grateful to each of them. However, I remain personally responsible for all interpretations in this biography. Copies of these interviews have been given to the Archives of the University of Notre Dame.

Cecily Hastings Bennett, London
Tom Cornell, Marlboro, N.Y.
Maria (Missie) Darlington, Efland, N.C.
Jack Dermoty, West Nyack, N.Y.
Geraldine Cunningham Elwes, London
Eileen Egan, New York
Marie De Stena, Jersey City, N.J.
Marigold Hunt, Somerset, Mass.
Robert Langbaum, Charlottesville, Va.
Pat and Owen McGowan, Somerset, Mass.
Abigail McCarthy, Washington, D.C.
John McMeel, Kansas City, Mo.
Mary Jo Middleton, London
Neil Middleton, Dublin
Rosemary Middleton, London
Gabrielle Murray, London
Marjorie Murphy, Baltimore, Md.
Mildred Neville, London
Ann Reinicke Peabody, New York
Martin Redfern, London
David Reeves, Princeton, N.J.
Bill Scanlon, S.J., Lagos, Nigeria
Bruno Schlesinger, South Bend, Ind.

Christina Dawson Scott, London
Frank Sheed, Jr., Washington, D.C.
Wilfrid Sheed, Sag Harbor, N.Y.
Lance Thwaytes, Appleby, Cumbria
Michael Walsh, London
Mary Jo Weaver, Bloomington, Ind.
Erika Fallaux Young, Richmond, Surrey

Archival Material

Dorothy Day Catholic Worker Collection, Marquette University Archives. Letters From Maisie Sheed to Dorothy Day. Series D-1, D-2.

Sheed and Ward Family Papers, 1832–1982. This collection includes Correspondence 1864–1981, the Papers of Frank Sheed, the Papers of Maisie Ward, the Papers of Frank Sheed and Maisie Ward, and Other Family Papers. Printed and manuscript materials found in these Papers will not be cited separately in the bibliography.

Books Edited, Translated, or Authored by Maisie Ward

Chesterton, G. K. *The Coloured Lands*. Introduction by Maisie Ward. London: Sheed & Ward, 1938.
LaGrange, M. J. *Christ and Renan*. Translated by Maisie Ward. London: Sheed & Ward, 1926.
Newman, John Henry. *Apologia Pro Vita Sua: Being a History of His Religious Opinions*. Introduction by Maisie Ward. New York: Sheed & Ward, 1946.
Oliver, Mary. *Mary Ward, 1585–1645*. Introduction and epilogue by Maisie Ward. New York: Sheed & Ward, 1959.
Ward, Maisie. *Anthony of Egypt*. New York: Sheed & Ward, 1950.
———. *The Authenticity of the Gospels*. New York: Sheed & Ward, 1956. This is an abridged edition of *They Saw His Glory*.
———, ed. *Be Not Solicitous: Sidelights on the Providence of God and the Catholic Family*. Introduction, "Plea for the Family," by Maisie Ward. New York: Sheed & Ward, 1953.
———. *Caryll Houselander: That Divine Eccentric*. London: Sheed & Ward, 1962.
———. *Catherine of Siena*. New York: Sheed & Ward, 1950.

——, and Frank Sheed, comp. *The Catholic Evidence Training Outlines.* New York: Sheed & Ward, 1934. This was first published by the Catholic Truth Society in London, 1925, with Maisie as sole compiler, and has been reissued recently by Servant Publishers, Ann Arbor, Mich., 1992.

——. *The Early Church Portrait Gallery.* London: Sheed & Ward, 1960. This is the English edition of *Saints Who Made History.*

——, ed. *The English Way: Studies in English Sanctity from St. Bede to Newman.* London: Sheed & Ward, 1933.

——, ed. *Father Maturin: A Memoir with Selected Letters.* London: Longmans, Green, and Co., 1920.

——. *France Pagan? The Mission of Abbé Godin.* New York: Sheed & Ward, 1949.

——. *Francis of Assisi.* New York: Sheed & Ward, 1950.

——. *Gilbert Keith Chesterton.* New York: Sheed & Ward, 1943.

——, and Josephine Ward, ed. *Last Lectures by Wilfrid Ward.* With an introductory study by Mrs. Wilfrid Ward. London: Longman, Green, and Co., 1918.

——, ed. *The Letters of Caryll Houselander: Her Spiritual Legacy.* London: Sheed & Ward, 1965.

——. *The Oxford Groups.* London: Sheed & Ward, 1937.

——. *Return to Chesterton.* New York: Sheed & Ward, 1952.

——. *Robert Browning and His World.* Vol. 1, *The Private Face, 1812–1861.* Vol. 2, *Two Robert Brownings?* Holt, Rinehart & Winston, 1967, 1969.

——. *S. Bernardino: The People's Preacher.* London: Herder, 1914.

——. *Saint Jerome.* New York: Sheed & Ward, 1950.

——. *Saints Who Made History: The First Five Centuries.* New York: Sheed & Ward, 1959. Published in England as *The Early Church Portrait Gallery,* 1960.

——. *The Splendor of the Rosary.* New York: Sheed & Ward, 1945.

——. *They Saw His Glory: An Introduction to the Gospels and Acts.* New York: Sheed & Ward, 1956. This appeared in abridged form as *The Authenticity of the Gospels.*

——. *This Burning Heat.* New York: Sheed & Ward, 1941.

——. *To and Fro on the Earth: The Sequel to an Autobiography.* New York: Sheed & Ward, 1973.

——. *The Tragi-Comedy of Pen Browning (1849–1912).* New York: The Browning Institute, 1972.

——. *The Wilfrid Wards and the Transition.* Vol. I, *The Nineteenth Century.* Vol. 2, *Insurrection versus Ressurection.* New York: Sheed & Ward, 1934, 1937.

———. *Unfinished Business.* New York: Sheed & Ward, 1964.
———. *Young Mr. Newman.* London: Sheed & Ward, 1948.

"Anti-Victorians Trapped in a Victorian Age." *Commonweal* 87 (23 February 1968), pp. 625–28.
"Casa Guidi, To Be Lost or Saved." *The New York Times Book Review,* 31 May 1970.
"Catholics and Novels." *Commonweal,* 8 January 1943, pp. 302–03.
"Changed World: Changed View?" *The Catholic Herald,* 21 October 1966, n.p.
"Changes in the Liturgy: Cri de Coeur." *Life of the Spirit,* October 1961, pp. 127–36.
"The Climate of Christian Hope." *The Catholic Mind* 48 (September 1950), pp. 554–58.
"Dag Hammarskjöld and Teilhard de Chardin." *The Dublin Review* 242 (Fall 1968), pp. 203–15.
"An Englishman's House." *Blackfriars* 43 (May 1962), pp. 204–13.
"English Spiritual Writers—William Basil Maturin, 1847–1915." *The Clergy Review* 45, no. 2 (February 1960), pp. 65–77.
"Ideas of God." Interview with Mr. and Mrs. Sheed by William F. Buckley, Jr. *Firing Line* TS 145, 1969. St. Paul, Minn.: 3 Mim Press, Microfiche, 5058, no. 2.
"The Indicating Number." *Clergy Review* 48, no. 3 (March 1963), pp. 139–53.
"A Kingly People: How is the Church Democratic." *Catholic Digest* 2, no. 7 (May 1938), pp. 71–73.
"Maisie Ward." In *Born Catholics,* assembled by Francis J. Sheed. New York: Sheed & Ward, 1954, pp. 123–44.
"Maisie Ward." In *The Book of Catholic Authors,* 4th series, edited by Walter Romig. Grosse Point, Michigan, n.p., n.d., pp. 324–30.
"Mary Ward." In *The English Way: Studies in English Sanctity from St. Bede to Newman.* New York: Sheed & Ward, 1933, pp. 242–67.
"The New French Revolution." Review of *To Every Man a Penny* by Bruce Marshall. *Books on Trial,* February 1950, pp. 193, 225–26.
"New Liturgy I: Give It a Chance." *America* 122 (30 May 1970), pp. 589–91.
"No Time to Read." *Today* 9 (February 1954), p. 17.
"Problems of the Apostolate." *Orate Fratres* 24 (December 1949), pp. 28–30.

"Proletariat Apostle." *Grail*, September 1952, pp. 1–6.

"Report From England." *Jubilee* 9 (February 1962), pp. 2–5.

"Restoring All Things." *Integrity* 7 (October 1952), pp. 14–24.

"Saint Paul the Apostle." *Sign* 39 (March 1960), pp. 21–23.

"Sharer of Life." *Today* 16 (April 1961), pp. 32–33.

"Speaking of Sex . . . and So Forth." *America* 124 (12 June 1971), pp. 613–15.

"Viewpoint." With Robert Robinson. TS from a television tape recording, 7 July 1965, pp. 1–6.

"Waste Land at Horley! Is This Typical?" *The Weekly Review*, 2 November 1939, n.p.

"When the Children Ask How? Why? What?" *Catholic World* 151 (April 1940), pp. 84–89.

SECONDARY SOURCES—BOOKS AND ARTICLES

Allitt, Patrick. *Catholic Intellectuals and Conservative Politics in America, 1950–1985*. Ithaca, N.Y.: Cornell University Press, 1993.

Benson, Robert Hugh. *Christ in the Church*. Reprint. London: Sheed & Ward, 1941.

———. *The Religion of the Plain Man*. New York: Benziger, 1907.

Blackburn, Thomas. "The Millstones of Genius: The Tragi-Comedy of Pen Browning." *The Tablet* (London) 227 (4 August 1973), pp. 730–31.

Blantz, Thomas E. *George N. Shuster: On the Side of Truth*. Notre Dame, Imd.: University of Notre Dame Press, 1993.

Bluett, Joseph J. "Current Theology: The Mystical Body of Christ: 1890–1940." *Theological Studies* 3 (May 1942), pp. 261–89.

Brien, Dolores Elise. "The Catholic Revival Revisited." *Commonweal* 106 (21 December 1979), pp. 714–16.

Brittain, Vera. *Testament of Experience: An Autobiographical Story of the Years 1925–50*. New York: Seaview Books, 1979.

Browne, Joseph. "Robert Browning and His World." *America* 117 (28 October 1967), p. 486.

Burns, Jeffrey M. "Catholic Laywomen in the Culture of American Catholicism in the 1950s." *U.S. Catholic Historian* 5, nos. 3 and 4 (Summer/Fall, 1986), pp. 385–400.

Burns, Tom. *The Use of Memory: Publishing and Further Pursuits*. London: Sheed & Ward, 1993.

Campbell, Debra. "Breaking the Laity's Silence." *Liturgy,* Fall 1989, pp. 59–65.

———. "The Catholic Evidence Guild: Towards a History of the Laity." *Heythrop Journal* 30 (July 1987), pp. 306–24.

———. "The Gleanings of a Laywoman's Ministry: Maisie Ward as Preacher, Publisher and Social Activist." *American Catholic Historical Society of Philadelphia* 98 (November/December 1987), pp. 21–28.

———. "The Heyday of Catholic Action and the Lay Apostolate, 1929–1959." In *Transforming Parish Ministry: The Changing Roles of Catholic Clergy, Laity, and Women Religious,* edited by Jay Dolan et al. New York: Crossroad, 1989, pp. 222–52.

———." 'I Can't Imagine Our Lady on an Outdoor Platform': Women in the Catholic Street Propaganda Movement." *U.S. Catholic Historian* 3, no. 2 (Spring/Summer 1983), pp. 103–14.

———. "The Laity in the Age of Aggiornamento, 1960–69." In *Transforming Parish Ministry: The Changing Roles of Catholic Clergy, Laity, and Women Religious,* edited by Jay Dolan et al. New York: Crossroad, 1989, pp. 253–66.

———. "Part-Time Female Evangelists of the Thirties and Forties: The Rosary College Catholic Evidence Guild." *U.S. Catholic Historian* 5, nos. 3 and 4. (Summer/Fall 1986), pp. 371–83.

———. "Reformers and Activists." In *American Catholic Women,* edited by Karen Kennelly. New York: Macmillan, 1989, pp. 152–81.

———. "The Rise of the Lay Catholic Evangelist in England and America." *Harvard Theological Review* 79, no. 4 (1986), pp. 413–37.

Carey, Patrick. "American Religious Thought: An Historical Review." *U.S. Catholic Historian* 4, no. 2 (1985), pp. 123–42.

Chesterton, Ada Elizabeth. *The Chestertons.* London: Chapman & Hall, 1941.

Chinnici, Joseph. *Living Stones: The History and Structure of Catholic Spiritual Life in the United States.* New York: MacMillan, 1989.

Ciernick, Helen Marie. "Cracking the Door: Women at the Second Vatican Council." In *Women & Theology,* edited by Mary Ann Hinsdale and Phyllis Kaminski. Maryknoll, N.Y.: Orbis Books, 1995.

Coulter, Moureen. " 'A Mirror Set Before the Face of God': Art and Mysticism in the Work of Caryll Houselander." *Studia Mystica,* Autumn 1990, pp. 83–95.

———. " 'A Terrific Bond': The Spiritual Friendship of Caryll Houselander and Maisie Ward." *The Downside Review,* April 1989, pp. 106–18.

Cramer, Maurice. "Irvine and Honan, and Maisie Ward Sheed: The New Standard Browning Biographers." In *Studies in Browning and His Circle: A Journal of Criticism, History and Bibliography* 3, no. 1 (July 1975), pp. 9–31.

———. "Maisie Ward and Browning Biography: A New Era." *Modern Philology* 68 (February 1971), pp. 294–300.

Culler, A. Dwight. "Browning: The Traditional Portrait." *The Yale Review,* 1968, pp. 589–92.

Cuthbert, Father, ed. *God and the Supernatural: A Catholic Statement of the Christian Faith.* New York: Longmans, Green, and Co., 1920.

Dawson, Christopher. Introduction to *Essays in Order.* London: Sheed & Ward, 1931.

———. "Introduction to Maisie Ward." TS in possession of Christina Dawson Scott, 1950.

Day, Dorothy. *The Long Loneliness: An Autobiography.* New York: Harper & Row, 1952.

De la Bedoyere, Michael. "The Intellectual Level of British Catholicism." *The Catholic World* 188, no. 1,125, pp. 233–37.

Dolan, Jay. *The American Catholic Experience: A History from Colonial Times to the Present.* Notre Dame, Ind.: University of Notre Dame, 1992.

———, et al., eds. *Transforming Parish Ministry: The Changing Roles of Catholic Clergy, Laity, and Women Religious.* New York: Crossroad, 1989.

Duquin, Lorene Hanley. *The Life of Catherine de Hueck Doherty: They Called Her the Baroness.* New York: Alba House, 1995.

Edwards, David L., ed. *Priests and Workers: An Anglo-French Discussion.* London: SCM Press, 1961.

Ellis, John Tracy. "American Catholicism in 'An Uncertain, Anxious Time,' " *Commonweal* 98 (27 April 1973), pp. 177–84.

Farley, Jane Mary. "Maisie Ward Sheed Urges Women to Thought, Action." *Milwaukee Journal,* 28 February 1955.

Fisher, James Terence. *The Catholic Counterculture in America, 1933–1962.* Chapel Hill: University of North Carolina Press, 1989.

"Frank Sheed Talks with Christopher Dawson." *Sign,* December 1958, pp. 34–36.

Gleason, Philip. "In Search of Unity: American Catholic Thought, 1920–1960." *The Catholic Historical Review* 65, no. 2 (April 1979), pp. 185–205.

Greene, Dana. "Maisie Ward as 'Theologian.' " *Women & Theology,* edited by Mary Ann Hinsdale and Phyllis Kaminski. Maryknoll, N.Y.: Orbis Books, 1995, pp. 50–61.

Greene, Graham. *Collected Essays*. London: Bodley Head, 1969.

Halsey, William M. *The Survival of American Innocence: Catholicism in an Era of Disillusionment, 1920–1940*. Notre Dame, Ind.: University of Notre Dame Press, 1980.

Hastings, Adrian. *A History of English Christianity, 1920–1990*. London: SCM Press, 1991.

———. "Some Reflexions on the English Catholicism of the late 1930s." In *Bishops and Writers: Aspects of the Evolution of Modern English Catholicism*, edited by Adrian Hastings. Wheathampstead, England: Anthony Clarke, 1977, pp. 107–25.

Hastings, Cecily. "Cecily Hastings." In *Born Catholics*, assembled by F. J. Sheed. New York: Sheed & Ward, 1954.

Heilbrun, Carolyn. *Writing a Woman's Life*. New York: Ballentine Books, 1988.

Hislop, Ian. "A Century of Catholic Intellectual Life." *Blackfriars* 31, no. 366 (September 1950), pp. 412–15.

Hitchcock, James. "Postmortem on a Rebirth: The Catholic Intellectual Renaissance." *American Scholar*, Spring 1980, pp. 211–25.

Hitchcock, James, and David O'Brien. "Dialogue: How Has American Catholic Intellectual Life Changed Over the Past Thirty Years?" *U.S. Catholic Historian* 4, no. 2 (1985), pp. 176–87.

Hornsby-Smith, Michael. *Roman Catholicism in England: Studies in Social Structure Since the Second World War*. Cambridge, England: Cambridge University Press, 1987.

Houselander, Caryll. "Caryll Houselander." In *Born Catholics*, assembled by F. J. Sheed. New York: Sheed & Ward, 1954.

———. *Guilt*. New York: Sheed & Ward, 1951.

———. *This War is the Passion*. London: Sheed & Ward, 1941.

Howes, John. "History of the Catholic Housing Aid Society." Unpublished manuscript written for CHAS, London, n.d.

Ineson, George. *Community Journal*. New York: Sheed & Ward, 1956.

Langbaum, Robert. "Robert Browning." *Yale Review* 57 (December 1967), pp. 303–08.

Lash, Nicholas. "Modernism, 'Aggiornamento' and the Night Battle." In *Bishops and Writers: Aspects of the Evolution of Modern English Catholicism*, edited by Adrian Hastings. Wheathampstead, England: Anthony Clarke, 1977.

Lawler, Justus George. "Catholicism in the Fifties: An Interview with Justus George Lawler." *U.S. Catholic Historian* 7, no. 1 (Winter 1988), pp. 1–13.

MacEoin, Gary. "Lay Movements in the United States Before Vatican II." *America,* 10 August 1991, pp. 61–65.

———. "Sheed: Businessman-Theologian." *National Catholic Reporter,* 23 March 1973, p. 6.

Martindale, C. C. *The Life of Monsignor Robert Hugh Benson,* 2 vols. London: Longmans, Green, and Co., 1916.

Mathew, David. *Catholicism in England, 1535–1935; Portrait of A Minority: Its Culture and Tradition.* London: Eyre and Spottiswoode, 1936.

McEnroe, James J. "Maisie Ward: Her Theory and Art of Evangelization." Doctoral dissertation, Dept. of Pastoral Theology, St. Michael's College, Toronto, 1986.

McGowan, Pat. "A Son Remembers." *The Anchor,* Fall River, Mass., 25 June 1982, p. 8.

McLucas, James W. "Frank Sheed Apologist." Doctoral dissertation, Pontifical University of St. Thomas, Rome, 1991.

Merriman, Brigid O'Shea. *Searching for Christ: The Spirituality of Dorothy Day.* Notre Dame, Ind.: University of Notre Dame Press, 1994.

Miller, Betty. *Robert Browning: A Portrait.* New York: Scribner, 1952.

Murray, Gabrielle. "A Housing Tale from the Parish of St. Saviour's, Lewisham." Unpublished article, n.d.

Newman, John Henry. *The Works of Cardinal Newman: Sermons Preached on Various Occasions.* Westminster, Md.: Christian Classics, 1968.

Norman, Edward. *Roman Catholicism in England from the Elizabethan Settlement to the Second Vatican Council.* New York: Oxford University Press, 1985.

Oliver, Mary. *Mary Ward, 1585–1645.* New York: Sheed & Ward, 1959.

Perrin, Henri. *The Priest-Workman in Germany.* Translated by Rosemary Sheed. London: Sheed & Ward, 1947.

Pryce-Jones, Alan. "Robert Browning and His World: The Private Face." *Commonweal* 87 (16 February 1968), p. 596.

Purtill, Richard. "Chesterton, the Wards, the Sheeds and the Catholic Revival." In *G. K. Chesterton and C. S. Lewis: The Riddle of Joy,* edited by Michael MacDonald and A. Tadie. Grand Rapids, Mich.: Eerdmans, 1989, pp. 20–32.

Redfern, Martin, ed. *The Slant Manifesto: Catholics and the Left.* London: Sheed & Ward, 1966.

Ruskin, John. *Essays and Letters Selected from the Writings of John Ruskin.* Edited by Mrs. Louis G. Hufford. Boston: Ginn and Company, 1894, p. 87.

Russell, W. H. "The Catholic Evidence Guild in the United States." *Lumen Vitae: Revue Internationale de la Formation Religieuse* 3 (1948), pp. 301–17.

Russello, Gerald J. "Christopher Dawson: Is There a Christian Culture?" *Commonweal* 123 (5 April 1996), pp. 19–20.

S. A. "The Personable Publishers." *Today,* October 1951, n.p.

Say, Elizabeth. *Evidence on Her Own Behalf: Women's Narrative as Theological Voice.* Savage, Md.: Rowman and Littlefield, 1990.

Scott, Christina Dawson. *A Historian and His World: A Life of Christopher Dawson.* New Brunswick, N.J.: Transaction Publishers, 1991.

"Sheed and Ward in New York." *The Catholic World* 136, no. 815. (February 1933), pp. 749–50.

Sheed and Ward Survey, 1934: An Anthology of Publication. New York: Sheed & Ward, 1934.

Sheed, F. J. *The Church and I.* Garden City, N.Y.: Doubleday, 1974.

——. *Communism and Man.* New York: Sheed & Ward, 1938.

——, trans. *The Confessions of St. Augustine.* New York: Sheed & Ward, 1943.

——. "The Future of Religious Publishing." *Religious Book Guide,* July-August 1971, pp. 2–4.

——. *The Instructed Heart.* Huntington, Ind.: Our Sunday Visitor, 1979.

——. *Is It the Same Church?* New York: Sheed & Ward, 1967.

——. *A Map of Life.* New York: Sheed & Ward, 1932.

——. "My Life on the Street Corner." *Saturday Review,* 10 May 1969, pp. 22–67.

——. *Sidelights on the Catholic Revival.* New York: Sheed & Ward, 1940.

——. *Theology and Sanity.* New York: Sheed & Ward, 1946.

——. *To Know Christ Jesus.* New York: Sheed & Ward, 1962.

Sheed, Wilfrid. *Clare Booth Luce.* New York: E. P. Dutton, 1982.

——. *Frank and Maisie: A Memoir with Parents.* New York: Simon and Schuster, 1986.

——. "Frank Sheed and Maisie Ward: Writers, Publishers and Parents." *New York Times Book Review,* 2 April 1972, pp. 2, 24.

——. *In Love With Daylight: A Memoir of Recovery.* New York: Simon and Schuster, 1995.

——. *People Will Always Be Kind.* New York: Farrar, Strauss and Giroux, 1973.

——. "What Frank & Maisie Did in America." *Commonweal* 112 (1 November 1985), pp. 601–07.

Siderman, Edward A. *A Saint in Hyde Park: Memories of Father Vincent McNabb, O.P.* London: Bles, 1950.

The Slant Manifesto: Catholics and the Left. London: Sheed & Ward, 1966.

Speaight, Robert. *The Property Basket: Recollections of a Divided Life.* London: Collins and Harvill Press, 1970.

Talbot, Francis. "The Sheed and Ward Imprint." *America* 48 (4 March 1933), pp. 532–33.

Unsworth, Timothy. "Catholic Publishing Dithers Between Business and Apostolate." *National Catholic Reporter,* 10 September 1993, pp. 25, 32–33.

Ward, Aileen. "Last Century's Literary Puzzle." Review of *Robert Browning and His World,* vol. 1. *The Saturday Review,* 4 November 1967, p. 41.

Ward, Elizabeth. *David Jones Mythmaker.* Manchester, England: University of Manchester, 1983.

Ward, Josephine. *Horace Blake.* London: Hutchinson, 1913.

——. *In the Way.* London: Burns and Oates, 1887.

——. *The Job Secretary.* London: Longmans, Green, and Co., 1911.

—— *One Poor Scruple.* London: Longmans, Green, and Co., 1899.

——. *Out of Due Time.* London: Longmans, Green, and Co., 1906.

——. *The Shadow of Mussolini.* London: Sheed & Ward, 1927.

——. *Tudor Sunset.* London: Sheed & Ward, 1932.

Ward, Leo R. *Nova Scotia: The Land of Co-operation.* New York: Sheed & Ward, 1942.

Ward, Wilfrid. *Aubrey De Vere: A Memoir.* London: Longmans, Green, and Co., 1904.

——. *Last Lectures by Wilfred Ward.* Edited by Maisie and Josephine Ward. London: Longmans, Green, and Co., 1918.

——. *The Life of John Henry, Cardinal Newman.* 2 vols. London: Longmans, Green, and Co., 1912.

——. *Men and Matters.* London: Longmans, Green, and Co., 1914.

——. *Problems and Persons.* London: Longmans, Green, and Co., 1902.

——. *Ten Personal Studies.* London: Longmans, Green, and Co., 1908.

——. *William George Ward and the Catholic Revival.* London: MacMillan, 1893.

——. *William George Ward and the Oxford Movement.* London: MacMillan, 1889.

——. *A Wish to Believe.* London, 1882.

Watkin, E. I. *Roman Catholicism in England from the Reformation to 1950.* Oxford: Oxford University Press, 1957.

Waugh, Evelyn. *Monsignor Ronald Knox.* Boston: Little, Brown and Company, 1959.

Weaver, Mary Jo. Introduction to *Letters from a Modernist.* Shepherdstown, W. Va.: Patmos Press, n.d.

——. "Wilfrid Ward's Interpretation and Application of Newman." In *Newman and the Modernists,* edited by M. J. Weaver. Lanhan, Md.: University Press of America, 1985.

White, John P. "The Winch of the Wine Press." Review of *Robert Browning and His World: The Private Face. The Tablet* 22 (19 October 1968), p. 1038.

Wicker, Brian. *Culture and Liturgy.* New York: Sheed & Ward, 1963

——. *Culture and Theology.* London: Sheed & Ward, 1966.

Wills, Garry. *Bare Ruined Choirs: Doubt, Prophecy, and Radical Religion.* Garden City, N.Y.: Doubleday, 1972.

Index

Agriculture Problem, The (Blundell), 87–88
alcohol, use of: by Herbert Ward, 60, 62, 136, 211 n.3; by Maisie Ward, 100–101, 190, 195
Andrews, Jim, 196, 229 n.1
Angelico, Fra, 119, 120
Arendt, Hannah, 198
Arendzen (Dutch priest), 55–56, 59, 170
Ashburnham, Catherine, 82
atomic bomb, Sheed's view of, 120
Aubrey De Vere: A Memoir (Wilfrid Ward), 28
Austen, Jane, 31, 203–4
authoritarianism: ecclesiastical and lay movements, 53; political movements' influence on the Sheeds, 92
autobiography: of Frank Sheed, 202; of Maisie Ward, 164, 180–82, 202, 227 n.21
awards, bestowed on the Sheeds, 141–42, 148, 150, 168, 169

Balfour, Arthur, 17
Balfour, Reginald, 40

Barth, Karl, 153
Belloc, Hilaire, 40, 59, 67, 112, 113, 221 n.27, 227 n.21; association with S&W, 69, 70–71, 106
Benedict XIV (pope), 43
Be Not Solicitous... (Maisie Ward), 144, 145–47, 152, 161, 163
Benson, Robert Hugh (priest), 33–34, 54, 125, 193
Bernardino, San, 43–44, 119
Bevan (priest), 55–56, 59, 148, 170
biblical scholarship, Maisie's interest in, 141, 144, 148, 155, 157–58
biography, theory of: Maisie Ward, 112–14, 138–39, 155; Wilfrid Ward, 113
Birdwood (Torresdale house), 98–99, 101, 114
Bloy, Leon, 86, 96
Blundell, Francis (Tetta Ward's husband), 48, 62, 88, 93
Blundell, Hester (niece), 123, 137, 196
Blundell, Theresa (Tetta) Ward, 48, 60, 64, 74, 77, 87–88,

Blundell, Theresa (Tetta) Ward
(continued)
102, 196; mental break-
down, 125, 136–37, 183, 211
n.3. See also Ward, Theresa
bookstores, Catholic, in America,
103–4
Bourne, Cardinal Francis Al-
phonsus, 42, 55, 88
Boy Ward. See Ward, Wilfrid
(brother)
Brennan, Niall, 149
Britain: housing after World
War II, 2, 153, 162–63, 167;
society after World War II,
123–24. See also Catholicism
Brittain, Vera, 36, 46, 94
Brontës, the, 31
Browning, Pen, 189
Browning, Robert: biography by
Maisie Ward, 177, 182, 184,
186–89; influence on Maisie
Ward, 31, 71, 112
Bruce Publishing Co., 85
Buckley, William F., Jr., 192
Bullitt, Maria Brown, 45, 76, 98
Burns, Oates and Washbourne
(publishers), 70
Burns, Tom, 56, 71; as managing
editor of S&W, 70, 73, 85

Camarra, Helder (bishop), 191
Cardinal Newman Award, 148
Caryll Houselander: That Divine
Eccentric (Maisie Ward), 127,
169, 178–80, 222 n.8
Casey, Eamonn (priest), 163, 206
Catholic Action, 166
Catholic Book of the Month Club,
72

Catholic Church and the Appeal to
Reason, The (Leo Ward), 64
Catholic Emancipation Act
(1829), 9
Catholic Evidence Guild (C.E.G.):
in America, 95, 142; connection with S&W, 70; decline of,
169–70; in England, 51–59,
61, 73, 134, 183
Catholic Evidence Training Outlines, The (Maisie Ward), 57
Catholic Housing Aid Society
(CHAS) (England), 2, 153,
162–63, 167, 225 n.19
Catholic Housing Association
(CHA) (England), 163
Catholicism
in America, 61, 85, 95–96,
197–98; Frank's war-
time reports on to Brit-
ish Intelligence, 101
in England: and authoritarian political Catholic
leaders, 92–93; histori-
cal and biographical tra-
dition, 158; influence of
Modernism movement,
29–30, 35–36, 50; in
post-Reformation years,
8–9; post-World War I
movements, 49–61, 85–
86
in France, 70, 106, 158;
priest-worker move-
ment, 2, 106, 130–34
Maisie Ward and intellectual
revival, 5, 90, 158, 160
Catholic Missionary Society, 53
Catholic ruralist movement, 79–
80
Catholic Soldiers Association, 45

Catholic Truth Society, 51, 53, 214 n.3

Catholic Worker movement (U.S.), 2, 95, 107, 109, 220 n.15; Houselander's views of, 126–27; wartime pacifism, 107–8

Cecil, Algernon, 50

C.E.G. *See* Catholic Evidence Guild

chapel, public, opened by Maisie and Frank in Surrey, 75–76, 77–78

Charlot, Jean, 115

CHAS. *See* Catholic Housing Aid Society

Chesterton, Elizabeth Ada (Mrs. Cecil), 110, 113

Chesterton, Frances, 40, 93

Chesterton, Gilbert, 40, 59, 77, 184; association with S&W, 70–71, 106; death of, 93

Chestertons, The (E. A. Chesterton), 111–12, 113

Chestnuts (Horley house), 75–76, 80, 86, 94

Christ and Renan (LaGrange, trans. Maisie Ward), 75

Christ in the Church (Benson), 33–34

Christ is King (Martindale), 67, 71

Church and I, The (Sheed), 202

church fathers, early, Maisie's interest in as research area, 141

"Church of the Poor" concept, 191, 193

class barriers, and the C.E.G., 55

Cockerill, Anthony G., 162

Coles, Robert, 189

Collingwood, Stuart Dodgson, 28

Collins, Dorothy, 93, 102, 123

Commonweal (magazine), 156

communism, Sheeds' views on, 92

Communism and Man (Sheed), 86

communities, Christian, Maisie's support of, 132, 144–45, 200, 230 n.12

Community Journal (Ineson), 145

Companion to Mr. Wells' Outline of History, A (Belloc), 71

Confessions (Augustine, trans. Sheed), 116, 205–6, 230 n.17

Connor, Edward, 70, 102

Conroy, Katherine, 119

conservatism: of Frank Sheed, 52, 173–74, 177; of Ward family members, 5, 10, 18, 29, 167

converts, literary skills of Catholic intellectuals, 70, 72

Cooke, Cardinal Terrence, 205

cooperative movement in Canada, 103, 220 n.10

Cornell, Tom, 202, 206

Cotter, William T. (bishop), 66

Coughlin, Charles Edward (priest), 101

Council, Reform and Reunion (Kung), 166

Cozens, Louisa, 55

Crosby Hall (Tetta's home), 87–88, 93, 196

Culture and Liturgy (Wicker), 172

Cuthbert (priest), 30, 50

Dameo, Claire, 195

Daniel, Yvan, 131

D'Arcy, Martin (priest), 50, 71

Darlington, Jean Bullitt, 76–77, 98

Darlington, Missie. *See* Sheed, Missie Darlington
Darlington, William (Bill), 76–77, 98
Davis, Charles (priest), 170, 191–92
Dawson, Christopher, 50, 71–72, 90–91, 102, 112, 158, 164, 227 n.21
Day, Dorothy, 104, 107–8, 147, 192, 205, 213 n.13; Houselander's views of, 126–27
De Chardin, Teilhard, 193
depression of the 1930s, effect on S&W, 79, 83, 91
D'Escoto, Miguel (priest), 194
De Stena, Marie, 195, 203
Dickens, Charles, 31, 74, 112, 205
Distributist movement, in England, 59, 79–80, 88, 112
divorce: as opposed to nullity, 79; of Sheed children, 183–84, 228 n.1
Dohen, Dorothy, 144
Doherty, Eddie, 107
Drexel, Mother Katherine, 99
Dru, Alice, 71–72
Drummond, Lister, 53
Duchesnese, Abbé, 158

education, higher: family attitude towards Rosemary's attending university, 116–17; Frank's pursuance of law degree, 60, 61, 64, 66–67; Maisie's attempt to enter Oxford, 36–37, 116; of Wilfrid Sheed, 121, 134, 136, 149
Edward VII (king, Great Britain), 29

Egypt House, Isle of Wight, 1, 48, 67, 213 n.11
encyclical, papal, on Modernism movement, 29–30, 42
English Way, The: Studies in English Sanctity from St. Bede to Newman (ed. Maisie Ward), 87, 164, 193
equality, social, viewed among Catholic allies, 30
Essays in Order (S&W series), 72
Eucharist, emphasis on, revival by C.E.G., 50, 57
Évangile et L'Église, L' (Loisy), 35

Fallaux, Erika, 151, 156, 224 n.20
family: housing as prerequisite for Christian living, 163; role in Christian life, 146–47
farming: Distributists' goal of agrarian life, 59, 79–80; Maisie Ward's interests, 80, 86, 94, 124, 130
France, Pays de Mission? (Perrin and Daniel), 131
France Pagan? The Mission of Abbé Godin (trans. Maisie Ward), 131, 134
Franco, Francisco, as seen by Catholic intellectuals, 92–93
Friendship House (U.S.), 2, 95, 109–10
Froude, Richard Hurrell, 129

Gauthier, Paul (priest), 193
Gill, Eric, 71–72
God and Mammon (Mauriac), 86
God and the Supernatural... (essay collection), 50, 62, 71, 72
Godin, Abbé, 131–32, 145
Goodier (priest), 43

Gosse's Farm (Essex), 124, 130, 155
grandchildren, 157, 183, 205
Greene, Graham, 112–13
Grisewood, Harmon, 71–72
Guild. *See* Catholic Evidence Guild
Guilt (Houselander), 126

Hammarskjöld, Dag, 193
Hartigan, John (priest), 80
Hasley, Lucille, 126
Hastings, Cecily, 134, 166, 170
Healy, John (priest), 78
Hewins, Gravernor, 66
Hoffman family, 98
Hope, James (maternal grandfather), 13
Hope, Josephine. *See* Ward, Josephine Hope
Hope, Theresa (aunt), 15
Hope, Victoria Howard (maternal grandmother), 13
Horace Blake (Josephine Ward), 40
Horley (Surrey, England), Catholic community in, 75–76, 77–79, 172
Houselander, Caryll, 98, 102, 109, 110–11, 119; death of, 127, 149; influence on Maisie Ward, 124–27, 180
House of Hospitality (Day), 107
Howard, Henry (uncle), 20, 47
Howard, Hubert, 85
Howard, Lady Catherine, 66
Howard, Margaret (aunt), 20
Howard, Mary (aunt), 20, 25, 32
Howard family: role in English Catholicism, 13–14; Ward children's preference for, 20

Hueck, Baroness Catherine de, 104, 109–10, 147
Hügel, Anatole von, 17–18, 28
Hügel, Baron Fredrich von, 12, 17, 26; and the Modernism movement, 29–30, 35, 42
Hügel, Isy Froude von, 17, 25, 32, 37
humanism, Christian, 153, 187
Hunt, Marigold, 102, 115, 196

Ideal of the Christian Church, The (William George Ward), 9
Ilgar (Essex house), 149, 150, 152
Incarnation, the, as restoration of human integrity, 153
India, Maisie's support for untouchables, 2, 190–91
Ineson, George, 145
Ingleby, Helen, 76
Institute of the Blessed Virgin Mary, founded by Mary Ward in the seventeenth century, 32
integralism, philosophy of, 26
Integrity (magazine), 144
intellectuals, Catholic: 1920s revival, 69; S&W as literary outlet, 70; view of Franco and Mussolini, 92–93
In the Way (Josephine Hope Ward), 14
Is It the Same Church? (Sheed), 174

Jackson, Carol, 144
James, Henry, 188
Jane's Marriage (poem, Kipling), 203–4
Jersey City, N.J., Sheeds' apartment in, 194, 195

Job (biblical personage), as symbol of human suffering, 198–99
Job Secretary, The (Josephine Ward), 40
John XXIII (pope), 165
Jones, Alexander (priest), 148, 149
Jones, David, 71–72
Journal d'un prêtre-ouvrier en Allemagne (Perrin), 131
Jubilee (magazine), 156
Julian of Norwich, 87, 119, 193, 199

Keble, John, 129
Kennedy, Chris (priest), 156
Kerr, Anne (aunt), 32
Kerr, Minna (cousin), 32
"Kingly People, A" (Maisie Ward), 94
Knox, Ronald, 50, 71, 127
Kung, Hans, 166

Lagrange, Père, 158
land allotments, during World War II, 94
Last Lectures (Wilfrid Ward), 112
Lay Apostolate, World Congresses, 164, 226 n.21
lay movements, 53, 95, 145, 164; activity in England, 86; involved in Horley chapel community, 77; and Vatican Council sessions, 165–66. *See also* Catholic Evidence Guild
lecturing: C.E.G. members, 53, 54, 56–57, 58; the Sheeds in America, 76–77, 80, 97, 103–4, 142; Wilfrid Ward, 44–45
Leo XIII (pope), 12, 29

Leo XIII Medal, 141–42
Life of John Henry Cardinal Newman (Wilfrid Ward), 28–29, 40–41, 43, 89
Little Crosby (village), 87–88, 93, 196
liturgy, changes in following Vatican Councils, 172–73
Loisy, Abbé, 35
London Society for the Study of Religion, 35–36
Lotus (house), as Ward family home in Dorking, 24, 28, 30, 48
Lowell, Robert, 115, 221 n.29
Luce, Claire Booth, 136, 174, 218 n.15

McCarthy, Eugene, 168, 193, 226 n.30, 229 n.19
McMeel, John, 196, 229 n.1
McNabb, Vincent (priest), 59, 80
Madeleva, Sister M., 150
Manning, Cardinal Henry Edward, 10
Map of Life, A (Sheed), 79, 86
Maritime cooperatives (Canada), 2
marriage
    of Brownings viewed as ideal, 184, 186, 187–88
    of Maisie and Frank, 1–2, 4, 61–63, 67
    of Sheed children, 143, 148–49, 152, 156, 183; divorces, 183–84, 228 n.1
Marriage: A Dialogue (pamphlet, Josephine Ward), 63
Martindale, C. C. (priest), 55–56, 59, 170, 227 n.21; early association with S&W, 67, 71

Marycrest community, 144–45, 155

mass (sacrament): English memorial service for Maisie, 206–7; Maisie's delight in active participation, 78–79, 195

Maturin, William (priest), 26, 28, 45, 50, 164, 165

Maurin, Peter, 107

Men and Matters (Wilfrid Ward), 40

mental illness: Houselander's vocation to help sufferers, 125–26, 179; in the Ward family, 60, 125, 136, 137, 183, 211 n.3

Middleton, Neil (son-in-law), 148, 174–75, 176; as editorial director of S&W, 156–57, 183–84, 218 n.15; separation and divorce from Rosemary, 183–84, 228 n.1

Middleton, Rosemary Sheed. *See* Sheed, Rosemary

Middleton, Simon Francis Wilfrid (grandson), 151

Mile End (settlement house), 39

Miller, Betty, 186

Min. *See* Sheed, Mary (Min) Maloney

Moberly, Walter, 44, 129, 215 n.29

Modernism movement, 70; effect on Wilfrid Ward, 41–42, 89; influence on English Catholics, 29–30, 35–36, 50

Morton, J. B. (Beachcomber), 73

Mosley, Walter, 129

Mussolini, Benito, 61, 92

Mystical Body of Christ doctrine: Houselander's view of, 109, 110–11, 125, 179; late nineteenth century interest, 34; post-World War I interest in England, 53–54, 57; priest-worker movement as living, 133–34; S&W's publications on, 107

Nagasaki, Japan, atomic bombing of, 120

Newman, John Henry, 10, 18, 35, 71
    biography: by Maisie Ward, 121, 127–30, 134, 186; by Wilfrid Ward, 28–29, 40–41, 43, 89
    canonization attempts, 178
    on the nebulous position of Catholics in England, 8–9

Newman (American publishing company), 85

Nolan (Msgr.), 33, 36

Not Known Here (Josephine Ward), 61

Nullity of Marriage (Sheed), 79

Oakwood Court (Kensington flat), 123, 130, 149

O'Conor family, 40

One Poor Scruple (Josephine Hope Ward), 15, 19

Orbis Books (publisher), 194

Order (magazine), 71–72

Orlandi, Don Nazareno (Italian priest), 43

"Outer Circle," interracial Christian hospitality, 109–10

Outline History of the World (Wells), 71

Out of Due Time (Josephine Ward), 25, 36

Oxford Groups, The (booklet, Maisie Ward), 93–94

Oxford Movement (1833–1845), effect on English Catholicism, 8, 9, 12, 128–29

Oxford University: Maisie Ward's attempt to enter, 36–37; Wilfrid Sheed's graduation from, 149

pacifism, views on during World War II, 107–8, 220n.15, 221 n.29

People Will Always Be Kind (Wilfrid Sheed), 229 n.19

Perrin, Henri (priest-worker), 124, 130–31, 133

Petre, Maude, 25

philosophy, Thomistic, in America, 95

Piggott, Sybil Smyth, 39

Pius X (pope), 35

Pius XI (pope), 166

Pius XII (pope), 133, 164

Plague of His Own Heart, The (Josephine Ward), 61

political activity: changes in Maisie's attitude toward, 163, 167–68, 226 n.30; and the priest-worker movement, 132–33; of the 1930s and the Sheeds, 91–92

priest-worker movement (France), 2, 106, 130–34

Priest-Workman in Germany (Perrin), 131

Problems and Persons (Wilfrid Ward), 28

race relations, in Catholic circles, 109–10

Redfern, Martin, 176, 218 n.15

Redwood, Vernon, 53

Reeves, David, 143

Reilly, Sidney, 127, 179

Religion and Culture (Maritain), 72

Religion of the Plain Man (Benson), 33–34

retreat movement (U.S.), 108, 220 n.17

Return to Chesterton (Maisie Ward), 114, 134, 137–38

Revue Biblique, 158

Robert Browning: A Portrait (Miller), 186

Robert Browning and His World (Maisie Ward), 186

Ruskin, John, 19

Saints in Pictures (series, Maisie Ward), 138, 160

Saints Who Made History (Maisie Ward), 158, 160

Salome, Rev. Mother Mary, 33

Satin Slipper (Claudel), 86

Sayers, Dorothy L., 36

Scharper, Philip, 143, 156, 174, 175–76, 194, 218 n.15

Scottish Catholic Land Association, 80

scripture studies, as Maisie's post-World War II interest, 141, 144, 148, 155, 157–58

Shadow of Mussolini, The (Josephine Ward), 61–62

Shaw, George Bernard, 71

Sheed, Andrews and McMeel, as successor to S&W, 229 n.1

Sheed, Francis (Frank) Joseph
and Maisie Ward: meeting,
51–52; marriage, 1–2, 4,
61–63, 67; her death, 205–6
personal life: accidental fall
in 1956 and decline in
health, 156, 189; attach-
ment to mother, 74–75,
143; pursuance of law
degree, 60, 61, 64, 66–
67
public life: awards and honors, 141–42, 148, 150,
156, 169; involvement in
the C.E.G., 53, 55–57,
79; lecturing tours in
America, 76–77, 80, 86,
104, 142; wartime activi-
ties for British Intelli-
gence, 101, 108, 120. See
also Sheed & Ward
reaction to post-Vatican theology, 173–74, 177
social status of, 65–66, 216
n.47
works, 240. See also individual
titles
Sheed, John (Frank's father), 52
Sheed, Mary (Min) Maloney
(Frank's mother), 51, 52, 73,
82, 95; death of, 143; as
housekeeper for Maisie and
Frank, 74–75, 98, 99–100
Sheed, Missie Darlington
(daughter-in-law), 152, 156,
183, 205
Sheed, Rosemary Luke (daughter), 73–74, 76, 136, 156,
205; family attitude towards
attending university, 116–
17; life in America, 95, 99,
115; marriage to Neil Middleton, 143, 148–49; separation and divorce, 183–84,
228 n.1; as translator, 117,
130, 131, 221 n.30
Sheed, Wilfrid John Joseph
(son), 77, 205, 229 n.19; education of, 99, 134, 136,
149; engagement and mar-
riage, 152, 156, 183; illness
of, 97, 98, 117–18; life in
America, 95, 99, 101, 115;
role in S&W, 175–76; separation and divorce, 183;
works by, 240
Sheed & Ward (S&W), 141, 142,
148
American branch, 82–83,
85–86, 91–92, 143–44,
218 n.15; Maisie Ward's
office visits, 115–16
conception of, 64–65
financial problems, 176–77,
194; sale of, 196–97,
229 n.1
London office: destruction
during 1940 air blitz,
102; early days, 69–73,
217 n.1; financial shape
during mid-1960s, 183–
84; rivalry with New
York, 175–76; Sheeds'
flat in building, 150–51
stock holdings, 174–75, 218
n.15
theology published by, 70,
166, 172, 176
Sheed & Ward's Own Trumpet
(company publication), 115,
143, 196
Sheen, Fulton (bishop), 156

Sheil, Bernard (bishop), 141–42
Slant Group (postwar Britain),
175
Smith, General, 45, 76
Smith, Grace, 76, 99, 151
social questions
emphasis in S&W publica-
tions, 91
Maisie's commitments, 2,
141; Catholic housing,
153, 162–63, 167; un-
touchables of India,
190–91
priest-worker movement,
106, 130–34
Slant Group's views, 175
social status: among Catholics
working together, 30; of
Frank Sheed, 65–66, 216
n.47
Speaight, Robert, 92–93
Splendor of the Rosary, The (Maisie
Ward), 98, 118–20, 160, 225
n.8
Strachey, Lytton, 90
Strauss, Eric, 126, 127
Suhard, Cardinal, 131
Supernatural Life, as central
doctrine of Catholicism, 57
Synthetic Society, 17

Taena community, 145, 155
Tennyson, Alfred Lord, 15
Ten Personal Studies (Wilfrid
Ward), 40
Tetta Ward. See Blundell,
Theresa; Ward, Theresa
That Divine Eccentric. See Caryll
Houselander: That Divine Ec-
centric
theology: C.E.G. teachings on,
57–58, 170; as defined by

Father Maturin, 165; as ex-
pressed in the rosary, 119;
Frank Sheed's reaction to
Vatican II changes, 173–74;
of Houselander, 125–27;
Josephine Hope Ward's use
of novels to espouse, 19;
published by S&W, 70, 166,
173, 176
Theology, Doctorate of, granted
to Frank Sheed, 151
Theology and Sanity (Sheed), 116,
130, 175
They Saw His Glory... (Maisie
Ward), 149–50, 151, 155,
157–58
Third Order Dominicans, Maisie
Ward as member, 56, 205
This Burning Heart (Maisie
Ward), 97, 102–3, 110
This War is The Passion (House-
lander), 110, 125
Thomistic philosophy, in Amer-
ica, 95
Thwaytes, Lance, 162
To and Fro on the Earth (Maisie
Ward), 193, 196, 198–202,
228 nn.3, 10
To Know Jesus Christ (Sheed), 174
Tragi-Comedy of Pen Browning
(Maisie Ward), 189
translations: of continental
works, 70, 72, 158; by Frank
Sheed, 116; by Maisie Ward,
75, 131, 134; by Rosemary
Sheed, 117, 130, 131, 221
n.30
Tristram, Henry (priest), 128–29
Trumpet, The (Sheed & Ward's
Own Trumpet), 115, 143, 196
Truth About Publishing, The (Un-
win), 69

Tyrrell, George (priest), 35, 42

Unfinished Business (autobiography, Maisie Ward), 164, 180–82, 202, 227 n.21
untouchables, India, Maisie's support for, 2, 190–91
Unwin, Stanley, 69
Upper Prestwood (England), farming attempts by the Sheeds, 80, 86

Van der Valk (priest), 190, 191
Vatican Council sessions, changes in the church, 165–66, 169, 170
Vaughan, Cardinal Herbert Alfred, 10, 12
violence, street, in Jersey City, 199
visions, experienced by Houselander, 125

Wade, Edward (Ted) W., 162, 163
Walker, John (cousin), 98
Wall, Bernard, 71–72
Walsh, Molly, 102, 146, 152; postwar housing efforts in Britain, 155, 161, 162, 170
Ward, Agnes (aunt), 10
Ward, Bernard (uncle), 10, 35, 44, 47
Ward, Edmund (uncle), 11, 14–15; death of and controversial will, 46–47, 213 n.11
Ward, Emily (aunt), 10, 47
Ward, Frances (grandmother), 10
Ward, Gertrude (aunt), 10
Ward, Herbert (brother), 17, 23, 26, 37, 43, 66; alcoholic addiction, 60, 62, 136, 211 n.3;

death of, 183; at Egypt House, 48, 76, 88, 213 n.11; service in World War I, 45, 47
Ward, John, 213 n.11
Ward, Josephine Hope (mother), 1, 12–14, 35, 37, 42, 62; death of Boy, 25; illness and death, 80, 82; as instigator of S&W, 64–65; involvement in C.E.G., 55; novels by, 14, 15, 18–19, 36, 40, 61–62; views on Mussolini, 61, 92
Ward, Leo (brother), 17, 23, 26, 37, 48, 76; death of, 97, 114; interest in religious renewal in England, 50; as missionary in Japan, 88; nervous collapse, 60, 211 n.3; perceived role in proposed Sheed & Ward, 64–65; service in World War I, 47–48
Ward, Maisie (Mary Josephine) and Frank: grandchildren, 157, 183, 205; life in America, 94–95, 114–15, 177, 194, 195; pregnancies and births of children, 73–74, 75, 77, 86–87, 146; return to post-war England, 120–21; wedding of, 1–6, 67
biographic style, 112–14, 138–39, 155. *See also individual biographies by title*
influences in her life, 71–72, 90–91; Caryll Houselander, 124–27, 180; Catherine de Hueck, 109–10; Christopher Dawson, 71–72, 90–91,

Ward, Maisie (Mary Josephine)
(*continued*)
    112, 124, 164; Dorothy
    Day, 106–9, 192; Father
    Maturin, 26, 28, 50, 164,
    165; Gilbert Chesterton,
    112–13; Robert Brown-
    ing, 31, 71, 112
personal life: attachment to
    parents, 22, 23, 39–40;
    attempt to enter Oxford,
    36–37, 116; birth, 15;
    convent schooling of,
    32–34; final illness and
    death, 204–6; health,
    74, 117, 157, 167, 189–
    90, 196, 202–3; as mem-
    ber of Third Order of
    Dominicans, 56, 205;
    use of alcohol, 99–100,
    190, 195; view of En-
    glish society after World
    War II, 123–24
public life: awards and hon-
    ors, 141–42, 148; hous-
    ing in postwar Britain,
    152–53, 155–56, 160–
    63; interest in farming,
    80, 86, 94, 124; interest
    in French priest-worker
    movement, 2, 106, 130–
    34; involvement in
    C.E.G., 55, 56–59, 76;
    lecturing tours, 76–77,
    80, 97, 103–4, 106; as
    nursing aide during
    World War I, 45–46, 47;
    support for India's un-
    touchables, 2, 190–91;
    support of Christian
    communities, 132, 144–
    45, 200, 229 n.12; as
    traveling companion of
    her father, 40; visits to
    S&W offices in New
    York City, 115–16; in
    wartime America, 95,
    100–101
published books and articles,
    232–35. *See also individ-
    ual titles*
Ward, Margaret (aunt), 10, 15
Ward, Mary (aunt), 10
Ward, Mary (seventeenth-
    century nun), 33, 34, 87,
    161, 164–65, 213 n.12, 227
    n.18
Ward, Theresa (Tetta) (sister),
    15, 20, 23, 211 n.3; service
    in World War I, 45, 47. *See
    also* Blundell, Theresa
Ward, Wilfrid ("Boy") (brother),
    15, 20, 23, 25–26
Ward, Wilfrid (father), 1, 9, 11–
    12, 28, 37
    death of, 47
    as editor of *Dublin Review*,
        35–36, 42
    influence of Newman and
        biography of, 28–29,
        40–41, 43, 89
    lecturing tours in America,
        44–45, 98
    Modernism movement, ef-
        fect on, 41–42, 89
    theory of biography, 113
    works, 241. *See also individual
        titles*
Ward, William George (grandfa-
    ther), 8, 9–10, 11, 20
Watkin, E. I., 50, 71, 129, 158
Weaver, Mary Jo, 204–5

Wells, H. G., 71

Wicker, Brian, 172

Wight, Isle of, Ward family's properties on, 1, 10, 46, 213 n.11

Wijnhausen, Louise, 142, 143

Wilfrid Wards and the Transition, The (Maisie Ward), 87, 88–89, 90

William George Ward and the Catholic Revival (Wilfrid Ward), 12, 17

William George Ward and the Oxford Movement (Wilfrid Ward), 12

Willock, Dorothy, 146

Willock, Ed, 144, 146

Wiseman, Cardinal Nicholas Patrick, Wilfrid Ward's biography, 12, 17, 28

Wish to Believe, The (Wilfrid Ward), 14

Woman Who Was Poor, The (Bloy), 86

women: audience reaction to as lecturers, 104, 106; Catholicism in America, 96; employed at S&W, 91; Maisie's achievements as, 209–10; participation in the C.E.G., 55; role in Christian communities, 145, 164–65; role in the family, 146–47

Worker Priests, The (manuscript), 133

World War I, Ward family members' efforts during, 45–47

World War II: Frank's work with British Intelligence, 101, 108, 120; Sheeds' removal to America in 1940, 94–95

Wyndham, George, 40

Young Mr. Newman (Maisie Ward), 127–30, 134, 186